thin within

Presents

Rebuilding God's Temple

Thin Within Workbook Series

Discovering God's Master Plan

Twelve Week Foundational Program

I came that they may have life, and have it abundantly.

John 10:10, NASB

Your journey toward an abundant life starts today...

© 2003, Thin Within, All Rights Reserved

Products Available From Thin Within...

Rebuilding God's Temple Workbook Series

Discovering God's Master Plan—Twelve Week Foundational Program

Discovering God's Master Plan—Audio Tapes

Laying A Godly Foundation—Workbook Two

Laying A Godly Foundation—Audio Tapes

Building On God's Truth—Workbook Three

Building On God's Truth—Audio Tapes

Celebrating God's Glory—Workbook Four

Celebrating God's Glory—Audio Tapes

Thin Within: A Grace Oriented Approach to Lasting Weight Loss

Hardcover Book by W Publishers

Thin Again: A Biblical Approach to Food, Eating, and Weight Management

Softcover Book by Revell Publishers

Special Thanks...

A special thanks to Sally Rackets from all of us at the Thin Within team for her wonderful work in creating the illustrations in this workbook series. God has definitely given her a wonderful gift.

A Note About Scripture References . . .

Unless otherwise identified, all Scripture quotations in this publication are taken from the HOLY BIBLE, NEW INTERNATIONAL VERSION ® (NIV®) Copyright © 1973, 1978, 1984 by International Bible Society. Use by permission of Zondervan. All rights reserved.

Scripture taken from the following versions noted alongside the Scripture reference:
New American Standard Bible (NASB), Copyright © 1960, 1962, 1963, 1968, 1971, 1972, 1973, 1975, 1977 by The Lockman Foundation. Used by permission.
Amplified® Bible (Amplified), Copyright © 1954, 1958, 1962, 1964, 1965, 1987 by the Lockman Foundation. Used by permission.
Holy Bible—New Century Version (NCV), Copyright © 1987 1988, 1991 by Word Publishing.
The Message. Copyright © 1993, 1994, 1995, 1996, 2000, 2001, 2002. Used by permission of NavPress

© 2003, Thin Within, All Rights Reserved

Contents

Discovering God's Master Plan – Twelve Week Foundational Program

Appendix

© 2003, Thin Within, All Rights Reserved

© 2003, Thin Within, All Rights Reserved

Thin Within workshops began in a basement in Berkeley, California, in 1975 by Judy Wardell Halliday and Joy Imboden Overstreet. Both had struggled with food and weight-related problems, and from their experience and research they developed a revolutionary approach that has helped thousands of people in this country and abroad..

Joy left Thin Within in 1980 to pursue an advanced degree in public health education while Judy continued to develop and expand the original concepts of the program. Thin Within grew to ten offices in the western United States.

In 1985, the book *Thin Within: How to Eat and Live As a Thin Person* was published by Crown Publishers and was on the West Coast best-seller list for sixteen weeks.

After a major Thin Within financial crisis, Judy received Jesus Christ as her Lord and Savior. As a result of God's instruction through the Living Word and spiritual insights, biblical concepts were incorporated into the Thin Within material and workshops.

In 1994, Baker Revell published *Silent Hunger*, republished in 1999 as *Thin Again*, republished in 2008 as *Get Thin Stay Thin*, which reflects the essential elements of God's transforming grace and the power of the Holy Spirit as the source of strength in conquering food and weight problems.

In January 2002 a biblical version of Thin Within was developed and made available in both workbook and online formats.

In May 2002, W Publishing reissued a biblical and revised version of Thin Within entitled *Thin Within: A Grace-Oriented Approach to Lasting Weight Loss.*

Thin Within is a non-diet, grace-oriented approach to weight, food and eating issues. It involves no calorie or fat-gram counting, nor weighing or measuring food. Thin Within teaches how to choose wisely when eating a variety of foods in response to the natural God-given signals of hunger and satisfaction. As a result, participants eat less food, make beneficial food choices and naturally melt down to the size that God intended. Success is not in following food rules, but rather in experiencing the transforming power of God's grace which empowers individuals to live the abundant life in Christ.

© 2003, Thin Within, All Rights Reserved

First Things First

A Healthy Start: Physician Approval

Be sure that you have received the permission of your physician before beginning any dietary or exercise program.

Why Approach a Practical Problem from a Biblical Point of View?

We believe that the focus must be on the Bible and the power of the Holy Spirit rather than on self-effort in order for lasting change to take place.

Why? Latest statistics indicate that we fail to change our behavior if we rely on external rules or food formulas. In the last decade, there has been a 30 percent increase in the number of overweight Americans of all age groups including children. At any one time, 50 percent of females and 24 percent of males are on diets. A Food and Drug Administration study indicates that 95 percent of people who diet fail, usually regaining all of the lost weight plus some. So we conclude from these statistics that the secular efforts have not solved but intensified the problem.

At Thin Within we know that with God's strength, biblical insights and discerning choices we can overcome temptation and effectively deal with everyday frustrations. God provides permanent solutions rather than quick fixes. When we approach weight loss, food, eating and body image issues from God's perspective and the power of the Holy Spirit we are transformed from within so that we do not continue to go from one addiction to another.

Scales: To Weigh or Not to Weigh?

In most weight-loss programs the scale is used to record each individual's progress. The scale is a helpful tool for measuring the amount of weight a person has released. However, it can be a stumbling block when it is used compulsively or when it becomes an idol or measure of "acceptance." Thin Within recommends using the scale occasionally only as a reality check. There are many other means to "measure" released weight, including how clothes fit, percentage of body fat, or measuring the waist/hip ratio. Prayerfully consider using the scale sparingly.

Benefits of a Support Group

Studies show that individuals have a much greater rate of success in weight loss when they have personal accountability and contact with others. Thin Within offers support groups to participants for discussion, video segments, sharing, and prayer. We encourage you to consider joining a group in your local area. If there is not one available, allow us to help you plan and prepare to lead a group. We also offer online support groups through our Thin Within website: www.thinwithin.org.

© 2003, Thin Within, All Rights Reserved

The Thin Within Workbook Series called *Rebuilding God's Temple* consists of four workbooks, *Discovering God's Master Plan*, *Laying a Godly Foundation*, *Building on God's Truth*, and *Celebrating God's Glory*, each containing inspirational lessons and motivational exercises. *Discovering God's Master Plan* presents the foundation for the physiological and spiritual components of the program. The remaining workbooks enrich and elaborate on the essential themes presented in the foundational material. Note the course of study:

Discovering God's Master Plan

- Week One: Hope

- Week Two: My Body—God's Temple

- Week Three: Identity in Christ

- Week Four: Celebration of God's Grace, Part One

- Week Five: Restoration

- Week Six: Counting the Cost

- Week Seven: The Fight of Faith

- Week Eight: Celebration of God's Grace, Part Two

- Week Nine: Building Godly Boundaries

- Week Ten: Forgiveness

- Week Eleven: Prayer

- Week Twelve: Celebration of God's Grace, Part Three

Laying A Godly Foundation – Workbook Two

Building On God's Truth – Workbook Three

Celebrating God's Glory – Workbook Four

Once you have completed this foundational workbook and are ready to continue your study with the supplementary workbooks, you may order them by calling our toll-free number 877.729.8932.

© 2003, Thin Within, All Rights Reserved

How to Use This Workbook

Daily Use:

- **Weekly Lesson** – These lessons are designed to teach the basic tools and concepts leading to the abundant life free from enslavement to overeating. It is your choice whether you read the whole lesson at the beginning of the week before doing the daily exercises, or read a portion of the lesson each day while you complete the exercises.

- **Daily Exercises** – The daily exercises and practical tools will take approximately 15 to 20 minutes per day. They will provide spiritual and practical reinforcement for what you are learning in the lessons. Within each week, there are seven daily sets of exercises with two optional days. They contain the following categories:

  - Going Deeper – journaling questions for a deeper understanding of the lesson

  - Bible Study – delving deeper into what the Bible says on the topic

  - Getting Practical – making the physiological principles real in daily life while keeping the focus on God

  - Knowing God by Heart – getting to know God more fully by studying who He is

  - Memory Challenge – memorizing God's truth in order to renew the mind and be ready for daily spiritual battle

  Consider starting a special notebook or journal as a place to record your prayers, thoughts, and insights from God as you work through the daily exercises. Both a Bible dictionary and thesaurus will be helpful (although not required) in the Knowing God by Heart study.

- **Review of the Week** – Look over what God has taught you during the week and use it as preparation for your support group meeting.

- **Support Group Meeting Notes** – A place to take notes during the support group meeting for your personal use in the following week.

Appendix:

- **Stop, Look, Listen, and Obey: Temptation Buster** – A battle plan to fight temptation through God's Word.

- **Reentry After Fallout** – For those who have fallen behind or have not moved at the anticipated pace.

- **Thin Within Care Center** – You are not alone on the Thin Within journey. In this section you will find a variety of ways to get support when you need it most.

   © 2003, Thin Within, All Rights Reserved

The Hunger Scale is presented in the first lesson. It defines the levels of hunger and fullness on a scale from 0 to 10. At the bottom of the scale is 0, which is physiological hunger—an absolutely empty stomach. At the top of the scale is 10—completely stuffed—what we call "Thanksgiving Day" stuffed. And in the middle of the scale is 5—a place of comfortable satisfaction. As you read lesson one, you will begin to determine your "0" (truly hungry) and your "5" (that place of just enough). Here are some basic guidelines that outline the Thin Within program:

- At any given point in time, notice where you are on the Hunger Scale and recognize when your body is truly hungry.

- Ask God for strength to wait until you are stomach hungry (0 on the Hunger Scale) before you eat.

- When you reach that point of stomach hunger (0), eat the foods you enjoy without being preoccupied with the diet rules of the past (for example, counting calories, fat grams, carbohydrates, or protein).

- As you eat, be attentive to that point of satisfaction, 5 on the Hunger Scale, and respectfully stop eating.

- Allow your conscience and the Holy Spirit to convict you of misusing food as you are being conformed to the likeness of Christ.

- Take time daily for Bible study and prayer and invite God to speak to you through His Word.

The Illustrated Hunger Scale

Zero	Five	Ten

Consider these basic keys as you incorporate the Thin Within principles into your life:

Keys to Conscious Eating

1. Eat only when my body is hungry.

2. Reduce the number of distractions in order to eat in a calm environment.

3. Eat when sitting down.

4. Eat when my body and mind are relaxed.

5. Eat and drink the food and beverages my body enjoys.

6. Pay attention to my food while eating.

7. Eat slowly and savor each bite.

8. Stop before my body is "full."

These are not to become "rules" only guidelines to conscious eating.

© 2003, Thin Within, All Rights Reserved

Helpful Hints

Essentials to Start:

- Think in terms of how <u>little</u> you can eat in order to be satisfied—rather than how <u>much</u> you can get away with in hopes of not gaining weight.
- Pray before you eat and invite God to have the final word as to when to stop at the point of satisfaction.
- Realize that beverages (including coffee, tea, soda, milk, sports drinks, and juices), mints, hard candy, and chewing gum all change your hunger number because your body takes everything into account. Consuming these things while waiting for hunger will keep you from reaching 0 or will often give false hunger signals. Water, on the other hand, will only change your hunger number for a very short period of time. We encourage you to replace habit-forming beverages with water.
- Eat from smaller plates and bowls in keeping with "fist-sized" 0 to 5 eating. (When your stomach is empty, it is about the size of your fist, which means that approximately a fist-sized amount of food is all that is required to take you from a "0" to a comfortable "5").
- Start out with half portions of the food you normally eat and determine if that satisfies you.
- If you are interrupted during your meal by the doorbell, the phone, or some other distraction, consider that this might be God's way of escape from the temptation to overeat (1 Corinthians 10:13).
- When you reach the point of satisfaction, do whatever it takes to get the food out of your reach: move it away from you; give it to someone else; wrap it up; put it in the refrigerator, freezer, or pantry; or place it in a carryout container.
- It is better to stop at 5 and throw away the excess food than store it in your body in the form of excess weight. Is it better that it goes to *waste* rather than your *waist?*
- It is really OK to skip a meal. Nothing terrible will happen. You will not die. God has designed our bodies to endure the lean times. This is evidenced in situations where people have been stranded or caught in unforeseen circumstances for days and survived. However, let it be clear that we are not advocating intentional long-term deprivation.
- You can plan your hunger by:
  - ▶ not eating all the way to a 5. If you reach a 0 at 2:00 P.M. in the afternoon and dinner is at 6:00 P.M., you can wait or perhaps have a very small amount of food (for example, half of a banana or a few almonds) that will take you off of 0. By dinner you will be empty and ready to enjoy a nice meal.
  - ▶ delaying when you eat for a period of time.
  - ▶ adjusting the kind of foods you eat. Different foods vary in how well they satisfy you.

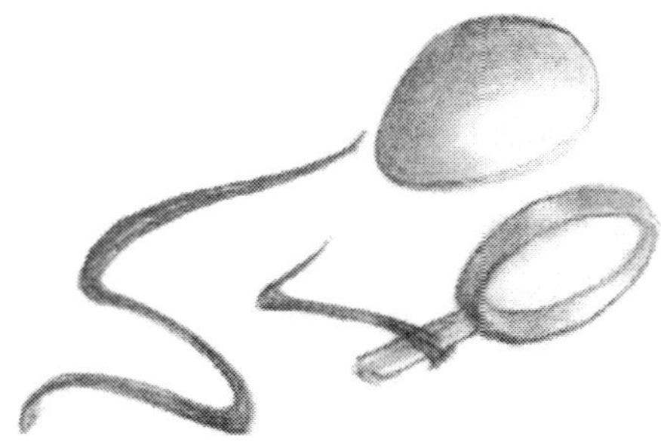

   © 2003, Thin Within, All Rights Reserved

As you begin your Thin Within journey, you will be entering into God's grace where He will meet all of your needs. These needs may include changing unhealthy eating patterns that have not served you, along with desiring to walk closer with God in order to experience the abundant life. The goal of this foundational workbook is to incorporate practical and biblical solutions to this cycle of disordered eating in which you have found yourself. After completing this twelve-week workbook, you will have the basic tools needed to

- foster a deeper relationship with God through Bible study and prayer;
- find hunger and satisfaction;
- experience hope in God's plan for your life;
- establish that your body is God's temple of the Holy Spirit;
- know your true identity is not in external appearance but in the identity you have been given in Christ Jesus;
- avoid the trap of legalism-following worldly dieting laws and rules for success-which lead to failure;
- set your mind on the Spirit in order to be aware of and make responsible choices that honor your body—God's temple;
- walk step by step in faith and begin to experience the abundant life in Christ even before it may be completely visible in your physical body;
- explore how to set proper boundaries in your life;
- find true freedom in forgiveness;
- access God's incredible tool of prayer as your lifeline to Him; and
- experience the transforming power of God's grace.

God will be with you each step of the way helping you to change your life and overcome your battle with food and weight. Be open to the leading of the Holy Spirit as He guides you. He will be the source of strength and comfort as you pursue an abundant life in Christ.

Commitment Prayer

Dear Father God:

I come to You with a needy heart. I confess I struggle to know how to live out the plan you have for my life in the area of food, eating, and weight. My heart is often drawn to the message that comparison and perfectionism is the answer. I can easily become overly preoccupied with wanting to look "perfect" externally rather than wanting You and Your perfect will to conform me from within. In the name of Jesus, I stand against all of Satan's lies that seem to be the answer to my deepest needs. I resist all the forces that would tempt me to give up or distract me from who I really am in Christ and what You desire for me regarding my body and my walk with You. I oppose every attempt that would keep me from knowing and experiencing full fellowship with You. I commit to completing the Thin Within foundational material with an open heart so that You might conform and mature me to the likeness of Jesus Christ. Amen.

© 2003, Thin Within, All Rights Reserved

Phases of Thin Within

We often speak of Thin Within (TW) as a journey where you travel from one phase to another. These phases are not rigid but a progression along a personal path that God has designed for you. The three phases are the Freedom Phase, the Discernment Phase, and the Mastery Phase based on I Corinthians 6:12,

"Everything is permissible for me" - but not everything is beneficial. "Everything is permissible for me"
– but I will not be mastered by anything.

Phase I - Freedom Phase: "All things are permissible"

Here you experience a wonderful freedom from dieting laws, enjoying a variety of foods including foods declared "bad" by the dieting world. Jesus said all things are permissible and you were meant to enjoy that freedom as you become attentive to your body and experience the reliable hunger/satisfaction mechanism that God has carefully crafted within you. Therefore, in TW there are no good foods or bad foods, however it is important to keep in mind any dietary restrictions designated by your physician.

Phase II - Discernment Phase: "not all things are beneficial"

God reminds us that, "all things are permissible, but not all things are beneficial". So now it's time to discern or tune in to your God-given body and the Holy Spirit's desire to teach you. Yes, you can have any food you choose but consider the best choice regarding your total well-being.

This is the phase where you begin to evaluate how you feel when you eat certain foods. You may discover you have more energy and sleep better when making certain food choices and the reverse may also be true. So your choices are not simply about a "taste bud" sensation but about caring for your body as a temple of the Holy Spirit!

In the discernment phase you will come to realize that you have the responsibility to choose wisely taking into account that your God-given freedom is not to be misused as "license" to eat whatever looks, smells or sounds good; our freedom has been purchased at a very high price. Therefore, enjoy your freedom wisely, with a grateful heart!

Phase III - Mastery Phase "I will not be mastered by anything"

Our Thin Within journey points us to the only one who is to have mastery over our lives and our every choice….the Lord God himself. It's so easy to turn to food for comfort or escape from whatever troubles us, but God is our only refuge! He is our way of escape.

Oreos or cheese enchiladas are not to have mastery over us! We are to enjoy food yet we are called to discern when we are hungry and by the power of the Holy Spirit, make wise food choices. God knows what our energy requirements are, since He designed us, and it's exciting to learn to ask Him, to obey His lead, and to depend on Him to direct our choices.

This is the most exciting journey of your life because it really isn't simply about the food, eating or weight. It's about a life that is surrendered to an all-powerful, all-loving God who desires nothing but the best for you in all things….His beloved! Freedom with responsibility produces a life of deep abiding joy!

© 2003, Thin Within, All Rights Reserved

Month One

Lessons &

Exercises

© 2003, Thin Within, All Rights Reserved

© 2003, Thin Within, All Rights Reserved

Hope

Welcome to Thin Within. We rejoice that you have accepted God's invitation to join us. His Word says in Jeremiah 29:11 that he has a plan, purpose, hope, and a future for you. Together we will discover the blessings of His plan as He longs for you to be at peace with food, eating, your body, and your life.

Over the next twelve weeks and beyond, you will discover practical tools to assist you in this exciting adventure as you melt down to your natural God-given size. You will hear motivational testimonies and read about real men and women who have experienced God's faithfulness in overcoming obstacles and accomplishing the impossible. You will search the depths and riches of God's Word and excavate the vastness of His treasure found in the Bible.

The fact is many of us try one diet after the other, but discover the hard way that when we "lose" weight we often "find" it again—plus some! In fact, 95 percent of all diets fail. If you have experienced failure in dieting or other efforts regarding food and weight, you are definitely not alone. We will investigate this phenomenon and discover that by utilizing biblical principles you can become the thin, healthy person God intended you to be—from within. As you do, you will be able to rest in God's embrace and not live in fear of "finding" your extra weight.

Our hope is in Him, not in ourselves.

Spiritual Foundation

You are about to experience the beginning of something new and wonderful! Even now, God *is doing* a new thing. The prophet Isaiah encourages us with the following:

Forget the former things; do not dwell on the past.
See, I am doing a new thing!
Now it springs up; do you not perceive it?
I am making a way in the desert and streams in the wasteland.
Isaiah 43:18–19

The fact that you are here with this material in front of you indicates that God is at work doing something new in your life.

For many, the past has been filled with frustration regarding food, body, and dieting failures. Often we jumped on the latest bandwagon, committing ourselves to fads, counting points, fat grams, or calories. We plunged headfirst into the latest rigorous workout program only to burn out. We may have even lost weight—sometimes a lot of weight—but couldn't manage to keep it off.

Many have been caught in the pendulum swing from one extreme to the other. On the one side we basked in our glory and ability to "do it all ourselves." Unable to keep up the performance, we swung to the other extreme, bailing out of the diet and eating with wild abandon. In essence we went from law to license, rules to recklessness. The one side of the pendulum swing is a place of self-righteousness where we took credit for the weight we lost and for following the diet regulations. But when we couldn't hold it together over time, we swung to the other side, beating ourselves over the head with the club of condemnation for yet another failure. All the while, we buried our pain in a half-gallon of ice cream. With this pendulum way of living, we move back and forth from one side to the other. This is the worldly path of my performance. On this path we discover the hard way that it leads only to frustration and discouragement.

The great news, however, is that God never intended for life to be a swinging pendulum. The finished work of the cross of Christ is our stabilizing force. We rest in the fact that the grace of God is immeasurable and steadfast, which transforms and grounds us through His Word. When we stumble and fall, we rely on God's amazing grace and the power of the Holy Spirit as He gently leads us back onto the path of His provision (Isaiah 40:11).

Our God is amazing! He who set the stars in the heavens and measured all of the waters of the earth in the palm of His hand desires intimacy with you (Isaiah 40:12). You are His beloved and He draws you with loving-kindness (Jeremiah 31:3). All the heavens declare His glory yet He esteems you (Psalm 8:3–8). It is this God who provides the grace, mercy, and strength needed for you to persevere as you trust and obey.

© 2003, Thin Within, All Rights Reserved

LESSON

Life on the swinging pendulum is dominated by fleshly lusts and fleshly pride, but a life surrendered to the cross of Christ leads directly to the Father. It may be a process of moving forward and sometimes faltering back, but the course is set; our hope is in Him, not in ourselves. Our direction and progress are assured. Slowly but surely, step-by-step, we make headway.

This is a path with a hope and a future that God has ordained for you because He loves you. Although He is highly exalted above all things, God chooses to love you because it is His nature to love. It gives Him pleasure to do so (Ephesians 1:5; Hebrews 12:2).

Christ died to set you free even while you were still rebellious, sinful, and without a care for Him (Romans 5:8). He has rescued you. He bought you with His blood. He has paid the price and you have been redeemed. It is finished. Because of His great love for you, God, who is very rich in mercy, chose to make you alive in Christ, even while you were dead in sin. His amazing grace has saved you (Ephesians 2:4–9).

God's love is relentless and immeasurable. His compassion knows no end. He is personally aware of your every breath and thought (Psalm 139:1–5). He shares your joys and victories as well as your pain and heartache. Let's look at the way He has approached His people in the past.

Our God is unchanging. He has always dealt with His people with mercy and grace. Even in the garden when Adam and Eve were given only one directive, which they broke, God Himself provided the first "sacrifice" by slaying the animals for the skins from which their clothing would be made.

With the Israelites, God again clearly made known His desires for His people in the Ten Commandments. Ten laws. Ten rules to break. The Israelites were like many of us. They struggled with a sin-repent-sin cycle. In His amazing love and mercy, God provided grace and forgiveness by instituting the sacrificial system. Ultimately it culminated in the sacrifice of Christ, the Lamb of God, who came and took away the sins of the entire world.

Eventually the people began to make a mockery of the very system God used to cover their sin. When they continued unashamedly in their idolatry, God gave them over to that which they wanted so much—to live like pagans. After years and years of warning, God allowed His people to be taken into captivity by the pagan Babylonians. Israel was handed over to a foreign king, removed from the land of promise, and taken into exile with no sense of identity, hope, or purpose.

Have you ever felt as if you were in captivity? Many of us have and do even now. Some of us feel captive inside a body that does not function well or that does not look like we would desire it to look.

Have you ever felt as if your very identity was stripped from you? Have you caught a glimpse of your reflection in a photograph or storefront window and gasped, "Who is that? That can't be me! I am not that size, that shape, or that large!" If this has happened to you, you probably wondered how you got to be that way. It may break your heart, but it also breaks God's heart for you because He wants you to experience His hope, His joy, and His peace. Jesus came that we might have life and have it abundantly (John 10:10).

As He spoke to the Israelites years and years ago, He speaks to us today. There were natural consequences as a result of their choices. Those consequences led to their captivity in Babylon. We, too, as a result of our poor choices, face a "captivity" of sorts. This may be physically manifested in the form of high blood pressure, breathlessness, heart problems, or diabetes. It may also be exhibited in a variety of emotional or spiritual strongholds such as a low self-image.

However, even to those in captivity God offers a promise that the captivity *will* end. For the Israelites, it was seventy years. It can end for us today!

"For I know the plans I have for you," declares the LORD, "plans to prosper you and not to harm you, plans to give you hope and a future."
Jeremiah 29:11

He has plans for you. He has plans to *prosper you* to make you like Himself and to give you a *hope* and a future. We can rest in this

> Many people never allow themselves to experience true stomach hunger.

© 2003, Thin Within, All Rights Reserved

promise. He who has promised is faithful. He is able. He is willing. He says He will do it and He will.

A choice is laid before us. As the Lord spoke to the Israelites through the prophet Jeremiah, He also speaks to us in words that are timeless.

"Then you will call upon me and come and pray to me, and I will listen to you. You will seek me and find me when you seek me with all your heart. I will be found by you,"
declares the LORD,
"and will bring you back from captivity."
Jeremiah 29:12–14a

Consider the number of times the word "will" is used in this brief passage. Look at the things that God desires us to do as well as the things He says He will do. It is God who is at work in us to will and to do according to His good pleasure (Philippians 2:13). In fact, no one comes to Jesus unless the Father draws him (John 6:44). The word translated "draws" can also be translated "drags." No one seeks after God at all according to Romans 3:11. Not even one. We must be "dragged" by the Father in order even to begin to be *willing* to do our part. Because He initiates, He puts it in our heart to will and to do His good pleasure. We love because He first loved us. Our seeking comes in response to a God who pursues.

As we cease from running and respond to God's outstretched arms, we experience the joy of His presence as we choose to say yes to His will for us. He brings the captive out of captivity and restores us to a "land" of hope and promise. We are transformed from *within* by the renewing of our mind according to the Word of God.

Even now, He begins this work in us. Even now we sense that He draws us to Himself. Out of His love for us, He begins a new work.

The LORD appeared to us in the past, saying:
"I have loved you with an everlasting love;
I have drawn you with loving-kindness.
I will build you up again and you will be rebuilt, O Virgin Israel. Again you will take up your tambourines and go out to dance with the joyful.
Jeremiah 31:3–4

We will be free from our captivity. He has a plan, a future, and a hope for us. Let us cast off every hindrance and lay hold of that for which Jesus laid hold of us.

Physiological Information

Your physical transformation will occur primarily through the God-designed mechanism of hunger. Did you know that the Bible teaches that you are one of God's masterpieces (Ephesians 2:10)? It is true. You are His work of art. Psalm 139 teaches that you are fearfully and wonderfully made, an intricate design of mastery and creativity. Therefore you can trust that a loving God who made you knew what He was doing when He placed the natural signals of hunger and satisfaction within you.

Throw out the old ways of thinking about food and your body. Discard the diet laws and fat gram counters, the food measurers, and so on. We will not be constrained by human-made rules (Colossians 2:20–23). Instead, we have at our disposal God's own perfectly designed and fail-proof approach to combating overeating and excess weight.

The Hunger Scale

Those on the Thin Within journey will learn to define their hunger with a tool we call the Hunger Scale. While marvelously simple, we believe you will find utilizing this scale very effective.

To illustrate what the Hunger Scale is, let's walk through the hunger reading exercise. Prayerfully invite God to give you sensitivity to what He wants to show you about your body during this exercise.

Concentrate on your mouth, your throat, your stomach, and your abdomen. In succession, ask yourself the following questions: "What do I hear, feel, taste, or think that I associate with hunger? Is there anything going on in my mouth, throat, stomach, or abdomen that I think indicates I am hungry?"

After focusing on the areas of your body that represent a part of your digestive system, take all of the information that you have just gathered and evaluate whether you are physically hungry. We call this "taking a hunger reading." Are you empty? Are you satisfied? Are you somewhere in between? Are you beyond satisfied? Are you stuffed? In Thin Within, we use the Hunger Scale to define our levels of hunger and fullness.

Although true hunger is physiologically complex, it is consistently associated with a stomach pouch that is empty. The only place you experience true hunger is your stomach. The other sensations that we may call hunger are usually related to other bodily processes. For instance, one participant upon taking a hunger reading realized that if she had a "bad *taste*" in her mouth, she considered it "hunger." It is also a misunderstanding to believe that hunger is only a sound or a "growl." It is a feeling of emptiness in the stomach that may or may not be accompanied by a growl. Hunger sensations emanate from just below your rib cage.

When your stomach is empty, we call that a 0 on the hunger scale. This week you will learn to recognize when you are at your 0.

When you are hungry and choose to eat only to a point of comfort, we call it a 5 on the Hunger Scale. It is when you have had "just enough" and your body does not need more food. A 5 is not "full" or "stuffed." It is "satisfied."

A 10 is that very uncomfortable feeling of needing to unbutton your pants and to lie horizontally. This occurs when we continue to eat beyond the point when our body signals that we have had enough food. This feeling may occur at least every year during Thanksgiving dinner if not more frequently.

As you consistently take hunger readings, you will find your body accurately indicating when it is hungry and full. Your goal will be to eat between 0 and 5 and thereby release excess weight. If you eat between a 3 and a 7, you will most likely stay your current weight and size. If you routinely eat between a 5 and a 10, you will gain weight.

Many people never allow themselves to experience true stomach hunger. It may take up to twenty-four hours or longer to experience a true 0. Just know that the wait will be worth it.

Before you eat, we suggest that you take a hunger reading to determine whether you are, in fact, at a 0. If you find yourself uncertain, we say, "When in doubt, leave it out." If you aren't sure you are hungry—at a 0—we encourage you to wait a while longer until you are certain.

When your body reaches its 0, you have the freedom to eat the food you desire unless your doctor has indicated otherwise. In the days and weeks ahead, you will develop more discernment regarding what most agrees with your body and enables you to feel your best. For now we suggest

that when you eat, sit down, focus on your meal, and eat slowly so that you will be able to recognize when you are approaching that point of "comfort" that we call a 5 on the Hunger Scale.

As you confine your eating to the parameters that God intended when He created you, you will discover many things about yourself and about your relationship with your Creator. Continue to take hunger readings prayerfully throughout the week. Note what your hunger levels are and pray that God will continue to help you to become better acquainted with the amazing biological machinery that is your body!

Integration

One of the most wonderful things about Thin Within is that we rely on the One who has a plan, future, and a hope for us. When we follow God's lead through the Holy Spirit, we can know without a doubt that He never intends harm, but desires only that which is good. While waiting for a 0 may seem challenging, we can gaze steadfastly on our Lord and Savior Jesus Christ who redeemed us from the empty life of endless dieting failures, weight gain, rigid rules, and self-condemnation. The pendulum swing is over. He brought us out of slavery and captivity. He purchased us not with perishable things such as silver or gold, but with His very own precious blood (1 Peter 1:18–19). *What, then, shall we say in response to this? If God is for us, who can be against us? He who did not spare his own Son, but gave him up for us all— how will he not also, along with him, graciously give us all things?* Romans 8:31–32

The Lord does not want you to experience hunger as something negative. Instead He wants you to experience hunger so that you will see your need for Him and experience His awesome ability to meet <u>all</u> your needs according to His purposes. He longs to show you compassion and to pour out His blessings that will come to you as you choose to follow His plan, purpose, and hope. Your future begins now with

---

Definitions:

- <u>Hunger Scale</u> – numbers given to define levels of hunger, 0 for hungry (absolutely empty stomach), 5 for satisfied, 10 for stuffed.
- <u>Hunger Number</u> – used to define a specific level of hunger.
- <u>0 to 5 eating</u> – eating between the parameters of hungry (absolutely empty stomach) and satisfied.

© 2003, Thin Within, All Rights Reserved

Him. Cling to the hope that He offers.

In closing this week's lesson, we want you to know we have prayed and are praying for you:

May the God of hope fill you with all joy and peace as you trust in him, so that you may overflow with hope by the power of the Holy Spirit.
Romans 15:13

I pray also that the eyes of your heart may be enlightened in order that you may know the hope to which he has called you. . . .
Ephesians 1:18a

My Notes

© 2003, Thin Within, All Rights Reserved

LESSON

Introduction To The Exercises

The daily exercises are divided into the following sections:

- **Going Deeper:** This section asks questions that will lead you to a deeper understanding of the material and how the lesson relates to you personally.

- **Bible Study:** This will range from asking you for simple observations of a passage to having you explore the depths of Scripture with comparisons and contrasts.

- **Getting Practical:** In this section you will be given the tools to make the physiological principles of Thin Within real in your daily life.

- **Knowing God by Heart:** Within each week of the foundational material, this section will cover two different attributes of God. You will have opportunity to look for their definitions and synonyms, find them in the Word of God, and finally, allow God to use this study to increase your knowledge, understanding, and trust in Him.

- **Memory Challenge:** God's Word is a lamp unto our feet and a light unto our path. By memorizing pertinent Scriptures you will never find yourself without His light to guide you when times become difficult.

- **Review of the Week:** Space is provided at the end of the week to prepare for your support group meeting. Since the majority of Thin Within members will be actively involved in a group, our hope is that this review will help you make the most out of your meeting.

- **Support Group Meeting Notes:** Use this section to make notes during your support group meeting and refer to it during the following week.

Knowing God

Our desire at Thin Within is to point you to the only One who can make a permanent and eternal difference in your life. He is the TRUE God and He wants to have a deep and close relationship with each one of us. Part of building that closeness is getting to know our Creator and allowing the knowledge and understanding of who He really is to permeate our hearts as He transforms us from the inside out. Many of the problems that we face with food or weight come from an inaccurate picture of who God is and of our relationship to Him. By gaining clarity on the character of God, it is our hope that the core issues that underlie our struggles with food and weight may be resolved.

The attitude of your heart is critical as you approach each day's exercise. This is not about working to earn favor, nor is it a contest to see who can do the most. It is about walking closer with God each day and following His will—spiritually, emotionally, and physically. You might want to pray this as a prayer each day before starting the exercises to help keep your motives pure and your focus on God.

Please don't condemn yourself for questions you don't answer or charts you don't fill out. If your schedule forces you to skip a day, that is OK. Yield your will to God and He will guide you in this process and you will not be disappointed as you trust in Him.

© 2003, Thin Within, All Rights Reserved

Day One

Starting Today...

- At any given point in time, notice where you are on the Hunger Scale and recognize when your body is truly hungry.
- Ask God for strength to wait until you are stomach hungry (0 on the Hunger Scale) before you eat.
- When you reach that point of stomach hunger (0), eat the foods you enjoy without being preoccupied with the diet rules of the past (for example, counting calories, fat grams, carbohydrates, or protein).
- As you eat, be attentive to that point of satisfaction, 5 on the Hunger Scale and respectfully stop eating.
- Allow your conscience and the Holy Spirit to convict you as you are being conformed to the likeness of Christ.
- Take time daily for Bible study and prayer and invite God to speak to you through His Word.

Going Deeper

Hope is defined in the dictionary as "desire accompanied by expectation of or belief in fulfillment." Into what kinds of things have you been putting hope?

Hope that my eating + appearance don't matter to God, Myself or anyone else. Hope my eating will "fix itself" w/ out my effort.

Bible Study

Promote the renewing of your mind by making time each day to open the Bible and study it, even if you read only a couple of verses. Romans 15:4 says that the Scriptures were written to teach us and give us hope. Read Jeremiah 29:11 and replace the word "you" with your own name, then write down what God's Word says to you. (Example: "For I know the plans I have for 'Linda,' plans to prosper 'Linda')

God can bring me back from the captivity of my own doing of over eating, emotional eating, drinking too much, avoiding reality + truth. He can and wants to show me the prison doors are open for me to walk through into freedom.

© 2003, Thin Within, All Rights Reserved

EXERCISES

Knowing God by Heart: Love

We know also that the Son of God has come and has given us understanding, so that we may know him who is true. And we are in him who is true—even in his Son Jesus Christ. He is the true God and eternal life.
1 John 5:20

For the next three days, we are going to look at how God is love so that you can experience understanding and knowing God in a tangible way. The goal is to have a change of heart so that you might come to know the One who loves you, forgives you, and promises not only eternal life but abundant life! The more we discover who He is and discover His ways, the deeper we can grow in Him to reflect His glory.

Look up the word "love" in the dictionary and write down a definition that you believe is consistent with God being love. Read 1 John 4:16 and relate your definition to this Scripture.

Fond affection, commitment to someone or something, loyalty to. God is love. He loved us 1st + sent His precious Son as a sacrifice for us, our sins, our redemption, our eternity.

Getting Practical

Look at the section in this week's lesson that explains the Hunger Scale. Find your hunger number right now and evaluate whether or not you are physically hungry. Decide if you are empty, satisfied, beyond satisfied, or somewhere in between. Write down what you discover.

I'm empty but it isn't overwhelming or something I should satisfy b/c I want to eat a good dinner in a couple hrs. I want to be hungry then.

Memory Challenge

In an effort to begin dwelling on the new work that God has planned for you in the weeks ahead, start memorizing Isaiah 43:18–19. Take time to see the message proclaimed in this Scripture. Read the verses out loud several times and then look away and say them from memory. (Note: For your convenience, a separate sheet of memory verse cards are included along with this workbook to cut out and carry with you throughout the week.)

Forget the former things; do not dwell on the past. See, I am doing a new thing!
Now it springs up; do you not perceive it? I am making a way in the desert and streams in the wasteland.
Isaiah 43:18–19

Thin Within Tip

Once you reach 0, sit down and pay attention to your food so that you won't be distracted from the Lord's provision for you. This will also help you recognize when you are approaching that point of "comfort" that we call 5 on the Hunger Scale.

   © 2003, Thin Within, All Rights Reserved

Day Two

Going Deeper

This week's lesson refers to a performance-based pendulum swing. One side represents the pride associated with an ability to lose weight through sheer self-effort, and the other side depicts the extreme of giving up on the weight loss effort and eating everything in sight. Have you had any experience with these two extremes? How does this cycle contribute to a feeling of hopelessness?

Yes, Every year of my adult life basically. I feel like everything I do ends up not working to help me feel satisfied. I am never at peace w/ eating and

Bible Study *and my weight.*

Along with daily Bible study, go to God in prayer and invite Him to speak to you through His Word and the Holy Spirit who indwells all who belong to Christ (Romans 8:9). God uses His living and active Word to convict and call us to righteous choices (Hebrews 4:12). Read Ephesians 2:4–9. Note the things that God has done for you. According to verse 4, why has He done all this? Read Ephesians 1:3–8 and replace the word "us" with your own name. Try to put into words how all these verses speak to your heart.

I have been saved from always doing what my body + mind want me to do, I'm to obey God — not my fleshy mind when its contrary to

Knowing God by Heart *God's will.*

We continue to grow in our knowledge of God by looking at 1 Corinthians 13. Since God is love, replace the word "love" with God in verses 4–8. Record how God reveals Himself to you. Use this revelation of God to guide you in worship of Him.

____
____
____
____

Getting Practical

Journal as you reflect on the last twenty-four hours. As you have paid specific attention to your body and your hunger numbers, what have you discovered? Have you been able to find 0? Write down your body's specific indications of hunger. If you are having difficulty finding hunger, pray right now and ask God to help you wait it out until you have most definitely found hunger (provided you have no health conditions that would cause any adverse effects).

empty stomach, hard to stop thinking about it,

Memory Challenge

Continue memorizing Isaiah 43:18–19 by saying or writing it several times. After some repetition, try repeating it from memory. Take the memory verse card with you and refer to it throughout the day.

© 2003, Thin Within, All Rights Reserved

EXERCISES

Day Three

Going Deeper

Do you feel as if you are held captive by food and eating? How has this area of your life kept you from doing all that God has planned for you?

Control by my desires, out of control. I have been disobedient, felt guilty, hid myself due to shame over appearance, been irritable + cranky

Bible Study

Read Jeremiah 29:12–14a. What does it show you about God's deliverance from any captivity that you may be experiencing? Read Jeremiah 31:3, Ephesians 1:5, and Zephaniah 3:17. Write down what these Scriptures say about God's view of you and His plan for your life.

God chose me, he celebrates + sings because of me. I can be trusted to work good in my life even thru discipline

Knowing God by Heart

Find synonyms for the word "love" in a thesaurus or at end of the definition in the dictionary (abbreviated as syn.). How do these words give you a deeper understanding of God as love? Read 1 John 4:8–10, 19 and John 3:16. What do these Scriptures tell you about God?

He shows true joy by giving of himself for us

Getting Practical

Keep the phrase "when in doubt, leave it out" in mind as you wait for hunger. It is easy to convince yourself that you are hungry when you may in fact be a 1 or 2 on the hunger scale. Prayerfully invite God to direct you when you are uncertain or in doubt. Make a prepared plan for those times of doubt, so that you will be ready when you are bombarded by the overwhelming desire to eat.

2–5 pm + after dinner high stress w/ kids, school. Verse cards good reminders.

Memory Challenge

Review Isaiah 43:18–19 until you can repeat it from memory.

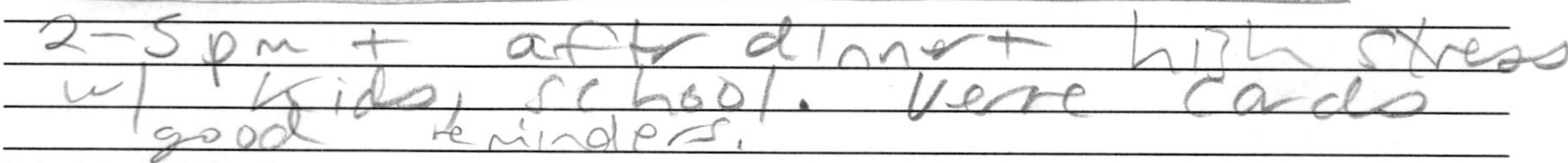

Thin Within Tip

Start out with half portions of the food you normally eat and determine if that satisfies you.

© 2003, Thin Within, All Rights Reserved

Day Four

Going Deeper

What brings you satisfaction? Write about the times when food does and does not satisfy you, and why you think this is true.

When truly hungry / when I go to it for "comfort" or when I'm not physically hungry

Bible Study

Read Psalm 145:14–16. Where does true satisfaction come from? What do these verses reveal to you about how God is concerned with the intricate details of your life? Psalm 63:1–5 paints vivid word pictures to illustrate what God wants us to experience in Him. Write your thoughts.

when the time is right you provide them w/ food. By your own hand you satisfy desires of living thing

Knowing God by Heart: Jealous

Look up the word "jealous" in the dictionary and write down a definition that you believe is consistent with God being jealous. (We often think of jealous in the negative terms of resentment and envy. But God's attribute of being jealous is one of not tolerating rivalry, competition, or unfaithfulness. It is being vigilant to guard a precious possession.) Read Exodus 34:14 and relate your definition to this Scripture.

He wants my love. He doesn't want me to love God like I should love Him. Wants me to turn to Him not food when in need of help

Getting Practical

In your quest to find hunger, have you discovered anything about yourself and your desire for food and eating? Journal on this topic. Make note of anything new you have discovered regarding your body's response to hunger.

All day I consider running to food or al cohol. Constant mental + spiritual battle. I have hard time stopping. Easier waiting.

Memory Challenge

Repeat Isaiah 43:18–19 from memory. Turn these verses into a prayer for yourself or someone you know.

© 2003, Thin Within, All Rights Reserved

EXERCISES

Day Five

Going Deeper

Identify the benefits of waiting for hunger.

____
____
____
____

Bible Study

Read Romans 5:8 and replace the word "us" and "we" with your own name. Write a prayer of response to God for the love He has shown you. In Psalm 139:1–6, find the extent of God's care and knowledge of you and journal your thoughts.

____
____
____
____

Knowing God by Heart

Continue to grow in your knowledge of how God is jealous by reading Exodus 20:5–6 and write your thoughts.

____
____
____
____

Getting Practical

Why do you think that diets don't work and have such a high failure rate? Name some diets that you have done, or seen others do, and note if you considered any of them a success.

____
____
____
____

Memory Challenge

Meditate on Isaiah 43:18–19 throughout the day and allow it to draw you closer to God. Ask Him to help you truly believe this Scripture so that it can set you free from all the deceptive lies of the world.

Thin Within Tip

Realize that beverages (including coffee, tea, soda, milk, sports drinks, and juices), mints, hard candy, and chewing gum all change your hunger number because your body takes everything into account. Consuming these things while waiting for hunger will keep you from reaching zero or will often give false hunger signals. Water, on the other hand, will only change your hunger number for a very short period of time. We encourage you to replace some of the other habit-forming beverages with water.

© 2003, Thin Within, All Rights Reserved

Day Six – Optional Exercises

Note that two days of each week's exercises are labeled "optional" exercises. These are provided for times when your schedule gets the best of you and you need a break. While we encourage you to work through all of the daily exercises, if you feel you need a break, take one. However, a break from these optional exercises does not mean a break from conscious eating. Continue to invite God to be part of this area of your life as you eat from 0 to 5.

Going Deeper

How would you define "abundant life"? Have you ever experienced it?

____

____

____

____

Bible Study

Read John 10:10. What do you think Jesus meant by "abundant" or "full" life? According to Hebrews 10:22–23, where can we find the hope of abundant life? Journal about hope after reading Romans 15:13 and Colossians 1:27.

____

____

____

____

Knowing God by Heart

Find words that are synonyms with the word "vigilant" and "guard" in a thesaurus or at the end of the definition in the dictionary. How do these words give you a more complete understanding of God as jealous? Read James 4:5–6. What do these Scriptures tell you about God?

____

____

____

____

Getting Practical

What is the hardest part of finding hunger? Take this to the Lord in prayer. What is the best part of finding hunger? Rejoice in the Lord at this observation.

____

____

____

____

Memory Challenge

Repeat Isaiah 43:18–19 out loud and ask God to make these verses real in your life. What might God be leading you to "be" or to "do" in response to this passage?

© 2003, Thin Within, All Rights Reserved

EXERCISES

Day Seven – Optional Exercises

Going Deeper

Have you ever felt like you sought God and He didn't answer you? Jeremiah 29:12–13 promises that He will listen and answer. Why you do suppose there are times when God seems distant?

____

____

____

____

Bible Study

Do you believe God's promise in Jeremiah 29:12–13? If not, take your unbelief to Him. According to John 8:32, how will we be set free? Journal on what you would like to see happen in the days and weeks ahead concerning "truth" in your life.

____

____

____

____

Getting Practical

Now that you have had a whole week of practice, define hunger (0) according to your own body's response. You do not need to be concerned with or to compare yourself with another's experience. Simply come to understand your body and how God has crafted you. Pray that God will establish a consistent pattern within you of eating when your body is truly hungry.

____

____

____

____

Memory Challenge

Share your memory verse with a friend or family member, telling him or her how it relates to your Thin Within journey.

Thin Within Tip

You can plan your hunger by:

- not eating all the way to a 5. If you reach a 0 at 2:00 P.M. in the afternoon and dinner is at 6:00 P.M., you can wait or perhaps have a very small amount of food (for example, half of a banana or a few almonds) that will take you off of 0. By dinner you will be empty and ready to enjoy a nice meal.
- delaying when you eat for a period of time.
- adjusting the kind of foods you eat. Different foods vary in how well they satisfy you.

  © 2003, Thin Within, All Rights Reserved

Review of the Week

Take time at the end of each week to review what God has taught you and how it is impacting your life. This will give you a great overview to take to your Thin Within Support Group Meeting.

The most significant thing God taught me this week:

The scripture memory verse this week said: "See I am doing a new thing!... Do you not perceive it?" The "new thing" God is doing in my life is:

This gives me hope because:

My experience in waiting for and finding hunger (0) this first week of Thin Within:

The most significant thing that God helped me to observe this week that I will focus on correcting next week:

What I have learned about the character of God as love and jealous, and how I have come to know and be drawn closer to him:

My prayer requests and praises:

© 2003, Thin Within, All Rights Reserved

LESSON

My Body—God's Temple

Introduction

Last week we had the opportunity of hearing God whisper His song of love and freedom to our hearts. We discovered that, like His people in ages past, God has promised us a hope, a plan, and a future. We can choose to begin to live that plan now—in this present moment. We don't need to wait to begin to experience the fullness of the resurrected life that He desires for us.

We also discussed that as we trust Him, we will begin to discover that the body He has given us is reliable. He directs us to freedom from captivity to food and eating through the cues of hunger and satisfaction as we continue to listen to Him. Last week you were introduced to the Hunger Scale and challenged to wait for a 0 before eating.

You will have the joy of seeing your body transformed by responding to these God-given cues of 0 to 5 eating. Perhaps you have already begun to experience some exciting changes as well as the melting away of excess weight. Additionally, you will be transformed from within by the renewing of your mind according to the living Word of God.

Spiritual Foundation

Your body is, in fact, the temple of God Almighty—His dwelling place on earth!

Do you not know that your body is a temple of the Holy
Spirit, who is in you, whom you have received from God?
You are not your own; you were bought at a price.
Therefore honor God with your body.
1 Corinthians 6:19–20

We want to cooperate with God in His work to restore this temple—your body—to its God-ordained splendor so that it truly reflects His glory. Your body is fearfully and wonderfully made (Psalm 139). It is also a container of the glory of God. In fact, your hope and future described in Jeremiah 29:11 are intricately linked to this truth: Christ in you *is* the *hope* of *glory* (Colossians 1:27).

Christ indwelling each of us is both the provision and the power of God's transforming grace. Christ came that we might have life—His life in us. He wants us to have His abundant life, His resurrection life pressed down and overflowing. Remember Thin Within is not just about your weight; it's about your life. He gave up

His life so that you could experience the fullness of His resurrection life within you.

As you receive this truth that Christ is in you, you will be on your way to experiencing reconciliation with your God-given body. As you are led away from the empty flesh-filled way of life to relying on Spirit-filled eating, you will begin to see your physical body as an amazing container for God's glory.

First, however, if we are to lay a solid foundation for stewardship of our bodies, we must evaluate and clear away any rubble—anything in our lives that might stand in the way of building and restoring these temples with honor to the Lord. One thing that can act as "rubble" in our restoration process is "heart hunger."

Heart hunger can be experienced as an even stronger pull than stomach hunger. Its roots go much deeper. Our glorious Creator made us in His own image. God exists in three persons—in close intimate fellowship that is beyond the full comprehension of the human mind—as Father, Son, and Holy Spirit. Having been made in God's image, we also *need* intimacy with *Him*. He designed us to be containers for His presence and glory as we have just discussed. Many of us hunger for God, but we don't realize that He alone can fill our needs. We often don't make the connection between what is drawing us to food and our compelling need for intimacy with God.

The psalmist identified that the Lord would totally and completely satisfy our inner longing:

My soul thirsts for God, for the living God.
When can I go and meet with God?
Psalm 42:2

O God, you are my God, earnestly I seek you;
my soul thirsts for you, my body longs for you,
in a dry and weary land where there is no water.
Psalm 63:1

The psalmist uses the imagery of thirst, a universal image to which most of us can relate. Later the image of hunger is used and God is his food—his "portion."

Whom have I in heaven but you?
And earth has nothing I desire besides you.
My flesh and my heart may fail,
but God is the strength of my heart and my portion forever.
Psalm 73:25–26

Yes, our Sovereign Lord is truly the living water that will quench our deepest thirst. He is the bread of life that satisfies the silent, relentless hunger of our souls and our hearts.

© 2003, Thin Within, All Rights Reserved

God intends that all our needs be met in relationship with Him. Until we are born again through faith in Christ (John 3:16), we go through life desperately trying to meet our own needs through our own strength or resources. Even after accepting Christ, three enemies—the world, the flesh (our selfish desires), and the devil—constantly call us to live independently from God, to continue to try to meet our own needs through our own resources. They tempt us to seek fulfillment apart from a relationship with the God who is the only One who can truly satisfy us. There is an incessant pull from these enemies, enticing us to do our own thing. They lure us to settle for a counterfeit fulfillment that is disconnected from our only true Source. Heart hunger is a deep demand that screams to be met, but food can't fill the place that God created to be filled by Him.

As you continue to embrace the truth that your body is the temple of God's Holy Spirit, you will want to be aware of the privilege, as well as the responsibility, that stewardship entails. We see in the Old Testament that God held the kings responsible for the physical temple. He called King Solomon to build the temple in Jerusalem. God gave a detailed, intricate plan for its design and mandated the finest and choicest of metals and materials to go into making His chosen dwelling place on earth. The temple of God was an elaborately beautiful structure—precious and valuable, just as each of us is today!

Following Solomon's reign, Israel was divided into a northern kingdom (Israel) and a southern kingdom (Judah), each with a king. The temple was located in Judah. God called the leaders of His people to be responsible for the temple and to maintain the worship of the one true God. He measured the success of each king accordingly. Did the king lead the people into worship of Jehovah God or did he lead them into rebellion? By these standards, the northern kingdom was without a godly king throughout its history. Judah, however, was blessed with several kings who sought to honor the temple as well as to establish and maintain godly worship.

Manasseh was considered one of the worst kings in the history of Judah. He rebuilt all the high places of idol worship that his father,

Hezekiah, had torn down, and even desecrated the temple with his idols. He neglected the house of the Lord and the things of God, and led the people of Judah into idolatry, rebellion, and sin. He was contemptuous of the things of God and allowed God's temple to fall into complete ruin.

Unfortunately, if we are honest, some of us can identify with this attitude of contempt toward our bodies, not recognizing that we are indeed the temple of a Holy God. Some have neglected, even desecrated or abused their bodies by the choices they have made. And some, like Manasseh, have built "high places" of idol worship that consume the attention, adoration, and devotion which was intended for God. We often think of idols as only Old Testament poles or bizarre-looking statues to which people bow down. But anything we constantly think about or run to for comfort and companionship is an idol. Anything we put before Almighty God. A long and yet incomplete list of twenty-first century idols includes: accumulation of possessions, pornography, overspending, alcohol, preoccupation with food, sports, television, body image, and the praise of people. So do you have an idol in your heart? "Therefore, my dearly beloved, shun (keep clear away from, avoid by flight if need be) any sort of idolatry (of loving or venerating anything more than God." I Cor. 10:14 AMP)

You see God does take this business of idolatry very seriously! In fact, idolatry is akin to spiritual adultery: as if we're married to God but trying to bring into the marriage bed another lover. This must not be!

The Book of Hosea is a beautiful illustration of how God longs to have our hearts devoted solely to Him, a pure and beautiful bride that yearns for Him alone. He wants us to separate ourselves from our idols so we are free to worship and adore Him! "What agreement (can there be between) a temple of God and idols: For we are the temple of the living God; even as God said, I will dwell in and with and among them and will walk in and with and among them, and I will be their God, and they shall be my people."(2 Cor. 6:16 AMP)

As sad and convicting as Manasseh's

> He is the bread of life that satisfies the silent, relentless hunger of our souls and our hearts.

© 2003, Thin Within, All Rights Reserved

story is, we can be encouraged that in the end even he was humbled and brought to repentance because ultimately God will have His way. The Lord, in His mercy and grace, heard Manasseh's prayer, and he was allowed to repair the temple, and bring Judah back to worshiping the Lord. We learn that it is never too late, no matter how low we have sunk, if we turn to God in authentic repentance. He gives grace to the humble and cleanses us by the precious blood of the Lamb.

Herod the Great, King of Israel at the time of the birth of Christ, spent forty-six years building a magnificent temple in Jerusalem. His motive in building the temple, however, was not for the glory of God, but rather for his own glory and recognition.

Herod was a cruel, jealous, power-hungry madman. He ordered the slaughter of all the male children in Bethlehem under the age of two after Jesus was born, seeking to eradicate the promised Messiah who was to be born "King of the Jews" (Matthew 2:16). He built the temple to appease the Jews whom he had alienated by his cruelty.

He idolized the temple, took great pride in it, and spent the major part of his life constructing it, but not for the worship and glory of God. In fact, when God sent His only Son to dwell among us, Herod saw Him as a rival to his throne and sought to have Him killed.

This was quite a different attitude than we observed in Manasseh. Rather than contempt for the temple, Herod was prideful of his own accomplishment. We can easily go from one extreme of contempt to the other extreme of pride. This is where the pendulum of the flesh will naturally swing, causing us to miss that place of humility, repentance, and dependence on God to which He calls us. Can you relate? We may be painstakingly attending to our bodies but not acknowledging the fact that God Almighty indwells us and we are not our own. In order to honor God with our bodies, it is essential that we humble ourselves and seek a godly perspective.

Josiah, Manasseh's grandson, had an attitude of humility and repentance that is an excellent example for us. We find his story in 2 Chronicles 34 and 35. He was only eight years old when he became king, and he reigned in Jerusalem for thirty-one years.

When Josiah came to the throne, there was much rebellion and idolatry in the land. In the eighth year of his reign, however, he began to seek the Lord and in the twelfth year, he began to purge the temple and land of all idols. In the eighteenth year of his reign, the Book of the Law was found in the temple. When Josiah heard of it, he tore his clothes and wept. He then went about restoring true worship of God in the temple, leading all the people back to the Lord to observe Passover. Here we see an attitude of humility and repentance as well as maturity. Josiah first recognized the ruin of the temple, began to seek the Lord, and purged the land and the temple of idols. He then heard the law read, was convicted, tore his clothes and wept, and brought the nation back to the Lord.

This is the heart attitude we must seek. It all begins with the recognition of the idols in our lives and the ruin of the temple. Let us humbly seek a gracious God, knowing He desires restoration through the power of the Holy Spirit. Are you ready to ask God to search your heart dear one? Listen to the voice of your Father calling you back into His arms. If you have put any earthly thing in His rightful place in your heart, be it food, lust, praise of man, etc then you have an idol in your heart and this must not be! You can not cling to an idol and cling to God at the same time. God wants to be your one and only. He longs to fill all of the empty places you've tried to fill with other things. He alone can satisfy ALL of your needs.

What are the idols in your life? What is your attitude toward your body, God's dwelling place? Have you treated it with the honor and respect due the temple of God?

Our bodies are God's intricate, miraculous creation into which He chooses to breathe His sovereign breath (Genesis 2:7). Each of us is uniquely created by the hand of God, and we are fearfully and wonderfully made (Psalm 139).

Do you desire to embrace this truth, to come to terms with it, and to be at peace with what God has declared *is true?* We can choose to believe Him and what He says about us. As we do, we will be reconciled to our physical body.

Those who consider their body to be more of an enemy than a friend may find this process of reconciliation to be a real challenge—perhaps, an unrealistic expectation. However, be encouraged, for all things are possible with God.

A Thin Within participant shares her story:

"At the time I attended the one-day workshop, I had regained about a third of the sixty

© 2003, Thin Within, All Rights Reserved

pounds I had lost in another program. Although I was very familiar with the message of waiting for true hunger and stopping when satisfied, I hoped to glean some additional insight that God would use to somehow turn on the light and enable me to get stable once again. I was not to be disappointed! There were several new insights that the Holy Spirit hit my heart with that day which truly impacted my life.

"Early in the workshop I was asked to participate in the 'Body Awareness Exercise.' This exercise is printed in the back of the *Thin Again* book. I had read it and promptly dismissed it, thinking it was nothing I needed to do. It seemed sort of weird. Well, I was sitting in the front row at the workshop and didn't want to appear to be uncooperative, so when I was asked to stand and close my eyes, I went along with it and didn't feel too dumb, because everyone else was doing it too. We were asked to consider each area of our bodies. Starting with our feet, we slowly proceeded reflecting on our thoughts and feelings about how each part of our body had served us over the years, and then to express gratitude to God for each part. I have to tell you—I entered into this very skeptical, but soon found myself completely broken before my God.

"As I continued the exercise I realized that my first thought was one of finding fault, ingratitude, or disgust. I had never looked the way I wanted, and I hated my body and myself for not being able to whip it into shape. When I was asked to focus on my calves, the Holy Spirit immediately brought to mind a lady at my church who had artificial limbs. I was completely overwhelmed with both a keen sense of gratitude that I had healthy strong legs and also a very real sense of shame and deep conviction that I had never thanked God for them. I had hated them and much of the rest of my body. For as long as I could remember I had focused on, magnified, and despised every flaw.

"The discussion that followed included how shame for our bodies entered humanity at the fall. However, God fearfully and wonderfully made our bodies in His image. To hate my body was to hate or have contempt for the things of God. Wow, that truth hit me with a mighty blow I'll never forget. I had held in contempt the things of God, the gift of God—my body, fearfully and wonderfully made by Him, created in His image and designed to be His temple—a display of His splendor! It's almost impossible to be a good

steward over something you hate, to take care of something you wish you didn't have.

"During this realization I was convicted of the abuse of bingeing, purging, and compulsive overeating that I had inflicted on my body. I had to separate that abuse and its effects from the vessel that God had lovingly created. God has created us in His image and purposed to dwell in each of us the moment we receive Christ as our Savior, whether we are a size 6 or a 26. He has placed tremendous honor and value on our bodies. I was inspired by the Spirit of God to gratefully embrace the body He uniquely designed especially for me, to lovingly take responsibility for it, and seek to honor God with it. I experienced a breakthrough, a new beginning with my body that day and God has begun to replace my negativity, criticism, and contempt with an attitude of gratitude—and in the process I have managed to release that weight I had regained!"

You, too, can experience the blessing of reconciling with your physical body as you walk through the Body Exercise below.

Physiological Information

Body Awareness Exercise

Begin by thanking God for reconciling you to Him through the sacrifice that Jesus made on the cross. Thank Him that your body belongs to Him and is a special container, a temple of the Holy Spirit. Take a moment to thank Him for the blessings of the gift of life. It may be a stretch for some; however, consider anything for which you can be thankful. Express this in a prayer of thanksgiving to God.

Turn your attention now to your body. Beginning at your toes and working your way up, ponder purposefully the way in which each part of your body has been hand-crafted and created by the Lord for your use in this world as you serve Him and others. Consider the function, structure, and formation of your toes, feet, lower legs, knees, upper legs, hips, thighs, stomach, chest, back, shoulders, neck, arms, hands, head, face, and hair. Consider all the ways in which your body has served you in order to perform tasks, recreational pursuits, worship, and service. Thank God specifically for each body part. You may find you have a lot to say about a specific part of your body. God wants to hear it all. Just remember that your main focus is thankfulness and praise to God for your body.

If you feel as if you can't do this because

© 2003, Thin Within, All Rights Reserved

LESSON

of the disdain you have for your body, pray that God will give you His perspective. He formed and made you. We know that He doesn't look at our outer appearance, but on the heart (1 Samuel 16:7). There is a lot to be said for doing something with an act of your will. We want to encourage you to step out in faith, demonstrating proper respect, regardless of size and shape, for the container that holds the priceless contents of God's own matchless presence.

As examples of what we have in mind, consider how much is required of your knees. How have they served you? Sustaining your weight, bending and straightening to propel you, springing you up when you played as a child or as an adult, and enabling you to sit down. There are many reasons to be thankful for functioning knees!

And your face—it is so expressive. It can reflect joy. It can express concern for a loved one. So many things can be said with a face.

Your hands have enabled you to serve others: your family, your friends, and your coworkers. In what ways have your hands been a blessing? Thank God for each and every way your hands have served you.

As you do this exercise, take careful mental note of your thoughts and feelings. We will ask you to journal about the Body Awareness Exercise this week.

During the past week, you focused on waiting for a 0 before eating. However, recognizing a 5, the place of just enough, may be even more of a challenge. Many of us routinely bypass this place of just satisfied.

Amazingly enough, your stomach when empty is about the size of your clenched fist. Consequently, eating that amount of food is often an effective measure for finding that comfortable point of satisfaction. This visual tool of a "fist" is a great aid in stopping at 5. As you adjust your portions to match the natural capacity of your stomach, you will take care of the needs of your body. When you eat past a 5, you have entered into overindulgence, otherwise known as the lust of the flesh. If we are honest, food begins to lose its appeal when we eat past a 5. It is the law of diminishing returns (Proverbs 27:7).

When you eat from a 0 to a 5, you will release excess weight until you reach your natural God-given size and you will maintain that size by continuing to eat 0 to 5. However, if you don't get in touch with your body and your internal scale and eat from a 3 to a 7, you will stay overweight.

Eating from a 5 to a 10 on the Hunger Scale will cause you to gain weight.

We can see how in touch and obedient we are responding to our internal hunger scale by looking at the results reflected in our bodies. We may think we have cut back in the amount of food we are eating, but if we are not releasing weight, then the truth is we are not waiting for a 0 or stopping at a 5. We are probably only waiting for a 2 or 3 on the Hunger Scale and eating beyond a 5 to a 6 or 7. The results will be reflected in your body and will be clear and undeniable. The good news is we can observe and correct as we get back on the road to godly eating at any given moment.

Integration

Having looked at and evaluated the attitude of the three kings toward the temple of God, we can choose which attitude we will adopt. Will it be one of disdain and contempt? This would be demonstrated by overeating and continuing in behaviors that maintain being overweight or being underweight, or other related health challenges.

Will it be one of pride, where our focus is on what *we* can accomplish in our own strength without recognition or regard for the power of God who enables us?

Or will we, like Josiah, a man of God, who chose an attitude of high regard and respect, honor the temple that God carefully crafted, as we eat with a mind and a heart that is surrendered to Him?

As you reconcile with your body, truly thank the Lord for the way it has enabled you to serve Him, serve others, and enjoy life. He has made your body a wonderful masterpiece, and He has chosen to live within you so that all may see Him through you.

God is faithful and His power and promises to us endure forever. He desires to transform our lives and we can be confident that He will do it by His amazing grace.

. . . He who began a good work in you will carry it on to completion until the day of Christ Jesus.
Philippians 1:6

Our God is a God who promises to remain true to His Word. He is at work in you even now. He has been faithful throughout all of history, keeping His promises to all generations. He will do the same for you as you allow Him to fall afresh on your heart and your life.

© 2003, Thin Within, All Rights Reserved

My Notes

© 2003, Thin Within, All Rights Reserved

EXERCISES

Day One

Going Deeper

What comes to mind when you think of the temple of God? Do you see your body as a temple honoring God? Why or why not?

____

____

____

____

Bible Study

Read 1 Corinthians 6:19–20. What is God's provision for you to have a temple that honors Him?

____

____

____

____

Knowing God by Heart: Sovereign

I keep asking that the God of our Lord Jesus Christ, the glorious Father,
may give you the Spirit of wisdom and revelation, <u>so that you may know him better.</u>
Ephesians 1:17

As we journey through the next eleven weeks and learn more about God, continue to seek what He specifically wants you to apply to your life from this knowledge so that it can transform you from within. Look up the word "sovereign" in the dictionary and write down a definition that you believe is consistent with God being sovereign. Read Isaiah 40:10–14, 21–26 and relate your definition to these Scriptures.

____

____

____

____

Getting Practical

At this point, how would you define satisfaction (5 on the hunger scale)? Ask God to give you wisdom on this during the week and reveal to you the amount of food that your body requires in order to experience being comfortable or satisfied. Commit your attitude and choices to God as you honor your body, God's temple.

____

____

____

____

Memory Challenge

Start memorizing 1 Corinthians 6:19–20. Take time to see the message proclaimed in this Scripture. Read the verses out loud several times, then look away and say them from memory.

Do you not know that your body is a temple of the Holy Spirit, who is in you, whom you have received from God?
You are not your own; you were bought at a price. Therefore honor God with your body.
1 Corinthians 6:19–20

Thin Within Tip

Get rid of legalistic diet books and diet paraphernalia so that you won't be tempted to return to them. Good solid books on nutrition and health, however, may be helpful for your reference.

© 2003, Thin Within, All Rights Reserved

Day Two

Going Deeper

Rather than wood or stone idols, there may be idols of the heart that replace your affections for God. Ask God to help you see and list anything in your life that is a barrier to accepting His love, provision, and correction.

____
____
____
____

Bible Study

Read 2 Chronicles 14:2–4 and 15:8. What do these verses say about the path of restoration and reform? What does James 4:8–10 say we are called to as this restoration process takes place? What do you think it means to be humble before the Lord?

____
____
____
____

Knowing God by Heart

Continue to grow in your knowledge of God by reading Psalm 135:5–6 and Daniel 4:35. What do these verses say to you about God's sovereignty?

____
____
____
____

Getting Practical

When you eat, begin to look intently at the different sensations you experience in your body from the point of hunger (0) to the end of each meal.   Stop at least once during the meal and evaluate your hunger number. Allow the Spirit to have the final say. If you are passing 5, pray and respond to the convicting call of the Holy Spirit.

____
____
____
____

Memory Challenge

Continue memorizing 1 Corinthians 6:19–20 by saying or writing it several times. After some repetition, try repeating it from memory. Take the memory verse card with you and refer to it throughout the day.

© 2003, Thin Within, All Rights Reserved

EXERCISES

Day Three

Going Deeper

If you have not taken the time to do the Body Awareness Exercise described in the Physiological Information section, please consider doing it today. Write down the observations and discoveries from the exercise.

____
____
____
____

Bible Study

Read 2 Chronicles 7:14 and reflect on what it says to do in order to receive God's healing.

____
____
____
____

Knowing God by Heart

Find synonyms for the word "sovereign" in a thesaurus or dictionary. How do these words give you a deeper understanding of God as sovereign? Read Ephesians 1:20–23 and Romans 9:20–23. What do these Scriptures tell you about God?

____
____
____
____

Getting Practical

As you anticipate a 5 (just comfortable or satisfied) in your eating this week, read Proverbs 27:7. What is one sure sign that you have gone past comfortable? Did you ever imagine that your taste buds were primed to enhance the flavor of food when you are hungry and then lose the desirable effect when you have reached satisfied? If you are having trouble refraining from going past 5, ask God to show you specifically where your stopping place is today, and record how He answers your prayer.

____
____
____
____

Memory Challenge

Review 1 Corinthians 6:19–20 until you can repeat it from memory.

Thin Within Tip

Pray before you eat and invite God to have the final word as to when to stop at the point of satisfaction.

© 2003, Thin Within, All Rights Reserved

Day Four

Going Deeper

Have you observed any thoughts of disdain or pride regarding your body, God's temple? Ask God for a healthy perspective of your body.

____

____

____

____

Bible Study

Read Psalm 139:1–16 and reflect on how God has made you. When God looks at you, what is He really looking at (1 Samuel 16:7)?

____

____

____

____

Knowing God by Heart: Good

Look up the word "good" in the dictionary and write down a definition that you believe is consistent with God being good. Read Psalm 31:19 and relate your definition to this Scripture.

____

____

____

____

Getting Practical

What is the most difficult part about stopping at the point of satisfaction? How can you overcome that challenge?

____

____

____

____

Memory Challenge

Repeat 1 Corinthians 6:19–20 from memory. Turn these verses into a prayer for yourself or someone you know.

© 2003, Thin Within, All Rights Reserved

EXERCISES

Day Five

Going Deeper

Journal on developing a godly perspective for the container (your body) that holds the priceless contents of God's own matchless presence.

____
____
____
____

Bible Study

Pray Psalm 51:10–12, asking God to purify your heart, giving you steadfastness and the willingness to do things His way.

____
____
____
____

Knowing God by Heart

Continue growing in knowledge of how God is good by reading Psalm 25:8 and Romans 2:4. Find out where His goodness leads. Write your thoughts.

____
____
____
____

Getting Practical

:Review the Keys to Conscious Eating. Determine if any of these might help you reach satisfaction

1. Eat only when my body is hungry.
2. Reduce distractions to eat in a calm environment.
3. Eat when sitting down.
4. Eat when my body and mind are relaxed.
5. Eat and drink the food and beverages my body enjoys.
6. Pay attention to my food while eating.
7. Eat slowly and savor each bite.
8. Stop _before_ my body is "full."

more easily.

____
____
____
____

Memory Challenge

Thin Within Tip

Notice the food on your plate and decide which appeals to you the most. Rather than "saving the best for last," why not "eat the best first"?

© 2003, Thin Within, All Rights Reserved

Day Six ~ Optional Exercises

Going Deeper

After looking at the attitude of the three kings mentioned in the lesson, which ones *do* you or *have* you emulated, and how might you become more like Josiah?

____
____
____
____

Bible Study

1 Corinthians 6:20 says to honor God with your body. Honor is defined as "to manifest the highest respect and reverence for, in words and actions; to entertain the most exalted thoughts of; to worship; to adore." What are ways that you can honor God with your body? Pray Psalm 86:11–13 to the Lord.

____
____
____
____

Knowing God by Heart

Find synonyms for the word "good" in a thesaurus or dictionary. How do these words give you a deeper understanding of God as good? Read Psalm 52:9, Psalm 107:8–9, and James 1:17. What do these verses tell you about God?

____
____
____
____

Getting Practical

Journal about your week of finding the point of satisfaction and any victories that you have experienced along the way. Give thanks to God for helping you get more in tune with your body's needs.

____
____
____
____

Memory Challenge

Repeat 1 Corinthians 6:19–20 out loud and ask God to make these verses real in your life. What might God be leading you to "be" or to "do" in response to this passage?

© 2003, Thin Within, All Rights Reserved

EXERCISES

Day Seven – Optional Exercises

Going Deeper

James 1:17 says that every good and perfect gift comes from the Father. This gives us a glimpse of God's perspective of His creation. What do you believe is God's view of your body? What adjustments can you make to line up with His perspective?

____
____
____
____

Bible Study

After reading Philippians 3:12–14, what will help you along the path even when you make mistakes and fail? What is the promise found in Philippians 1:6?

____
____
____
____

Getting Practical

Now that you have taken a whole week to look at satisfaction (5), look at your definition on Day One. Have you redefined or clarified it since then? Journal all that you have learned about how much your body requires to be comfortably satisfied.

____
____
____
____

Memory Challenge

Share your memory verse with a friend or family member, telling him or her how it relates to your Thin Within journey.

Thin Within Tip

Don't wait until you have achieved your goal to begin taking care of your body. Keep your hair and nails clean, as well as nicely trimmed. Wear clothes and colors that compliment you and not just "hide" your body. Maintain good dental hygiene. Put on a favorite piece of jewelry. Treating your body with respect and appreciation isn't just for people who have already reached their natural God-given size.

© 2003, Thin Within, All Rights Reserved

Review of the Week

Take time at the end of each week to review what God has taught you and how it is impacting your life. This will give you a great overview to take to your Thin Within Support Group Meeting.

The most significant thing God taught me this week:

____
____
____
____

My memory verse this week was I Corinthians 6:19-20.
> *Do you not know that your body is a temple of the Holy Spirit, who is in you, whom you have received from God? You are not your own; you were bought at a price. Therefore honor God with your body.*

Choosing from the phrases "you are not your own," "you were bought at a price," or "honor God with your body" the one I find most compelling to me is:

____

Because:

____
____
____

My experience in finding the point of satisfaction (5) in my eating this second week of Thin Within:

____
____
____
____

The most significant thing that God helped me to observe this week that I will focus on correcting next week:

____
____
____
____

What I have learned about the character of God as sovereign and good, and how I have come to know and be drawn closer to Him:

____
____
____
____

My prayer requests and praises:

____
____
____
____
____
____

© 2003, Thin Within, All Rights Reserved

LESSON

Identity in Christ

Introduction

Amazingly enough, God has chosen to use your physical body as the place for His presence to dwell in the person of the Holy Spirit. Last week we recognized that this is an incredible privilege, but with it comes the responsibility of stewardship. We revere God by demonstrating proper respect for our physical bodies in which God chooses to dwell.

Obviously, we want to emulate the stewardship of King Josiah who, with a tender heart, acknowledged the ruin of the temple and upon discovery of the truth of the living Word, began diligently to rebuild it. His teachable spirit resulted in a transformation from within. The parallel between Josiah and us is that having now seen ourselves as God's temple, we can begin to allow the rebuilding process to take place according to the Word of Truth.

Before we get under way, let's be certain the necessary preparation work has been completed which will enable you to build on a solid foundation. Have you opened your heart to God and allowed Him to expose any idols or barriers that would hinder you from receiving all that He has for you? What is your attitude right now toward your body, God's Holy temple?

As you reconcile with your body and continue being filled with truth and hope, lets roll up our sleeves and get to work restoring the foundation. This is an essential place to begin, as a building is only as secure as the foundation on which it stands.

Spiritual Foundation

Your personal transformation will take place as you rest on the firm foundation of God's Word. Jesus taught a parable that illustrates this firm foundation.

Therefore everyone who hears these words of mine and puts them into practice is like a wise man who built his house on the rock.
The rain came down, the streams rose, and the winds blew and beat against that house; yet it did not fall, because it had its foundation on the rock.
But everyone who hears these words of mine and does not put them into practice is like a foolish man who built his house on sand.
The rain came down, the streams rose, and the winds blew and beat against that house, and it fell with a great crash.
Matthew 7:24–27

It is important not merely to hear the Word or simply know what it says. But to embrace it as our own, act on it, obey it, and build our life upon it.

This week you will have the opportunity to invite the Spirit of the living God to change your beliefs so that you can see yourself as you really are in Christ. Proverbs 23:7 defines a man in this way: "For as he thinks in his heart, so is he" (Amplified). You will live according to what you believe to be true about yourself. When you believe and think as Adam then you behave like Adam behaves, even though that is no longer your true identity.

What exactly is our identity? The world

Born In Adam

B-32   © 2003, Thin Within, All Rights Reserved

would have us believe that it is determined by our performance, our possessions, or our appearance. If we have money, position, and good looks, we have value in the eyes of the world. However, there is no security in this type of identity because all of these things are fleeting and can be lost at any one moment. To build our life on such things is to build on shifting sand. Let us discard this unstable foundation and build on the solid rock of God's Word.

When we are born into the world, we come into the family and lineage of Adam. The fifth chapter of the book of Romans tells us that in Adam, we all sin and die. We all come under judgment and are condemned.

But take heart! Jesus proclaims in John 3:3–21 that we can have a change in our identity. The only way identity can be changed is by rebirth. Jesus said you must be born again . . . whatever is born of the flesh is flesh and whatever is born of the Spirit is spirit. We see in 2 Corinthians 5:17 that "if anyone is in Christ, he is a new creation; the old has gone, the new has come!"

When we come to faith in Christ, we are taken out of the family of Adam and put into the family of God. Our identity is changed! According to Colossians 1:13, "[The Father] has delivered and drawn us to himself out of the control and the dominion of darkness and has transferred us into the kingdom of the Son of his love." (Amplified) We become a new creation, with a new heritage, and a new identity.

You were dead in your transgressions and sins, in which you used to live when you followed the ways of this world and of the ruler of the kingdom of the air, the spirit who is now at work in those who are disobedient. All of us also lived among them at one time, gratifying the cravings of our sinful nature and following its desires and thoughts. Like the rest, we were by nature objects of wrath.

But because of his great love for us, God, who is rich in mercy, made us alive with Christ even when we were dead in transgressions— it is by grace you have been saved. And God raised us up with Christ and seated us with him in the heavenly realms in Christ Jesus, in order that in the coming ages he might show the incomparable riches of his grace, expressed in his kindness to us in Christ Jesus. For it is by grace you have been saved, through faith—and this not from yourselves, it is the gift of God—not by works, so that no one can boast. For we are God's workmanship, created in Christ Jesus to do good works, which God prepared in advance for us to do.
Ephesians 2:1–10

How glorious is this truth! We were once condemned, without hope, and without God; now we have been placed in the family of God, born anew, and created in Christ Jesus for good works that God has prepared for us. We have been given a new identity, a new hope, and a new future! And we have been given all of this by grace through faith—not because we deserved it, but because He loved us and gave us faith to believe and receive all that He had purchased for us in Christ.

What a difference embracing a new

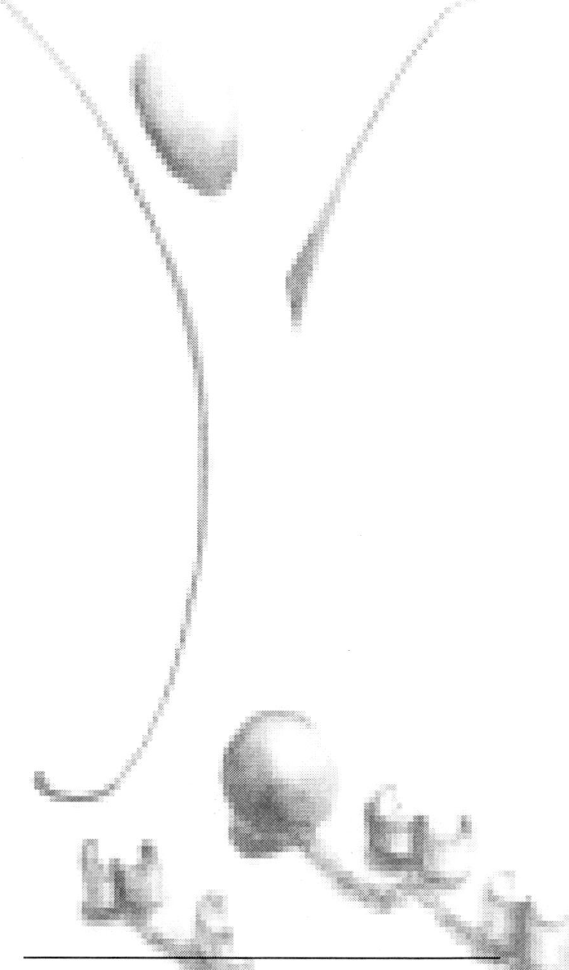

© 2003, Thin Within, All Rights Reserved

LESSON

identity can make! Romans 12:2 says that we are no longer to be conformed to this world, but we are to be transformed by the renewing of our minds. So let's examine our individual belief system with the following questions:

1. Is your value as a child of God based on your size?
2. Would you have a greater sense of self-worth if you were the size of an exceptional athlete or a fashion model?
3. Do you look in the mirror and say, "You're a hopeless wreck who will never conquer the battle of food, eating, and weight?"
4. Do you justify your behavior by saying, "But food is one of the few things I have left in life that I can really enjoy; it's just not fair to give up something that brings so much pleasure"?

Because so many of us can identify with one or more of these questions, we are going to deliberately and gently expose the lies and rubble of those faulty, unworkable beliefs. We are going to replace them with the *solid* truth of God's Word. As we do, we will create a firm, unshakable foundation on which to restore your body, God's temple.

Jerry Bridges expounds upon the need to embrace our new identity in Christ in his book *The Discipline of Grace*. Referring to the story of Viktor Ivanovich Belenko, a Russian MiG pilot, Mr. Bridges says the following:

- -

During the long years of the Cold War between the United States and the Soviet Union, a Russian air force pilot flew his fighter plane from a base in Russia to an American air force base in Japan and asked for asylum. He was flown to the United States where he was duly debriefed, given a new identity, and set up as a bona fide resident of the United States. In due time he became an American citizen.

The Russian pilot's experience illustrates to some degree what happened to us when we died to sin and were made alive to God. He changed kingdoms; he was given a new identity and a new status. He was no longer a Russian; he was now an American. He was no longer under the rule of what was then an oppressive and totalitarian government. Now he was free to experience all of the advantages and resources of living in a free and prosperous country.

This former Russian pilot, however, was still the same person. He had the same personality, the same habits, and the same cultural patterns as he did before he flew out of Russia. But he did have a new identity and a new status. As a result of a new identity and status as a citizen in a free country, he now had the opportunity to grow as a free person, to discard the mind-set of someone living under bondage, and to put off the habit patterns of a person living under the heel of a despotic regime. Furthermore, as a benefactor of our government's intelligence establishment, he was furnished all the resources needed to make a successful transition to an American citizen.

In effect, this Russian pilot "died" to his old identity as a Russian citizen and was "made alive" in a new identity as an American citizen. As an American, all the resources of our government were at his disposal to become in fact what he had become in status. But this could not have happened without first changing his status.

When we as believers died to sin, we died to a status wherein we were under bondage to the tyrannical reign of sin. At the same time we were granted citizenship in the Kingdom of God and, through our vital union with Jesus Christ, were furnished all the resources we need to become in fact what we have become in status. We have been given all we need to bring the imperative—"do not let sin reign in your mortal body"—into line with the indicative—"we died to sin." But this could not have happened without a change in our status. And it is through our legal union with Christ in His death and resurrection that our status has been forever changed.

We must count on this and believe it. We must by faith in God's Word lay hold of the fact that we have died to the reign of sin and are now alive to God, under His reign of grace. Unless we do this we will find ourselves seeking to pursue holiness by the strength of our own wills, not by the grace of God.[1]

- -

Many of us remain entrenched in the old identity of the flesh, even though we have been transported into a new kingdom and given a new identity similar to the pilot in Mr. Bridges' story. We walk as though we are still citizens of the old

© 2003, Thin Within, All Rights Reserved

kingdom even though our identity changed when receiving Christ as our Savior and Lord. Will you embrace your new identity and the freedom that was purchased on the cross at Calvary? Will you walk confidently as you claim all the rights, responsibilities, and privileges that come with being a citizen of a heavenly kingdom?

Jesus says, "You will know the truth, and the truth will set you free" (John 8:32).

The apostle Paul, in Romans 6 tells us what is true of us as new creatures in Christ. As we trust and submit to God He conforms us from within, and we melt down to our natural God-given size. Romans 6:2 tells us that we died to sin. Verse 3 encourages us that we were baptized into Christ by His death. In verse 4, we see that just as Christ was raised from the dead, we also walk in newness of life. In verse 5, we are united with Christ in His death, burial, and in His resurrection. In verse 6, our "old man" was crucified with Christ, so that the body of sin might be done away with, and so that we would no longer be slaves to sin. As we continue reading, we see a wonderful promise that he who has died has been freed from sin. In verse 8, we have that if we died with Christ, we believe we shall also live with Him. Verse 11 tells us to reckon ourselves to be dead indeed to sin, but alive to God in Christ Jesus our Lord.

Eight different times in this chapter we are told that we are dead to sin, no longer enslaved to sin, or that we've been set free from sin. *This* is our identity, the truth of who

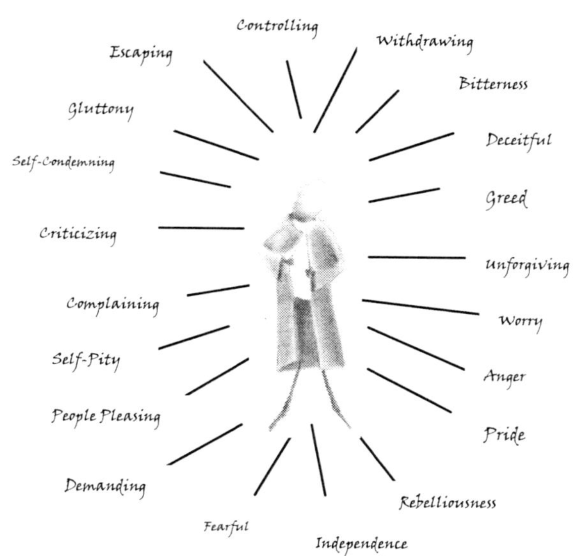

Putting Off the Old

we are in Christ.

We are told that our old man was crucified with Christ in verse 6. Who is our old man? Our old man is our old identity, our old creation in Adam. The old man as we saw in Ephesians 2 walked according to the world and the lust of the flesh, without hope and without God. The part of us that was enslaved to sin was crucified with Christ.

Furthermore, there is behavior that is consistent with the old man (who was crucified with Christ) and behavior that is consistent with the new man (who is the new creation in Christ). We are told in Ephesians 4:22–24 to put off the old man and put on the new and be renewed in the spirit of our minds. Again in Colossians 3:9–10, we're instructed to put off the old man and put on the new man renewed in knowledge.

This putting off old behavior and putting on new behavior takes place first in the mind as a result of restructuring our belief system. We were once hopeless and helpless. However, that part has been crucified (Romans 6:6; Galatians 2:20). We are now a new creation in Christ (2 Corinthians 5:17) and we can do all things through Him who strengthens us (Philippians 4:13). We have been born again to walk in newness of life. We are told to reckon this to be true and live according to this truth.

Practically speaking what will this look like? When tempted to eat an entire package of cream filled cookies we prayerfully stand by faith against that temptation. We choose to make a sacrifice and proclaim God's truth. "No

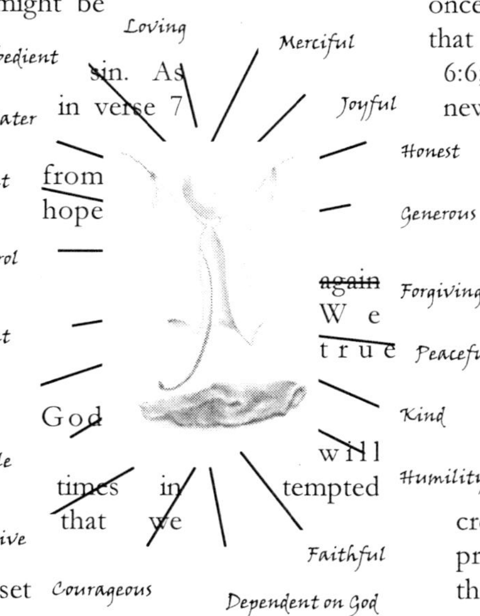

Putting on the New

© 2003, Thin Within, All Rights Reserved

thanks, I am dead to that" and I submit my will to thy will. We then experience the power of God as we resist temptation saying, "it has no power over me, I am dead to sin and alive to God in Christ." This is the rock on which we must build our temples. It is not enough just to hear it, we must embrace it by faith, rise up, and walk with confidence in this reality.

So why do we continue to live according to our "former citizenship mentality," not recognizing our new identity and our freedom from the bondage of sin? This is exactly what the world, the flesh, and the devil want us to do. We are constantly exposed to the messages of the world conveyed in magazines, movies, television commercials, and billboards. They say that our appearance is all that matters and that we must look like a world-class athlete or a fashion model in order to have any measure of worth, value, or good feelings about ourselves. But the truth according to God's Word is that our value was established at the cross. Our Father God considered us so priceless and precious that He gave the life of His only Son to bring us into His family and make us His own.

The enemy, who is a liar and the accuser, would also like to trip us up here with thoughts like:

- "You'll never have victory in this area of your life. You're a total failure when it comes to food, eating, and weight. You don't have what it takes. You're a hopeless wreck; you might as well just give up."
- "God isn't going to help you with this insignificant problem."
- "God is disgusted with you, and He has surely given up on you by now."

The truth of God's Word is that we are *not* hopeless. We are new creatures in Christ and saints according to His calling. (Ephesians 1:18-19) God has begun a good work in us, and He has promised that He will be faithful to complete it. He will never give up on any of us!

However, our self-focused, insatiable flesh chimes in with lies such as:

- "Food is one of the few things I have left to enjoy in life."
- "It's not fair. I'll be miserable if I can't have what I want."
- "Other people get to eat as much as they want."
- "Life will not be <u>any</u> fun without an abundance of food as my constant companion."

The truth is that we have been given the abundant life in Christ—a life of fulfillment, joy, and peace. We can be content with all the good things God provides, including foods we enjoy within the God-given boundaries of hunger and satisfaction. It is often a challenge to embrace God's truth when the enemy attacks with his lies, when our flesh wars against us, and when our emotions deceive us as we sin.

The life of a Christian, however, is a life of faith. We are called to believe and to act in faith even before we see the reality of what God has promised. In fact, Scripture tells us that God calls the things that are not as though they are (Romans 4:17). This is a totally opposite view from the world, which says, "Seeing is believing." The enemy whispers, "I'll believe you are dead to sin when you start acting like it." It is only as we embrace by faith our new identity in Christ and choose to sacrifice our fleshly desires that we experience the transforming power of God's grace. The Holy Spirit begins His work within us as our minds are renewed by the truth of God's Word. As in the story of the Russian pilot, our behavior will change in response to a change in our beliefs. Now we must allow that truth to empower us to walk in our new identity.

Let's cease from striving to change our outward actions of controlling our food, our body, our will, and our performance without first changing our beliefs because the results at best are temporary. It will look like an exterior whitewash rather than an internal transformation where the focus is on God, believing what He says, and choosing to do His will in His strength.

When man chose to sin in the Garden of Eden, he was disconnected from a Holy God who was to be his only source for his every need. This left man acting totally on his own, striving to meet his needs through his own effort, based on his own resources. This resulted in flesh behavior and prideful attempts to cope with life independent from God. Running to food and overeating are

God's work in you brings about a transformation from within.

   © 2003, Thin Within, All Rights Reserved

examples of learned flesh patterns or coping skills that keep us independent from God. They are behavior patterns of the old creation that we are told to put off!

So what do we mean by "Flesh Patterns"? In Thin Within we call this "Flesh machinery" which is learned behavior that keeps us running to food or engaged in flesh-filled eating—eating that is done in response to a stimulus other than true stomach hunger. For example, "It's 12 noon, so it's 'time' to eat." Each of us has some flesh machinery, which consists of faulty beliefs preventing us from being all God intends us to be. These unworkable beliefs do not support who we are in Christ or allow us to become victorious in Him.

Another kind of flesh machinery is conditioned or habitual responses. These are automatic triggers that stimulate us to eat, such as "I'm at the movies so I can't possibly enjoy it without some popcorn." Other conditioned responses can be triggered by our emotions, such as "I just love chocolate chip cookies, so that's my treat for a hard day," "I'm bored. I want pizza," or "I'm lonely. Where's the chocolate?"

Other forms of flesh machinery that can contribute to disordered eating include our past experiences and previous failures, especially dieting failures. Flesh machinery is the result of using food to medicate the pain in our lives. Pain plus misused pleasure results in addictive, repetitive behavior. Flesh machinery includes anything that signals us to eat when we are not hungry. A few examples are:

1. It's time to eat.
2. It's free. Never pass up free food.
3. Someone else paid for it. It would be rude not to eat.
4. It tastes so good and this is my only opportunity to eat.
5. I deserve a treat. I've worked hard all day.
6. Children are starving in Africa.
7. It's sinful to waste food.

It's time dear one to examine your life for those counterfeit signals that call you to the pantry day or night. Ask God to open your eyes and shed light on every destructive flesh pattern so that you can put off the old and put on the new.

We have found since this program began in 1975 that there is a core unworkable belief at the bottom of all our excuses for eating when we are not truly hungry. That bottom line belief is

"This is my body, and I can do with it as I please!"

Think about this for a moment. Can you see how this prideful and rebellious thinking has led you to continue to overeat or misuse food even though you know you want to reach your natural God-given size and be healthy? If this belief were not at the heart of the matter, we would not give ourselves permission, even unconsciously, to continue to overeat. If we even subtly hold on to this core belief, then our foundation is not established on truth.

But what does God's Word say?

*. . . Your body is a temple of the Holy Spirit who is in you.
. . . you are not your own; you were bought at a price.
Therefore, honor God with your body.
1 Corinthians 6:19–20*

The truth is that your body isn't yours to do with as you please. It is God's body that He bought and paid for with the precious life and blood of His only Son. Jesus said that our foundation must be truth and that "you will know the truth and the truth will set you free" (John 8:32).

You have a conscious choice to make. Will you acknowledge that your body belongs to God and relinquish your right to treat it anyway you want? Will you choose not to rebel but to submit to a God who loves you? This is a critical turning point in your walk with God. If you choose to surrender, God will be glorified in your body as His life and His will are lived out in you. This is the exciting Spirit-filled life that results in Spirit-filled eating. What joy and what freedom awaits you dear one!

Physiological Information

There are many reasons why we eat inappropriately. When you find yourself drawn to food or eating beyond a 5, stop and ask yourself these questions:

- "Is there a habitual response going on? What habit have I developed that makes me think I need to eat right now?"
- "Is my flesh rebelling against what is God's best for me?"
- "Is there a false belief or an idol of my own making that isn't serving my genuine desire to reach and maintain my natural size? What is the belief that is in operation right now?"

© 2003, Thin Within, All Rights Reserved

- "Is my present response to food rooted in my past? Am I trying to alleviate the pain of old wounds by turning to food at this time?"
- "Do I see myself as a failure? Is this why I just give up and eat even when I'm not hungry?"

Remember that food offers only a temporary satisfaction to our deeper, more legitimate needs. As the psalmist mentioned in last week's lessons, God wants you to discover that He alone can meet and satisfy all of your needs. Regardless of the reasons you may want to eat, if you eat outside of the 0 to 5 parameters, you will, at best, stay at your current weight. Depending on how far outside of those parameters you go, not only will your heart continue to cry out for what it really needs, but your body will respond by gaining weight.

Many suffer from health problems such as diabetes, high blood pressure, breathlessness, or other potentially dangerous conditions as a result of poor eating habits or from being overweight or underweight. God desires your entire body to be healthy from within—soul, spirit, mind, and body. He wants to eliminate those health problems that could be solved, or at least minimized, by Spirit-filled, present time, healthy eating choices. This is appropriate, healthy eating in the present time not influenced by anything from the past.

God cares about your body remaining as healthy as possible so that His glory may be reflected in and through you. You are His, bought at a price, and regardless of what you look like, He wants you to live a healthy vibrant Spirit-filled life!

"You will know the truth, and the truth will set you free"

blameless in His sight (Ephesians 1:4).

As you rest in and believe what God says about you in Christ, you begin to see that, yes, all things *are* possible in Christ (Philippians 4:13). He who promised is faithful to finish the work that He has begun in you (Philippians 1:6).

We are told in Ephesians and Colossians to choose to set aside the beliefs and fleshly behaviors of the old man and put on the new godly beliefs and behaviors of the new man. By replacing old thinking and belief systems with the new way of thinking, your behavior will change as you are conformed to the image of Christ.

In the week ahead, resolve to believe and obey God as you tune into your hunger signals and trust the body He has given you.

As God leads you into truth by the "nudging" of the Holy Spirit, you will continue to be conformed to the image of Christ by the renewing of your mind. Your faulty beliefs, your former citizenship mentality, the thinking of the world, and the lies of the enemy will be exposed and replaced by the truth of God's Word. God's work in you brings about a transformation from within. By God's grace and the power of the Holy Spirit, you will truly be Thin Within as you live abundantly in this new identity!

Endnotes
1) Jerry Bridges, *The Discipline of Grace* (Colorado Springs, CO: NavPress, 1994), 75–76. Used by permission of NavPress—www.navpress.com. All rights reserved.

My Notes

Integration

There may be real reasons that you have battled with issues related to food, eating, and your body. However, dear one, do NOT view these reasons as valid excuses, but as ploys to prompt you to eat in a way that is outside of God's plan for you. Exposing these lies and the workings of "Flesh-machinery" releases you from the draw of food when you are not truly hungry. You can now rest in the fact that God chose you from before the foundation of the world to be holy and

   © 2003, Thin Within, All Rights Reserved

© 2003, Thin Within, All Rights Reserved

EXERCISES

Day One

Going Deeper

Do you look in the mirror and say, "You're a hopeless wreck who will never conquer the battle of food, eating, and weight?" How do you think this belief affects your behavior?

____
____
____
____

Bible Study

Read Jonah 3:5–10 and Titus 1:15–16. What does belief produce? What does unbelief produce? Refer to Isaiah 43:10. List all the things you find in this passage that God desires for you to be or do. What is the difference between believing _in_ God and believing God?

____
____
____
____

Knowing God by Heart: Holy

> _His divine power has given us everything we need for life and godliness_
> _through our knowledge of him who called us by his own glory and goodness._
> _2 Peter 1:3_

Look up the word "holy" in the dictionary and write down a definition that you believe is consistent with God being holy. Read 1 Samuel 2:2, Hebrews 7:26, and Revelation 15:4 and relate your definition to these Scriptures.

____
____
____
____

Getting Practical

Today consider adding an accountability tool to your eating. Begin to keep an informal log of your hunger number at the start and finish of each meal. (Remember that this is only a tool to help you visualize your pattern of eating, and it is not meant to hinder or create a stumbling stone. Use this tool as the Lord leads.)

____
____
____
____

Memory Challenge

Start memorizing Galatians 2:20 today. Take time to see the message proclaimed in this Scripture. Read the verse out loud several times and then look away from it to say it on your own.

> _I have been crucified with Christ and I no longer live, but Christ lives in me. The life I live in the body, I live by faith in the Son of God, who loved me and gave himself for me._
> _Galatians 2:20_

Thin Within Tip

Think in terms of how little you can eat in order to be satisfied—rather than how much you can get away with in hopes of not gaining weight.

© 2003, Thin Within, All Rights Reserved

Day Two

Going Deeper

What exactly is your identity? Contrast the world's definition with the biblical definition.

____

____

____

____

Bible Study

Read John 3:1–21. Have you experienced a rebirth in your spirit that this passage talks about? If not, will you consider doing so today? Read through the following passages and see how the Lord moves your heart: Romans 3:23, Romans 6:23, Hebrews 9:27, Romans 5:8, John 1:12. Why not pray today to accept Jesus' free gift—payment for your past, present, and future sins and the gift of eternal life? He wants to be your Savior and Lord. (If you have given your life to Christ today for the first time, please contact your church or the Thin Within office so that you can be congratulated and learn how to grow in the Lord and follow His plan for you.)

____

____

____

____

If you have been born again in Christ, what is your identity according to Galatians 4:4–7? In Christ, what does 2 Corinthians 5:17–21 say that you are? What is Paul saying is gone and what has come?

____

____

____

____

Knowing God by Heart

Continue to grow in your knowledge of God by reading Job 34:10 and Isaiah 57:15. What do these verses say to you about God's holiness?

____

____

____

____

Getting Practical

Look over your hunger numbers from yesterday. Were there occasions when you ate between 0 and 5? Say a prayer asking God to help you establish a consistent 0 to 5 pattern. Continue to record your hunger numbers.

____

____

____

____

Memory Challenge

Continue memorizing Galatians 2:20 by saying or writing it several times. After some repetition, try repeating it from memory. Take the memory verse card with you and refer to it throughout the day.

© 2003, Thin Within, All Rights Reserved

EXERCISES

Day Three

Going Deeper

According to Romans 6:17–18, those who are reborn in Christ obtain a new spirit that is no longer a slave to sin, but rather a slave to righteousness. Make a list of the differences in those two slaves.

Bible Study

What is our new identity and hope according to Ephesians 2:1–10; 12–13? Read Romans 6:6–10, 17–18. From what has God freed you? As His child, to what are you now a slave?

Knowing God by Heart

Find synonyms for the word "holy" in a thesaurus or dictionary. How do these words give you a deeper understanding of God as holy? Read Leviticus 19:2 and 1 Peter 1:14–16. What do you glean from these verses regarding God's holiness and His plan for you?

Getting Practical

Keep recording your hunger numbers and praying for the desire and ability to eat 0 to 5.

Memory Challenge

Review Galatians 2:20 until you can repeat it from memory.

Thin Within Tip

When you reach the point of satisfaction, do whatever it takes to get the food out of your reach: move it away from you; give it to someone else; wrap it up; put it in the refrigerator, freezer, or pantry; or place it in a carryout container.

© 2003, Thin Within, All Rights Reserved

Day Four

Going Deeper

In this week's lesson, we read that flesh machinery is learned behavior that keeps us running to food or engaged in flesh-filled eating. It is eating that is done in response to a stimulus other than true stomach hunger. Each of us has some flesh machinery, which consists of faulty beliefs preventing us from being all God intends us to be. These unworkable beliefs don't support who we are in Christ or allow us to become victorious in Him. Make a list of some of your own flesh machinery that may be holding you back from God's victory in your life.

____
____
____
____

Bible Study

On Day Two we established that at the moment of your spiritual rebirth you were made new in Christ and given a new spirit. The old was buried with Christ, and a new spirit was risen with Christ (Galatians 2:20, 2 Corinthians 5:17). Even though we are new creatures and are no longer slaves to sin, but to righteousness (Romans 6:17–18), we do not suddenly cease to sin (Romans 3:23). In our daily walk we must deal with our old flesh patterns (flesh machinery). In Ephesians 4:22–24, what does Paul mean by putting off the old self and putting on the new self? What is the key to turning away from faulty beliefs that trigger our flesh machinery?

____
____
____
____

Knowing God by Heart: Self-Sufficient

Look up the word "self-sufficient" in the dictionary and write down a definition that you believe is consistent with God being self-sufficient. Read Psalm 50:7–12 and relate your definition to these Scriptures.

____
____
____
____

Getting Practical

Do you see any patterns in your eating? Do you always reach 0 before you eat? If not, pray that God would give you the desire to let go of those times when you want to eat but you are not at 0.

____
____
____
____

Memory Challenge

Repeat Galatians 2:20 from memory. Turn this verse into a prayer for yourself or someone you know.

© 2003, Thin Within, All Rights Reserved

EXERCISES

Day Five

Going Deeper

The bottom-line faulty belief is "This is my body and I can do with it what I please!" Ask God to show you if this is part of your belief and what is driving it. Replace the lie with the truth of God's Word. The one single truth that can refute every lie is "I am not my own. Christ bought and purchased me with His own blood and I now belong to Him. Therefore I will choose to honor God with my body."

____
____
____
____

Bible Study

You may be thinking, "Even though I know I am God's child, I still struggle with sin." What does Romans 6:11–14 say about this? Journal about God's provision for obedience after reading Philippians 4:13 and 19. Incorporate the Stop, Look, Listen, and Obey tool (found in the appendix) into your daily life in order to turn temptation into an opportunity to obey.

____
____
____
____

Knowing God by Heart

Continue to grow in your knowledge of God by reading Acts 17:24–25. What do these verses say to you about God's self-sufficiency?

____
____
____
____

Getting Practical

Are you finding that place of comfortable satisfaction at least a few times each day? If not, experiment with eating half as much as you usually do and see if you can find 5.

____
____
____
____

Memory Challenge

Meditate on Galatians 2:20 throughout the day and allow it to draw you closer to God. Ask Him to help you truly believe this Scripture so that it can set you free from all the deceptive lies of the world.

Thin Within Tip

Put your fork down between bites. Concentrate on enjoying the present bite instead of anticipating the next one. This will not only slow you down, it will give you time to _chew_ your food and enjoy the taste for a longer period of time without actually eating more.

 © 2003, Thin Within, All Rights Reserved

Day Six – Optional Exercises

Going Deeper

Resist the temptation to succumb to the influences of flesh machinery by praying or journaling. Invite the Holy Spirit to take control. Some participants have made tremendous strides by praying and recording their feelings instead of simply trying to grit their teeth and bear it in their own strength. Seek God regarding your struggles and relinquish control to the Holy Spirit.

Bible Study

Read John 8:32 again this week and be reminded of what will set you free. What part does obedience play in this freedom in Christ? After reading James 1:22–25, list the ways that God leads you to do what the Word says for today and this week.

Knowing God by Heart

Find synonyms for the word "self-sufficient" in a thesaurus or dictionary. How do these words give you a deeper understanding of God's self-sufficiency? Read Romans 11:34–36. What do these Scriptures tell you about God?

Getting Practical

Which is the hardest—waiting for 0 or stopping at 5? Take this to God and be open to His solutions.

Memory Challenge

Repeat Galatians 2:20 out loud and ask God to make this verse real in your life. What might God be leading you to "be" or to "do" in response to this passage?

© 2003, Thin Within, All Rights Reserved

EXERCISES

Day Seven – Optional Exercises

Going Deeper

You can now rest in the fact that God chose you from before the foundation of the world to be holy and blameless in His sight. The empowering of His indwelling Spirit will enable you to fulfill your new identity. . . . With the power of the Holy Spirit, you don't have to succumb to flesh machinery. List some ways that you have resisted the temptation to fall back into flesh machinery this week.

____

____

____

Bible Study

It is clear that you cannot do this in your own strength. Read 2 Corinthians 4:1–7. Be reminded of how the Truth (Light) brings you to the knowledge of the glory of God in the face of Christ. Where does this all-surpassing power come from? Rest in His provision (Proverbs 3:5–6).

____

____

____

Getting Practical

Rather than focusing on all that you failed to do right this week, note the positive changes that have occurred in your eating and allow God to use your missteps to mold you to His likeness. Take time to thank and praise God for your victories this week.

____

____

____

Memory Challenge

Share your memory verse with a friend or family member, telling him or her how it relates to your Thin Within journey.

Thin Within Tip

Practice leaving food on your plate, even if it is only a few bites. Remind yourself that you can be satisfied with 0 to 5 eating. When we are able to leave food on our plates, we take a big step in breaking the stronghold of overeating and the selfish demands of having our own way.

© 2003, Thin Within, All Rights Reserved

Review of the Week

Take time at the end of each week to review what God has taught you and how it is impacting your life. This will give you a great overview to take to your Thin Within Support Group Meeting.

The most significant thing God taught me this week:

____
____
____
____

In day 1 of this week's Bible study, I saw through the Ninevites that belief produces action (Jonah 3:4-10). This being said, the belief that I no longer live, but Christ lives in me (Galatians 2:20) affects my actions regarding food and weight by:

____
____
____
____

With respect to waiting for hunger (0) and stopping when my body was satisfied (5), I would describe my progress as:

____
____
____
____

The most significant thing that God helped me to observe this week that I will focus on correcting next week:

____
____
____
____

What I have learned about the character of God as holy and self-sufficient, and how I have come to know and be drawn closer to Him:

____
____
____
____

My prayer requests and praises:

____
____
____
____

© 2003, Thin Within, All Rights Reserved

LESSON

Celebration of God's Grace, Part One

Introduction

Welcome to the Celebration of God's Grace. This week we rejoice in all that God has done during the past three weeks. He has met us with His promise and plan for our future and hope. We delight that His grace pours out on us as we step out of the stigma of past failures, dieting laws, and rules and into the blessing that comes when we reconcile with our body and heed its God-given cues of hunger and satisfaction.

We bask in the joy of knowing that God is good and that His mercies are new every morning. The abundance of His grace is clearly displayed in the fact that He has chosen you to be His dwelling place on earth. He has given you an identity that is firmly established in Him. As you agree with God that you are the temple of His Spirit, your actions will line up with that transforming truth. You will begin to keep in step with the Spirit of God through Spirit-filled eating and will experience changes in your actions. Rejoice that God is good! He who has begun a work in you is faithful and will bring it to completion as you continue to surrender to Him (Philippians 1:6).

Instead of bringing out the club of condemnation and beating yourself over the head, apply God's amazing grace to your mistakes in the form of observation and correction. Seek the Lord's will so that you might move forward again. You are breaking free from self-condemnation, false guilt, and the need to perform in order to impress God. He desires for us to know the depth of His infinite love and the power of His Spirit as we wholeheartedly surrender all to Him and walk in obedience to the nudging of the Holy Spirit.

These past three weeks have been liberating, indeed, as we have completed the first phase of Thin Within by breaking free from the law. We have thrown off shackles of legalism, performance, and approval seeking. We are now walking with Christ in His profound love, grace, and transforming power.

In this week's lesson, we will see many of these very things illustrated in the life of Daniel.

Spiritual Foundation

Daniel was a teenager living in Judah at the time that King Nebuchadnezzar's large army stormed and destroyed the city of Jerusalem in 606 B.C. The temple was plundered and destroyed in honor of the Babylonian pagan god, Baal.

God's people were taken captive by the king of powerful Babylon and sent into exile. Daniel, like many others of noble blood, was trained in the way of the Babylonians and forced to enter into the service of this pagan kingdom. Daniel was even given a new name, Belteshazzar, in honor of their god.

The Babylonians sought to remove a sense of identity from the Israelites. If the captives adopted the lifestyle of their captors and contributed to the building of the pagan nation, they would be content to remain there and would never be a threat. In essence, they would be forsaking their God-given identity and begin to live as Babylonians.

Unfortunately, this strategy worked, as many of the Israelites forgot who they were and settled into their new life.

But at least one young man never forgot. Daniel knew that he was an Israelite called by God to be set apart. He maintained his sense of identity throughout his life in Babylon. He held on to the promises of God and knew that God was faithful.

This is beautifully illustrated in Daniel chapter 9 where we catch a glimpse into the heart and private devotional life of this man of God. Throughout his captivity, Daniel continued to maintain his habits of prayer and Scripture reading. No matter how things appeared on the outside, deep within he knew who he was and he clung to the Lord in whom he found hope.

Daniel recorded this for us:

In the first year of Darius son of Xerxes (a Mede by descent), who was made ruler over the Babylonian kingdom—in the first year of his reign, I, Daniel, understood from the Scriptures, according to the word of the LORD given to Jeremiah, the prophet, that the desolation of Jerusalem would last seventy years.
Daniel 9:1–2

Daniel read the Scriptures, specifically the book of Jeremiah. He held fast to God and His Word and maintained his hope even when circumstances seemed hopeless. This is the prophecy from the book of Jeremiah that Daniel most likely read:

This is what the LORD says: "When seventy years are completed for Babylon, I will come to you and fulfill my gracious promise to bring you back to this place."
Jeremiah 29:10

© 2003, Thin Within, All Rights Reserved

Oh, how Daniel's heart must have thirsted for the cool, clear refreshment of this promise from God! Notice the Scripture reference is Jeremiah 29:10, which precedes the following verse that we have become very familiar with:

"For I know the plans I have for you," declares the LORD, "plans to prosper you and not to harm you, plans to give you hope and a future."
Jeremiah 29:11

Daniel, who was in his eighties or nineties, found hope and encouragement as he read the Scriptures. It had been seventy years since the captivity began. At this moment, might he have felt an ache in his heart for the Lord? The land of promise seemed so far away. Was it all a distant memory? We see here that because of God's grace, He had not abandoned His people and He will not abandon you.

Daniel believed the promises found in Jeremiah. The captivity God had spoken of through the prophet Jeremiah had come true to the letter. So, too, would this promise of freedom. It had been seventy years. Daniel's mind may have raced with such thoughts: "Seventy years? Why, that's soon. That's now. The Lord is on the move. He is at work even now."

Did Daniel have any earthly reasons to think the captives would be allowed to return to Jerusalem? It didn't seem likely. No conquering army was present at the gates to defeat Babylon on behalf of Israel. Most of those who had been taken into captivity had died and their children were now acclimated to Babylonian culture. How many who remained hoped, like Daniel, that God would bring them back to the holy city? How many remembered that their identity was as God's chosen?

Over the past three weeks, perhaps your captivity to food and eating has seemed overwhelming. You may struggle with giving your desires to the Lord, feeling that you never string together "two good days" in a row. Because of God's grace, His promise to you still stands. He does have a plan, purpose, future, and a hope for you.

Hold fast to the promise of God. You may think you have no earthly reason to do so.

You may not have seen tangible changes or released any weight during these past three weeks. But as we will soon see, because of God's power and grace, He often does the impossible through impossible means. Even now He is at work in you. The fact that you are open to His Word is evidence that you have a heart that wants to be given over to the Lord.

Daniel's response was based on knowledge and faith in God's character. He didn't depend on the character of anyone else—not himself, not the king, not a neighboring nation. His confidence was in God alone. He knew that God pours forth grace on His children. He knew God always does what He says He will do. So he depended on His promises.

Let's continue reading in Jeremiah to see what else Daniel may have read that day.

"Then you will call upon me and come and pray to me, and I will listen to you. You will seek me and find me when you seek me with all your heart. I will be found by you," declares the LORD, "and will bring you back from captivity. I will gather you from all the nations and places where I have banished you," declares the LORD, "and will bring you back to the place from which I carried you into exile."
Jeremiah 29:12–14

Can you just see Daniel's heart pounding? The blood in his veins may have swelled with anticipation. The living Word of God was doing its work—dividing soul and spirit, joints and marrow (Hebrews 4:12). Daniel's "quiet time" was interactive with God as He spoke to him through the Scriptures. He listened and responded through prayer. We don't have to wonder what went through Daniel's mind when God spoke to his heart. He recorded it for us.

So I turned to the Lord God and pleaded with him in prayer and petition, in fasting, and in sackcloth and ashes. I prayed to the LORD my God and confessed. . . .
Daniel 9: 3–4a

Upon reading the promises that the exiles would be returned to the land of promise, Daniel believed. Let's look at the actions that demonstrated his belief.

1. Daniel turned to God. Often we say we believe, but how often do we turn to our Lord?

> What you choose to believe about God's promises and the identity He ascribes to you *will* affect the way you act.

© 2003, Thin Within, All Rights Reserved

LESSON

Our actions are true evidence of what we believe. Turning to the Lord implies that we turn away from something else vying for attention, such as the world, the flesh, or the devil. We turn away from the defective, the sinful, the impotent, and turn to the Lord. We turn to His ways, His will, and His solution. This is observation and correction. By welcoming the gracious leading of the Holy Spirit, we are convicted as to what is out of God's plan for us. We can then, in the power He provides, turn away from that and apply the needed correction. We turn to Him, His ways, and His will. This is applying God's grace in the everyday situations of our lives. He doesn't condemn when we are out of step, He corrects us by the powerful conviction of the Holy Spirit. This is precisely what Daniel did in the beginning of his prayer when he turned to God and away from whatever earthly things might distract him from belief and action.

▶**Personalize It:** You can experience the pouring out of God's grace in this moment. There is no condemnation in Christ (Romans 8:1). There is gentle nudging that convicts us regarding the need for change. Is there anything in the area of food and eating (or other areas in your life) you can observe and correct in the power of the Holy Spirit?

2. Daniel submitted his will to God. In response to the life-transforming message in Jeremiah, he began to plead, pray, petition, fast and confess to God.

- He asked God because God alone has authority.
- He confessed to God because God alone is holy.
- He exalted God because God alone is worthy.

What is your response to Jeremiah 29:11? Would that it be as wonderful as Daniel's? It is fascinating to look at the prayer Daniel recorded. We want to encourage you to journal your prayers because this can help you focus if you tend to become distracted. It can also act as a wonderful touchstone to refer to later, much as Daniel's prayer is for us today.

▶**Personalize It:** Is your will submitted to God? What

"Not by might, nor by power, but by my Spirit..." (Zechariah 4:6).

are you struggling with and not relinquishing to Him?

3. Daniel praised God. His prayer began by praising God for His character.

> "O Lord, the great and awesome God,
> who keeps his covenant of love with all who love him . . .
> Daniel 9:4b

- Here we see Daniel continue to point to God's sovereignty, power, love, and covenant. What kind of God would even make a covenant with us? He doesn't need us. This, too, is God's grace poured out on us.
- In verse 7, Daniel acknowledges God's righteousness.
- In verse 9 and 18, he exalts God for His mercy and forgiveness even of rebellious people—more grace displayed.
- In verses 14 and 16, Daniel remembers God's righteousness.
- In verse 15, he highlights God's power, might, and great deeds He has done.

▶**Personalize It:** Take time now to praise God for aspects of His character that most stimulate you to worship.

4. Daniel acknowledged the truth about his condition and his confidence in God's solution. After recalling the character of God, repenting of his own sin and acknowledging the sin of the people, Daniel makes a request asking God to "look with favor on [his] desolate sanctuary" (Daniel 9:17).

▶**Personalize It:** You have seen that your body is a temple of God, yet you may still struggle with unbelief. The fact that you are a tabernacle in which the Most High God dwells is clear from Scripture, but perhaps you feel less than "stately". Call out to God to look with favor on his desolate sanctuary. Join with Daniel in pleading with God that, according to his promises and his character, he will "open [his] eyes and see the desolation of the city that bears [his] Name" (verse 18). No matter how "scattered" or "desolate" you may feel today, God wants you to pour out your heart to him and call on him. Call on his character, his power, his mercy, and his grace to restore you to his glory. He will do it. In fact, he has already made you new in Christ.

© 2003, Thin Within, All Rights Reserved

5. Daniel anticipated and saw an answer to His prayer. Daniel was blessed with a visible experience that was evidence that God answers prayers prayed by His saints according to His Word. Gabriel, an angel, appeared to Daniel with this message:

As soon as you began to pray, an answer was given, which I have come to tell you, for you are highly esteemed.
Daniel 9:23

As amazing as it may seem, God used another pagan king to answer Daniel's plea to remember His promise and return the exiles to their homeland. The unbelievable would come through unbelievable means!

▶ **Personalize It:** Do you believe that God has already changed you from within and that you can melt down to your natural size and be revitalized in your body, soul, and spirit? Do you believe that He can satisfy your heart hunger? Ask God to help you with any unbelief that remains so that your actions are based on truth.

Ezra records God's response to Daniel's prayer:

In the first year of Cyrus king of Persia, in order to fulfill the word of the LORD spoken by Jeremiah, the LORD moved the heart of Cyrus king of Persia to make a proclamation throughout his realm and to put it in writing: "This is what Cyrus king of Persia says: 'The LORD, the God of heaven, has given me all the kingdoms of the earth and he has appointed me to build a temple for Him at Jerusalem in Judah.'"
Ezra 1:1–2

Cyrus, also known as Darius, was on the throne when Daniel read the Scriptures from Jeremiah. Cyrus became Israel's champion, a shepherd for God's people. He was a recipient of God's amazing grace, having had the blessing and privilege of participating in the fulfillment of God's promises to His people.

God often does the impossible in impossible ways through impossible means. Do you think you are as stuck as stuck can be? What about all those Israelites left in Babylon? They may have felt stuck too. Yet, faithful and according to plan and promise, God delivered them. Hallelujah!

Many of the exiles forgot their identity as Israelites and chose to stay behind. Many, however, chose to go back to the land of promise, Jerusalem, to restore the temple and to rebuild the wall around the city. What choice will you make? Will you allow God's grace to pour out upon you? Will you stand under it and let it drench you through and through?

Will you, like Daniel, believe the promises God has for you? When he read Jeremiah 29:11, he acted based on that belief. Daniel knew, based on God's character and promise, that God was at work now.

What about you? Do you know that now is the time?

Physiological Information

To more fully understand the power of beliefs, consider a person who thinks of herself as an endurance athlete. She runs road races, including marathons (26.2 miles), for "fun." When asked who she is, she shares what she considers to be her identity, "I am a long-distance runner." Because she thinks of herself as a runner, she acts in accordance with that belief. She runs. She may also eat certain foods and avoid others. She may eat while she runs, something that most of us don't usually do. The thought of how much water she drinks makes us float away. The fact is, believing that she is a marathon runner determines her actions.

Similarly, consider a person who thinks of himself as a couch potato. If he believes this to be who he is, how will he act? He isn't likely to eat while he runs—if he runs at all. Sadly, he is likely to sit all day, fiddle with the remote control, and eat like the person he thinks he is.

How do your beliefs about the promises of God affect your choices and your physical body? God has a plan for your freedom. He has drawn you here and given you material over the past three weeks to encourage and stimulate you. He has provided you with resources and has challenged you to believe in Him and what He wants to do in you.

If you believe that God wants you to experience freedom from overeating, food, and body issues, how will it affect your actions? If you believe that your body is reliable, that it will tell you what, when, how much to eat, and that God can satisfy your heart hunger, then gradually—perhaps almost imperceptibly—you will begin to make changes in keeping with those beliefs. Your actions will begin to reflect what you believe. Eventually you will be eating from 0 to 5. It may not all show up at once, but then we aren't talking about absolute perfection. We know that God is doing a work in our hearts and that it is by His grace that He changes us from within.

One hurdle to moving forward may be what you believe about yourself. Like the runner

© 2003, Thin Within, All Rights Reserved

LESSON

or "couch potato" in our previous examples, do you have a label for yourself? "I'm a human garbage can." "I'm bulimic." "I'm a food addict." "I'm anorexic." "I'm a hopeless failure." "I'm a Thin Within dropout." If you think of yourself as any of these things, it may be hard to break free from actions that coincide with this belief. Prayerfully evaluate this and submit it to God.

God says you have been set free from disabling labels. Start living as the person *He* says you are. What you choose to believe about God's promises and the identity He ascribes to you will affect the way you act. Daniel could have accepted his role as a captive. Instead, he chose to believe that what God said would indeed come true. He waited in faith for the decree of the king to be issued signaling the return to Jerusalem.

In any moment, you can observe and correct as Daniel did. You can turn away from *anything* that distracts you from God and His promises. Praise God for His character, confess to Him when you eat outside of 0 to 5, and beseech Him to accomplish His visible work in you that results in a thinner, healthier you. Spirit-filled eating, 0 to 5, is in agreement with what He has planned for you. He who has promised it will do it. Believe it!

Integration

Actions follow belief. Results follow actions. And with Daniel, we see the result of his actions was answered prayer—change.

The actual reality of the exiles' return to Jerusalem was just outward confirmation of something that Daniel believed in his heart. In the same sense, you releasing extra weight and being at peace with food, eating, and your body will be an outward confirmation of what you believe —that God is faithful. He has purchased and equipped you to walk in freedom and in truth.

The Holy Spirit empowers you. Your beliefs can be your worst enemy or one of your greatest allies. So take captive those thoughts that stand contrary to the Word of God and you will be victorious in living the truth of what God has promised.

According to your awesome and majestic Lord, it is "Not by might, nor by power, but by my Spirit . . ." (Zechariah 4:6).

This was promised to Zerubbabel, who was chosen to begin rebuilding the temple following the return of the exiles to Jerusalem. He may have had doubts as he faced what seemed impossible. Can you identify? God encouraged Zerubbabel with the promise that His Spirit would accomplish in him what his own flesh and strength could not.

You are like God's modern-day Zerubbabel, called to rebuild your body, the temple in which God now dwells. Hear the Word of the Lord to encourage you, His faithful Zerubbabel.

"Who are you, big mountain? In front of Zerubbabel you will become flat land, and he will bring out the topmost stone, shouting, 'It's beautiful! It's beautiful!'" Then the LORD spoke his word again, saying, "Zerubbabel has laid the foundation of this Temple, and he will complete it. Then you will know that the LORD All-Powerful has sent me to you. The people should not think that small beginnings are unimportant. They will be happy when they see Zerubbabel with tools, building the Temple. . . ."
Zechariah 4:7–10 (New Century Version)

Don't diminish your humble beginnings or be discouraged if you had difficulty getting started. God's promise is what matters. Your belief is to be based on what is factual and true. The results will be a changed life and a changed you from your heart outward!

As we conclude the first phase of the Thin Within program, we delight that by God's lavish love and amazing grace, our freedom has been purchased. We no longer need to be captives to sin, slavery, or the curse of the law. Like Daniel, we celebrate God's grace by taking Him at His Word so that we can walk in obedience to that which He has called us.

We learn from Scripture that God does not abandon His people, and He will not abandon you as His precious one. We rejoice in the fact that His promise still stands, regardless of how you have progressed during the past three weeks. It is *never* too late.

If you are bombarded with doubt or the

Our actions are true evidence of what we believe.

© 2003, Thin Within, All Rights Reserved

desire to "give up," refer to the Reentry after Fallout section of the appendix in this workbook. This is designed to encourage those who have not experienced the anticipated results.

Finally, our story in Daniel also serves as a reminder that God often does the *impossible* through *impossible* means. Expect Him to do amazing things and enjoy seeing His promises come to pass.

My Notes

© 2003, Thin Within, All Rights Reserved

EXERCISES

Day One

Going Deeper

The thought of how far you still have to go may seem overwhelming. You may wonder how it could be possible to find freedom when you have trouble stringing together "two good days" in a row. Journal what you have learned about God's grace and how He looks upon you despite your failures.

____
____
____
____

Bible Study

As you read Jeremiah 29:12–14, note the predominate theme from God. Journal about the declaration made in Romans 8:1 and how it affects God's response to you.

____
____
____
____

Knowing God by Heart: Hope

That is why I am suffering as I am. Yet I am not ashamed, because I know whom I have believed, and am convinced that he is able to guard what I have entrusted to him for that day.
2 Timothy 1:12

Look up the word "hope" in the dictionary and write down a definition that you believe is consistent with God being hope. Read Psalm 71:5 and relate your definition to this Scripture.

____
____
____
____

Getting Practical

Observe any trends you see in the hunger numbers you have logged this last week and ask God to help you grow through any mistakes you have experienced. Pray for God's grace to continue to transform you from within.

____
____
____
____

Memory Challenge

Start memorizing Jeremiah 29:11 today. Take time to see the message proclaimed in this Scripture. Read the verse out loud several times and then look away and say it from memory.
"For I know the plans I have for you," declares the LORD,
"plans to prosper you and not to harm you, plans to give you hope and a future."
Jeremiah 29:11

Thin Within Tip

Eat from smaller plates and bowls in keeping with "fist-sized" 0 to 5 eating.

© 2003, Thin Within, All Rights Reserved

Day Two

Going Deeper

Belief is defined in the dictionary as "conviction that certain things are true." What do you believe about God, yourself, and your future?

____

____

____

____

Bible Study

Read the prayer recorded in Daniel 9:3–19. What do Daniel's words reveal about his heart and his relationship to God? Daniel's response reflects a life submitted completely to God. Are you doing the same? Is there anything you are holding back from God out of fear or selfishness?

____

____

____

____

Knowing God by Heart

Continue to grow in your knowledge of God by reading Colossians 1:27 and Hebrews 6:19–20. What do these verses say to you about God being hope?

____

____

____

____

Getting Practical

When you eat this week, consider praying "Lord, what does starting at this hunger number tell me about what I believe about Your promises? . . . What does stopping at this hunger number indicate of my beliefs about Your promises to me?" Eating 0 to 5 is an action confirming your belief that what God says is true. Allow God to show you how your beliefs impact your actions and ultimately the end results.

____

____

____

____

Memory Challenge

Continue memorizing Jeremiah 29:11 by saying or writing it several times. After some repetition, try repeating it from memory. Take the memory verse card with you and refer to it throughout the day.

© 2003, Thin Within, All Rights Reserved

EXERCISES

Day Three

Going Deeper

Set aside some special time with the Lord as you pray and allow Him to fill those empty places in your heart. Like Daniel, consider journaling your prayers for a week and watch the hand of God move mountains.

____
____
____

Bible Study

Read John 1:1 and John 1:14. About whom are these verses speaking? Jesus came from the Father full of what two things? What is the significance of these two attributes being placed side by side in this passage?

____
____
____

Knowing God by Heart

Find synonyms for the word "hope" in a thesaurus or dictionary. How do these words give you a deeper understanding of God as hope?   Read Romans 15:13. What does it say about how God is hope and how does that affect you?

____
____
____

Getting Practical

Establish a goal of consistently finding 0 before you eat as you allow God to have His way with you.

____
____
____

Memory Challenge

Review Jeremiah 29:11 until you can repeat it from memory.

Thin Within Tip

Are there any foods or drinks that master you? When at 0, is there something that you "just gotta have" such as a candy bar, a hot fudge sundae, or a particular cookie? Do you find yourself lusting for hunger so you can dive into the thing that pleases your taste buds most? Try an experiment. Allow yourself to have that "favorite something" whenever you are hungry—in other words, morning, noon, and night until you get your fill. As strange as it may seem, as soon as you are free to eat the food that you enjoy, the "forbidden fruit" concept no longer controls you. Soon your body will call out for a wide variety of wholesome foods.

© 2003, Thin Within, All Rights Reserved

Day Four

Going Deeper

Do you believe that God has changed you from within and that you can melt down to your natural size, and be revitalized in your body, soul, and spirit? Do you believe that He can satisfy your heart hunger? Ask God to help you with any unbelief that remains so that your actions may be based on truth.

____
____
____
____

Bible Study

Read Mark 9:17–27. Describe the request of the father in verse 24. Regarding your unbelief, with what do you need Jesus' help?

____
____
____
____

Knowing God by Heart: Truth

Look up the word "truth" in the dictionary and write down a definition that you believe is consistent with God being truth. Read John 14:6 and relate your definition to this Scripture.

____
____
____
____

Getting Practical

Have you found a point of comfortable satisfaction (5)? Experiment with different amounts of food. You may discover that what you thought was a 3 is really a 5. In addition, you will become more attuned to your body and better able to plan to be at a zero when you so desire.

____
____
____
____

Memory Challenge

Repeat Jeremiah 29:11 from memory. Turn this verse into a prayer for yourself or someone you know.

© 2003, Thin Within, All Rights Reserved

EXERCISES

Day Five

Going Deeper

Do you have a label for yourself (such as "I'm a human garbage can," "I'm a food addict," "I'm a hopeless failure")? A label may make it hard to break free from the actions that go along with that belief. Prayerfully evaluate this and submit your labels and beliefs to God.

____

____

____

____

Bible Study

Read Isaiah 30:18–19. How does this comfort you today with your ongoing quest to submit to God as you eat from 0 to 5? Read John 14:12 and Matthew 17:20. What is required in order for impossible things to come to pass?

____

____

____

____

Knowing God by Heart

What do Psalm 31:5 and John 1:14 tell you about God?

____

____

____

Getting Practical

Have you dared to share your food with others to assist you in eating 0 to 5? How can you adjust when you eat, and how much you eat, so that 0 to 5 eating becomes a reality throughout the day?

____

____

____

____

Memory Challenge

Meditate on Jeremiah 29:11 throughout the day and allow it to draw you closer to God. Ask Him to help you truly believe this Scripture so that it can set you free from all the deceptive lies of the world.

Thin Within Tip

Prayerful fasting is permissible if you feel called by God to fast for a meal or two and you are under the leading of the Holy Spirit.

© 2003, Thin Within, All Rights Reserved

Day Six – Optional Exercises

Going Deeper

Jesus took the burden of all of our guilt and shame upon Himself when He died on the cross at Calvary. He freed us from all past, present, and future sin, so as believers, we are declared "not guilty" through this incredible act of love. If the "false guilt" of self-condemnation that comes from the enemy is burdening you, take this to God and you can with confidence accept the "not guilty" verdict.

____

____

____

____

Bible Study

Being free from the burden of "false guilt" does not, however, mean we should never feel any guilt whatsoever. There is "biblical guilt" that we experience when we sin. If we gossip, overindulge, or lust after things that are not in line with God's will for us, we experience "biblical guilt" when the Holy Spirit nudges us to repentance and humility before God. Read Hebrews 10:19–23. Ask God to show you any unconfessed sin remaining in your heart so that He might cleanse your guilty conscience and restore the broken fellowship with Him. After reading Romans 8:1, journal on your freedom from the "false guilt" of self-condemnation.

____

____

____

____

Knowing God by Heart

Find synonyms for the word "truth" in a thesaurus or dictionary. How do these words give you a deeper understanding of God as truth? Read John 14:16–17 and John 16:13 to know about the Spirit of truth and how He will guide you.

____

____

____

____

Getting Practical

Have you considered sharing your food with others to assist you in eating 0 to 5? How can you adjust when you eat, and how much you eat, so that 0 to 5 eating becomes a reality throughout the day?

____

____

____

____

Memory Challenge

Repeat Jeremiah 29:11 out loud and ask God to make this verse real in your life. What might God be leading you to "be" or to "do" in response to this passage?

© 2003, Thin Within, All Rights Reserved

EXERCISES

Day Seven – Optional Exercises

Going Deeper

What you choose to believe about God's promises and the identity that He ascribes to you will affect the way you act. God says you are free in Him. How can you start living as the person He says you are?

____

____

____

____

Bible Study

Read Zechariah 4:6 and identify how you can accomplish things that you have never been able to do in your own strength. Journal a prayer of how you have tried to do things in the past in your own strength and power, and then your surrender to a new plan of action according to this verse.

____

____

____

____

Getting Practical

Continue to monitor your hunger numbers throughout the day.

____

____

____

____

Memory Challenge

Share your memory verse with a friend or family member, telling him or her how it relates to your Thin Within journey.

Thin Within Tip

It is really OK to skip a meal. Nothing terrible will happen. You will not die. God has designed our bodies to endure the lean times. This is evidenced in situations where people have been stranded or caught in unforeseen circumstances for days and survived. However, let it be clear that we are not advocating intentional long-term deprivation.

© 2003, Thin Within, All Rights Reserved

Review of the Week

Take time at the end of each week to review what God has taught you and how it is impacting your life. This will give you a great overview to take to your Thin Within Support Group Meeting.

The most significant thing God taught me this week:

____
____
____
____

In this week's lesson and day 2 of the bible study, I saw Daniel as another illustration of beliefs producing actions. My memory verse this week states that God has plans for me. When I choose to believe this scripture my actions will be:

____
____
____

If I allowed my faith to truly impact my actions in the area of food and weight, my actions would be:

____
____
____

I have come to the conclusion of the first phase of Thin Within. Although I understand that there is still room to grow in this area of freedom, I have experienced freedom in:

____
____
____

I have not experienced freedom in:

____
____
____

The most significant thing that God helped me to observe this week that I will focus on correcting next week:

____
____
____
____

What I have learned about the character of God as hope and truth, and how I have come to know and be drawn closer to Him:

____
____
____

My prayer requests and praises:

____
____
____
____

© 2003, Thin Within, All Rights Reserved

© 2003, Thin Within, All Rights Reserved

thin within

Month Two

Lessons &

Exercises

© 2003, Thin Within, All Rights Reserved

You are now entering Phase II of your Thin Within journey. Consider the description of Phase II below as you seek to renew your mind.

Phase II - Discernment Phase: "not all things are beneficial"

God reminds us that, "all things are permissible, but not all things are beneficial". So now it's time to discern or tune in to your God-given body and the Holy Spirit's desire to teach you. Yes, you can have any food you choose but consider the best choice regarding your total well-being.

This is the phase where you begin to evaluate how you feel when you eat certain foods. You may discover you have more energy and sleep better when making certain food choices and the reverse may also be true. So your choices are not simply about a "taste bud" sensation but about caring for your body as a temple of the Holy Spirit!

In the discernment phase you will come to realize that you have the responsibility to choose wisely taking into account that your God-given freedom is not to be misused as "license" to eat whatever looks, smells or sounds good; our freedom has been purchased at a very high price.

© 2003, Thin Within, All Rights Reserved

Restoration

Introduction

Welcome to Phase Two of Thin Within. Last week we celebrated the transforming power of God's grace that is poured out abundantly on us through Christ. In the first phase of Thin Within we experienced God's amazing grace through unchaining the shackles of dieting laws and of the dieting mentality that may have bound you for years.

We recognized last week that God's grace has been demonstrated throughout history, including in the lives of the Israelite exiles. The Lord fulfilled His promises to them by doing the *impossible* through *impossible* means. He set them free after seventy years in captivity.

This historical account demonstrates God's unwavering devotion and love for His people. We can trust in His promises that He will free us from our captivity to disordered eating and ungodly behavior regarding our bodies. As we remember who we are in Him and the freedom He purchased by His blood, we can begin to experience the abundant life that we were born to enjoy in Christ Jesus (John 10:10).

During Phase One, we emphasized that your body is not your own. It is the very temple of the Holy Spirit that Christ purchased with His blood. You have begun to see that even if your temple is in ruins, in Christ you can rebuild it. We began laying a firm foundation for this restoration process by using the truth of God's Word.

We quickly discovered, however, that the rubble of our past flesh machinery is part of our old identity, the old man with all the old flesh patterns. Scripture identifies two types of people. We are either in Adam or in Christ (1 Corinthians 15:22). What we believe about our identity is reflected in the choices we make. So in order to see progress, we will have to examine our beliefs. Beliefs result in actions. Therefore, we put off those old habits and thought patterns and put on the new through the renewing of our minds

. . . Avoid looking at 0 to 5 as a law that will "fix" you.

(Ephesians 4:22–24). Our foundation will be firm and secure only as it is built on our new identity in Christ.

We recognized that we are no longer hopeless but more than conquerors through Him who loved us. As we embrace this truth by faith, we will begin to experience the reality of it in our lives. According to God's Word, this is the truth of who we are—dead to sin but alive to God in Christ! This is yet again a demonstration of God's amazing grace making it possible in Him to live a new life. We don't have to remain locked into our old way of living. We can walk in the ways of the new redeemed man. Oh, it may seem impossible, but take heart! The Lord has purchased your pardon, and He will show you the way to step out of captivity into the practical realization of the hope that He has stored up for you in Christ.

During the first phase of Thin Within , we discovered that there is glorious freedom from the law—from diet plans, man-made rules, and regulations—and we have rejoiced in this newfound freedom.

"Everything is permissible for me" —
but not everything is beneficial.
"Everything is permissible for me"
— but I will not be mastered by anything.
1 Corinthians 6:12

Coupled with the statement that everything is permissible is the acknowledgment that, while everything is "OK," "allowed," and "acceptable," not everything is beneficial.

During Phase Two of Thin Within , we will see the Lord lead us from the realm of merely rejoicing in our freedom from the curse of the law into a place of walking responsibly in that freedom. We are not building just any temple. We want to build a godly temple with only the choicest materials, just as the Lord required of Solomon when he built His temple. We are building that in which the Holy Spirit dwells. Our lives are to be a reflection of His holiness. Because of His mercy and grace, we begin to ask Him to direct us to make choices that reflect our awe and wonder of Him. We surrender our will and our rights unto Him who alone is able. In so doing, we

© 2003, Thin Within, All Rights Reserved

LESSON

are attentive to the leading of His Spirit within.

As you wait on the Lord, the Spirit will lead you to that which is good, pleasing, and acceptable. Does this sound far beyond your ability to accomplish? In your flesh it is. However, a tremendous source of supernatural power is available to you as you allow the transforming work of a holy God to restore your temple. Actually it is the only source of power sufficient for the work that is required.

Spiritual Foundation

It is only by the power of God's grace that we experience the fullness of the life we have been given in Christ. In Romans 6:14, Paul tells us that we have changed power sources. We are no longer under our own influence and strength. We are no longer under law. Grace is our new master. Herein lies the key: Grace is not simply a pardon from sin, but it is also a constant presence, power, and provision. It is the power source that enables us to live the crucified life, a life where we are dead to sin and alive to God. That is the resurrected life!

Grace is the *unmerited* favor and *unmerited* blessing of God in our lives. Grace provides the opposite of what we deserve. "Unmerited" means that it is not deserved and cannot be earned by anything we do. It cannot be bought by our performance nor is it withheld because of any lack of performance. Grace flows from the heart of God because of His great love for us. Grace is initiated by God and extended to us based on the finished work of Christ on the cross. It is available to us for the purpose of expressing the life of Christ in and through the believer by faith alone (Habakkuk 2:4).

Rather than abuse this unmerited favor by running rampant in sinful behavior we offer ourselves completely to Him out of a heart overflowing with gratitude and compelled by love. Paul speaks to this as well:

What then? Shall we sin because we are not under law but under grace? By no means!
Romans 6:15

Sadly, many never experience grace as the constant provision and power source that it was meant to be. God's grace is not meant to be boxed into a one-time moment whereby we are pardoned for all past, present, and future sin. Though that alone is a glorious gift, it is only part of the picture. Love beyond measure motivates God, who offers us favor and forgiveness through Christ's atoning death. It equips and empowers us through Christ's resurrection life in us (Titus 2:11–12). This is the Spirit-filled life.

We tend, however, to stay stuck in the familiar. We focus on our laws and rules and what we will "*do* for God." We miss the still small voice and the whisper that says, "Be still, My child. Rest in Me. I am here. I am present. My love, My power, My presence, and My provision are more than enough for you."

Letting go of our striving to *do* is so very difficult, isn't it? It comes so naturally to us. Society teaches that we gain approval by doing. With natural man, not yet born of the Spirit, this is true. But with God, this is not true. His provision, power, and pardon are all things that God does; those same things allow us to trust in Him. When we trust in Him, we then do what He calls us to do, which is to walk in obedience to His ways.

Paul tells us we have been released from the curse of the law—the outward list of dos and don'ts. "So, my brothers, you also died to the law through the body of Christ . . . so that we serve in the new way of the Spirit" (Romans 7:4a, 6b). Then Paul immediately speaks of the struggle he had in his flesh to live in this new identity according to the law. He explains how he strived to do because he knew all the dos and don'ts, but he couldn't live according to them. He verbalizes his frustration that his behavior didn't reflect his new identity in Christ. He still felt enslaved to sin. He says, "I do not understand what I do. For what I want to do I do not do, but what I hate I do" (Romans 7:15).

The New American Standard renders verse 18 this way: "I know that nothing good lives in me, that is, in my flesh. For I have the desire to do what is good but I cannot carry it out." In verses 23 and 24, he finds a law at work: "When I want to do good, evil is right there with me. For in my inner being I delight in God's law, but I'm a prisoner to the law of sin in my members. Oh, wretched man that I am who will rescue me from this body of death?"

Most of us can identify with the struggle of wanting desperately to do what is right, such as eating between 0 and 5. Yet at times we find that impossible to do. A part of us rises up in rebellion against that which our conscience and the nudging of the Spirit tells us is right. Do you feel that the good you want to do you cannot do and the evil you hate is what you do? Does it seem as if the

   © 2003, Thin Within, All Rights Reserved

more you try not to think of food, the more you actually think of food, and the more you think of food the more you want to eat? The result is that you may find yourself eating when you aren't hungry and maybe not even knowing why.

Do you ever feel like a great chasm exists between the knowledge of your new identity in Christ and the reality of living it? In a very real way, there is. The more we strive in our self-efforts to bridge that chasm, the more we see the law of sin at work. Only God's transforming grace can bridge that gap. As Paul admits in Romans 7, we can try to bridge it by law—by what we *do*—but the law is powerless to give us newness of life. The law is utterly impotent to make it happen, even when combined with our best intentions and self-effort. Only when we come to the end of ourselves in total defeat do we cry out in utter dependence on Him. It is a painful but necessary experience, a devastating brokenness that God uses to bring us to the point where we are ready and willing to receive His grace—God's unmerited, undeserved favor—to live the resurrected life by the power of His Holy Spirit within us.

Are you feeling victorious? If so, we thank God for what He is doing in you. Or are you feeling frustrated with yourself and with your lack of success? Have you given up even hoping to have a "normal" attitude toward food and your body? You may be struggling and failing, but God longs to teach you to observe and correct in the midst of your struggles and failures. Hopefully you are made humble, not hopeless, in this process, because God gives grace to the humble. If you want to throw up your hands and quit, throw them up to God! Ask Him to pour out on you what only He can. He will meet you in this place with His steadfast love. He will teach you what He wants you to know if only you will ask Him. He has and is all that you need.

The grace of God not only saves us from our sins but is the power by which we live moment by moment in newness of life in Him. In Romans 7, Paul, brought to this point of humility and brokenness, cries out, "Oh wretched man that I am. Who will deliver me from this body of death?" (Romans 7:24). This is observation. "Thanks be to God through Jesus Christ our Lord!" (Romans 7:25). This is the correction. Paul knew that trying in his flesh wasn't working. He realized the only solution was Christ who had given His life so that we may experience grace moment by moment, strengthening us to make choices in line with godliness. Can you see that grace is much more than a one-time pardon for sin?

Grace bridges the chasm of failure. Just as Paul discovered in Romans 8:1, "Therefore, there is now no condemnation for those who are in Christ Jesus" we, too, discover that God doesn't condemn us. However, we must admit our failures and our sins as we humbly take them to God. "If we confess our sins, he is faithful and just to forgive us our sins and will purify us from all unrighteousness" (1 John 1:9). What an awesome promise this is. Not only is forgiveness available to us, but God is also faithful to purify us from all unrighteousness. He doesn't just forgive us. He personally cleans us up as we humbly take our failures to him in faith. We can start with a clean slate, cleansed by his blood and empowered by his Spirit. It is only as we see our mistakes and look to him that we can learn, grow, and mature in our walk with God.

In Romans 8, Paul tells us that the law of the Spirit of life—the life of Christ living in us—sets us free from the law of sin and death. What is the law of sin? It is that constant pull we feel when we want to do good and realize that evil is right there with us. We may want to eat 0 to 5, for instance, but then we go to dinner and a movie with a group of friends. The popcorn, candy, and sodas at the theater seem to be part of the package. We give in even though we were at a comfortable 5 following that dinner we had just minutes before. It is only as we look to Christ and trust Him to live His life in us that our new identity in Him becomes a

> It is only by the power of God's grace that we experience the fullness of the life we have been given in Christ.

reality. Then giving in to the flesh is not a viable option.

The Russian pilot whose story we told in week three was able to embrace his new identity and citizenship as an American when he trusted in the legal status granted by the U.S. government. He flourished in the reality of his new identity and never returned to his old oppressive state. You, too, can live beyond the pull of your old fleshly nature that was crucified with Christ as you savor the resurrected life!

Physiological Information

We want to step out of the "former citizenship mentality" and realize that because of our identity in Christ we are God's people. We have been set free to live in the transforming power of God's grace. There may be obstacles, however, that keep us from seeing our true identity, which is based not on what we *do* but on who we *are* in Christ. We must remember that our status is changed forever, and we are free to flourish in that new identity.

In fact, if you have not yet released any weight so far, you may be tempted to blame it on the very freedom that Thin Within endorses. How are you to respond to this challenging situation?

Rather than look for more rules or to another program, recognize that the law in any form is powerless to restrain fleshly indulgence (Colossians 2:20–23, NASB). Instead, up the ante in your accountability regarding your hunger numbers. This is what we mean:

If you truly believe you have been eating between a 0 and 5 or less and are still not releasing weight, perhaps you need to refine your 0 and your 5. Do this by asking the Lord to give you discernment. Is there anything that is causing you to think you are hungry, when your stomach isn't actually empty? When you think you are at a 0, review your hunger numbers beginning with your mouth, throat, stomach, and then your abdomen. See what sensations are present. Then stop at an appropriate 5, which will make a big difference. Do you notice you want to continue to eat past the place of comfort to a 6, 7, or even an 8? Rather than see how many bites you can "get away with"

before reaching your 5, why not see how close to a 4 or a 3 you can remain, yet still be comfortable? Ask the Holy Spirit to direct and guide you.

Notice how your body responds to different foods. Are you eating 0 to 5 but feel as if you are hungry all the time? If so, maybe what you are eating isn't the wisest choice. Some people find that certain foods sustain them for longer periods of time. Some things may taste good but may not satisfy in the long run and may fool you into thinking that you are at a 0 even if you are not. Notice how your body responds to various foods. For example, eating a greasy hamburger and french fries may cause you to feel lethargic, where as fruits and vegetables may energize you for an enjoyable activity.

We encourage you to avoid looking at 0 to 5 as a law that will "fix" you. It will, however, lead you to the One who has the power through His transforming grace to change you from within. As you apply yourself to 0 to 5 eating, offer your appetite and your body to God as a living sacrifice. His grace alone will supply what is needed as you eat the food that your body requires in order to be nourished, healthy, and vibrant. Over the course of time, as you turn to the Lord to meet your needs, eating will become an integral part of your day rather than the most anticipated "event."

Believing that we can improve on what God has done is another obstacle to avoid. This kind of thinking is a way of reverting to fleshly patterns. For instance, some people think that if eating 0 to 5 is effective, then eating only fat-free foods 0 to 5 or using diet drinks in place of meals will *really* help to release weight more quickly. Still another ploy might be to eat between 0 and 5, and count those calories "just to be sure." Hopping on and off the scales and excessive exercising are other techniques that won't solve the issues of your heart that cause you to struggle with food, body, and weight-related issues.

When we apply a law to our condition and begin to put our hope in it, we fail to cling to the Savior and experience His grace as a constant provision and power for the change He wants to work from within. Your body truly is remarkable and God carefully crafted it with built-in hunger and fullness signals to guide and direct you. He will

Grace bridges the chasm of failure.

© 2003, Thin Within, All Rights Reserved

speak to you through the cues of your body as you listen for His voice and develop a discerning spirit that is yielded to Him.

Integration

This week your focus will be on how to avoid the tendency to revert to legalism, or laws in any form, if you find that you are stuck. You will want to avoid the temptation to try to "improve" on the work God is doing. Focus instead on the matchless face of Jesus, and then you will more easily discern your hunger numbers and His will for your eating. We have seen that the human tendency is to want rules that tell us what to do. It seems so much easier when someone tells us what to eat or not eat. You may feel as if you can't handle the freedom of choosing the foods that will work best for your body. You may think, "If I just had the right food rules to follow I could be successful. It is all of this freedom that is messing me up."

Avoid getting caught again in the pendulum of "trying harder" with the "right" set of rules and then "giving up" because it is impossible to make them work. As Paul writes in Romans 7, don't try to live by laws that can't straighten out your behavior. You may even be tempted to make 0 to 5 eating a law in your life. But remember, the law was never meant to fix us. Rather it was intended to demonstrate that we can't fix ourselves and to expose our need for Christ, who has given us all we need to become like Him.

So the law was put in charge to lead us to Christ
that we might be justified by faith.
Galatians 3:24

The law will fail you every time. There is no power in the law to enable you to obey. If you start struggling, avoid the temptation to think, "OK, *I* have to get a grip. *I'll* fast till lunch or *I'll* eat only protein today." If you succumb to that kind of thinking you place yourself again under the supervision and restraint of the law, hoping to straighten yourself out. You are looking to yourself and to "Do not handle, do not taste, do not touch" to "get it together," even though God's Word clearly says that these have absolutely no value in dealing with fleshly indulgence (Colossians 2:23, NASB).

There is only one way to get "straightened out": quit trying and start trusting by faith.

Avail yourself of the power of God's transforming grace rather than the powerlessness of the law. Make the Spirit, rather than the law, your default system. Allow the Spirit to be your fresh beginning each and every time you need it. Rather than looking for an external "do" or "don't," look to the internal power of God's transforming grace. "For it is God who works in you to will and to act according to his good purpose" (Philippians 2:13).

As you learn to look to God and trust Him with your body as you seek to melt down to your natural God-given size, you will experience times of testing, trial, and failure. But the good news is that as you draw upon God's provision of grace, you are going to grow through those times. As you observe and correct, or in biblical terms "confess and repent," you will have a change of heart and learn from your mistakes. Look to God's indwelling Holy Spirit to enable you to get back on track and grow in the process. Avoid the natural, fleshly tendency to look to your own resources as well as to the law for a quick fix.

Stand firm, then, and do not let yourselves
be burdened again by a yoke of slavery.
Galatians 5:1b

The law kills (Romans 4:15; Romans 8:2). It has no power to enable us to obey or to meet the requirements of a holy God. The Spirit gives life (John 6:63). The life of Christ within us is the power source of God's transforming grace. Trust Him to make you truly thin within!

My Notes

© 2003, Thin Within, All Rights Reserved

EXERCISES

Day One

Going Deeper

How would you define grace? Journal how grace has worked in your life. What role do you think grace has in finding victory in overeating and weight-related issues?

____

____

____

____

Bible Study

Read Titus 2:11–14. Consider how God's grace goes beyond salvation to help in your daily life. As Jesus has redeemed you and purified you through His sacrifice on the cross, what is your natural response according to verse 14?

____

____

____

____

Knowing God by Heart: Just

My purpose is that they may be encouraged in heart and united in love, so that they may have the full riches of complete understanding, <u>in order that they may know the mystery of God, namely, Christ,</u> in whom are hidden all the treasures of wisdom and knowledge.
Colossians 2:2–3

Look up the word "just" in the dictionary and write down a definition that you believe is consistent with God being just. Read Deuteronomy 32:4 and relate your definition to this Scripture.

____

____

____

____

Getting Practical

Journal what you have experienced with hunger numbers and eating between 0 and 5 over the last four weeks. Have you been successful eating within these parameters? If you haven't yet released much weight, consider refining or redefining your 0 and 5. You might even consider stopping at a 3 or a 4 one meal a day, just to see how your body responds. Record any new insights you have.

____

____

____

____

Memory Challenge

Start memorizing Titus 2:11–12. Take time to see the message proclaimed in this Scripture. Read the verses out loud several times, then look away and say them from memory.

For the grace of God that brings salvation has appeared to all men.
It teaches us to say "No" to ungodliness and worldly passions,
and to live self-controlled, upright and godly lives in this present age,
Titus 2:11–12

   © 2003, Thin Within, All Rights Reserved

Day Two

Going Deeper

Journal your thoughts on the idea that everything is permissible, but not everything is beneficial (1 Corinthians 6:12).

____
____
____
____
____

Bible Study

Read Romans 7:14–24. Do you have the tendency to do what you don't want to do? Can you relate with Paul in wanting to do what is good, but not being able to carry it out?   Journal how Titus 2:11–14 shares the answer to the tendency to do what is undesired.

____
____
____
____

Knowing God by Heart

Continue to grow in your knowledge of how God is just by reading Numbers 14:18 and 23:19. Write your thoughts.

____
____
____
____

Getting Practical

Pay attention to how your body responds to the foods you eat. Notice if some foods seem to satisfy your physical needs longer than others. Take mental note of this as your observation and apply it as godly correction. You will be using these observations in the next few weeks to find what are the most beneficial choices for your uniquely designed body.

____
____
____
____

Memory Challenge

Continue memorizing Titus 2:11–12 by saying or writing it several times. After some repetition, try repeating it from memory. Take the memory verse card with you and refer to it throughout the day.

Thin Within Tip

Create an appealing table setting. Leave the food containers on the counter and serve individual portions. This requires a moment of prayerful consideration as you get up from the table for a second serving.

© 2003, Thin Within, All Rights Reserved

EXERCISES

Day Three

Going Deeper

Observe and correct. Do you find yourself doing what you don't want to do? Prayerfully consider what the Lord directs you to do in those specific instances and execute that correction the next time a similar situation faces you. Record it in your journal.

____

____

____

Bible Study

As believers in Jesus Christ, we become new creatures. We are now "in Christ." The Holy Spirit indwells us so that through the power of the Spirit we put off old fleshly habits and put on new Christ-like behavior. Look at the chart at the bottom of this page showing examples of both walking according to the flesh and walking according to the Spirit. Which one is consistent with our true identity in Christ? Can you add to these lists? (Refer to the Month One – Week Three lesson entitled "Identity in Christ.")

____

____

____

Knowing God by Heart

Find synonyms for the word "just" in a thesaurus or dictionary. How do these words give you a deeper understanding of God as just? Read Psalm 89:14–15. What does it say about how God is just and how that will affect you?

____

____

____

Getting Practical

As you continue to log your hunger numbers, consider using the Flesh Machinery Log (found at the bottom of Day 7 page C-14). This is a great tool to observe reasons why you eat when you are not hungry. Look over the log and write down some flesh machinery that you see in you.

Memory Challenge

Review Titus 2:11–12 until you can repeat it from memory.

Walking According to the Flesh	Walking According to the Spirit
Abusing food, alcohol, drugs, sex, or work	Died with Christ and died to the power of sin's rule over my life (Romans 6:1–23)
Resisting and rebelling against my God-given conscience and nudging of the Spirit	Completely forgiven and made righteous, having peace with God (Romans 5:1–11; 2 Corinthians 5:21; Colossians 2:13)
Believing lies of worthlessness or stupidity	Freedom from self-condemnation (Romans 8:1)
People pleasing	Given the mind of Christ (1 Corinthians 2:16)

© 2003, Thin Within, All Rights Reserved

Day Four

Going Deeper

Grace is not simply a pardon for sin, but also a constant presence, power, and provision. It is the power source that enables us to live the crucified life, a life where we are dead to sin and alive to God. That is the resurrected abundant life! Are you beginning to see the connection between grace and the abundant life?

____
____
____
____

Bible Study

Go back to the Day Three Bible Study exercise and see if you can add to the two lists. As you look through the entries, pray about how God might transform you in areas where you walk in the flesh, so that you might begin to walk in the Spirit.

____
____
____
____
____

Knowing God by Heart: Righteous

Look up the word "righteous" in the dictionary and write down a definition that you believe is consistent with God being righteous. Read Psalm145:17 and relate your definition to this Scripture.

____
____
____
____

Getting Practical

Continue using the Flesh Machinery Log by adding items to the "Flesh Machinery in Others" category.

____
____
____
____

Memory Challenge

Repeat Titus 2:11–12 from memory. Turn these verses into a prayer for yourself or someone you know.

Thin Within Tip

In a restaurant, ask for a carryout container ahead of time so you can remove half of the food before you even get started.

© 2003, Thin Within, All Rights Reserved

EXERCISES

Day Five

Going Deeper

Is it tempting to revert back to the old way of eating when you are not losing weight as quickly as you would like? The human tendency is to want rules that tell us what to do. But rules and laws can't fix us. Journal about any temptation you may have to fall back on the rules. Pray for God to sever that temptation in your life.

____

____

____

____

Bible Study

Paul has let us know in Romans 7:24–8:4 that in ourselves failure is inevitable. What promise does God give us in our daily sin? (1 John 1:9; Hebrews 10:19–23)

____

____

____

Knowing God by Heart

Read Psalm 119:137, 142 and Hosea 14:9. How do these verses show you God's righteousness?

____

____

____

Getting Practical

Now look at the "Flesh Machinery in Media" category on the Flesh Machinery Log. Write down ways the media influences you.

____

____

____

Memory Challenge

Meditate on Titus 2:11–12 throughout the day and allow it to draw you closer to God. Ask Him to help you truly believe this Scripture so that it can set you free from all the deceptive lies of the world.

Thin Within Tip

If you consistently eat too quickly and find yourself beyond a 5, stop at a 3 or 4. Then you will find yourself at a comfortable 5 thirty minutes later.

© 2003, Thin Within, All Rights Reserved

Day Six – Optional Exercises

Going Deeper

Have you tried to "improve" on the hunger/satisfaction way of eating by adding something else to "help weight loss along"? (For example: eating only fat-free foods, diet shakes, or other diet foods within 0 to 5; counting calories along with hunger numbers; fasting for the purpose of speeding up the process; eating only protein for a time.) Consider how these actions might be adding a "law" to your body's natural way to eat.

____

____

____

____

Bible Study

Read Colossians 2:20–23 and reflect on all the world's eating rules to which you are tempted to submit. What does Galatians 3:21–25 say about the law and its present role?

____

____

____

____

Knowing God by Heart

Find synonyms for the word "righteous" in a thesaurus or dictionary. How do these words give you a deeper understanding of God's righteousness? Read 2 Timothy 4:8 and 1 John 2:1–2. What do these Scriptures tell you about God?

____

____

____

____

Getting Practical

Take one more look at the Flesh Machinery Log and see if anything else comes to mind that you might add. Take this list to the Lord and ask Him to show you truth compared to these lies that you are bombarded with every day.

____

____

____

____

Memory Challenge

Repeat Titus 2:11–12 out loud and ask God to make these verses real in your life. What might God be leading you to "be" or to "do" in response to this passage?

© 2003, Thin Within, All Rights Reserved

EXERCISES

Day Seven – Optional Exercises

Going Deeper

According to Galatians 5:1, what was Christ's reason for coming? It says we are to stand firm in this verse. How can we do this (Ephesians 6:10–18)?

____

____

____

____

Bible Study

Our strength to stand firm comes from the Lord. Isaiah 40:31 tells us that those who hope (place confidence in with an expectation or belief that it will be obtained) in the Lord will renew their strength. Reflect on the idea of hoping in the Lord and God's provision for you.

____

____

____

____

Getting Practical

Has it become automatic to think about your hunger number when eating comes to mind? If not, ask God to establish that practice in your life.

____

____

____

____

Memory Challenge

Share your memory verse with a friend or family member, telling him or her how it relates to your Thin Within journey.

Flesh Machinery Log

Below, record any of your personal flesh machinery ("I paid for it so I should eat all of it"), from others ("You have to clean your plate"), and from the media ("Feed the Need"). As you observe and correct your flesh machinery you will be amazed at the changes that will occur in your eating patterns.

Flesh Machinery in Me	**Flesh Machinery from Others**	**Flesh Machinery from Media**

Thin Within Tip

Stop looking for that magic moment when this will all fall into place. Remember, this is a process allowing God to have His rightful first place in your life.

 © 2003, Thin Within, All Rights Reserved

Review of the Week

Take time at the end of each week to review what God has taught you and how it is impacting your life. This will give you a great overview to take to your Thin Within Support Group Meeting.

The most significant thing God taught me this week:

According to this week's memory verse, grace teaches me to say no to ungodliness and worldly passions. I have learned to say no to:

This week I started phase 2 of the Thin Within journey—all things are permissible but not all things are beneficial. I need to make beneficial choices within my freedom.   One beneficial choice I made this week:

The most significant thing that God helped me to observe this week that I will focus on correcting next week:

What I have learned about the character of God as just and righteous, and how I have come to know and be drawn closer to Him:

My prayer requests and praises:

© 2003, Thin Within, All Rights Reserved

LESSON

Counting the Cost

Introduction

Last week we recognized the power source needed to restore our temples to their God-ordained splendor. "Christ in you the hope of glory!" summarizes what we have discussed. As the life of Christ is lived out in us, the glory of Christ will be revealed through us. We also learned the importance of observing and correcting, which is the way we actually mature through our mistakes and experience the transforming power of God's grace at work within us.

This week we will see how life that moves steadily forward on the path of God's provision is a life of choices—costly choices. As we investigate what this new level of commitment involves we are given an encouraging promise:

His divine power has given us everything we need
for life and godliness through our knowledge
of him who called us by his own glory and goodness.
2 Peter 1:3

As we discussed last week, the grace of God is a pardon that we receive once upon salvation. It is a "done deal," good now and forever. However, His grace doesn't stop there. It is also a constant power source, a presence, and provision for His people. Unfortunately, many of us do not walk fully in this grace. Either we aren't thoroughly aware of what it means, or we revert to the law, striving in our own strength to do that which we can't do apart from dependence upon His Spirit within. We hear about "living according to the Spirit" on Sunday mornings in church, but do we connect with what that really means in our day-to-day life?

This week we will make practical applications of the wondrous truths that we have had the pleasure to absorb over the past five weeks. We will see that one of the things God's grace provides is the desire "to will and to do" according to His good pleasure. In the moment when a choice is before us, we must turn to Him to discern what actually is His good pleasure. Then as we avail ourselves of His tender mercies and comprehend His amazing grace, He gives us a heart that wants to yield or surrender all to Him.

Spiritual Foundation

Christ's life lived in and through you provides the hope and the means of making a godly choice each and every time you have an opportunity. But how can you experience the reality of this Spirit-led life?

For those who are according to the flesh set their minds on
the things of the flesh, but those who are according to the
Spirit, the things of the Spirit.
Romans 8:5, NASB

If you desire to experience the victory that Christ purchased for you, and if you want to see the Lord be glorified in all you do, including in your eating and drinking (1 Corinthians 10:31), you must choose to *set* your mind on the things of the Spirit.

Conversely, if you experience consistent defeat, you need to evaluate where your mind is fixed. What are you thinking? What are your values or priorities? According to Romans 8:5, if your mind is set on the flesh, you will live accordingly. You choose what you set your mind on. It is a choice you make countless times throughout a day.

Although it may seem as if our minds are stuck in destructive or fleshly patterns, we actually can do something about this. We are not victims of our minds. In fact, Scripture says we can take our thoughts captive rather than allow them to take us captive.

If we follow the pattern offered to us in God's Word, our minds will be renewed and retrained in the way of the Spirit. Our behavior will fall in line accordingly, and we will live our lives by the Spirit as Romans 8:5 promises. We are to put off the old way of the flesh with its worldly mindset, and put on the new, in which we are created to be like God in true righteousness and holiness (Ephesians 4:22–24). Scripture also tells us on what to set our minds.

Set your minds on things above, not on earthly things.
Colossians 3:2

In order to set our mind on things above, things of the Spirit, instead of earthly things of the flesh, we must become very well acquainted with both. As we understand what the fleshly mindset looks like, we can begin to discern when it rears its ugly head and refuse to be taken in by it.

The fleshly mindset dwells on past disappointments, failures, or even past victories, which can result in puffed-up pride. Such thoughts can lead you down a slippery slope, so it is imperative that they be taken captive to Christ. Ask Him to open the eyes of your understanding so that you can learn from the past rather than condemn yourself for it. Pray that the Spirit of our living God will use

 © 2003, Thin Within, All Rights Reserved

such thoughts for His purposes to be accomplished in you.

Similarly, it can be fruitless to focus inappropriately on the future, thinking that life will *finally* be perfect and worth living when you reach your ideal size. This is a lie from Satan that keeps you from living in the present moment, which our precious Savior and Lord has given to you right now. As Psalm 118:24 says, "This is the day the LORD has made; let us rejoice and be glad in it!"

Instead of seeking the will of the Lord in the present moment, the mind set on the flesh is focused on my will, my plans, my agenda, doing things my way, attempting to cope with life independently from the Spirit of God. The fleshly mindset constantly compares itself to others, either for the purpose of being "puffed up" or "berating." A mindset that is obsessive and focused on oneself is not at peace. It churns, worries, and stews about food, eating, or body image rather than focusing on what God desires for us. Such consuming thoughts are not edifying or glorifying to Him, and they serve no useful purpose in the plan the Lord has for our lives.

What does a fleshly mindset look like? Examples include one that is constantly thinking about food when not hungry. Another might obsessively dwell on what one longs to eat the next time hunger comes around. It could also be manifested in being overly focused on calories and fat grams, or on how *much* food one can get away with. These specific thoughts are to be taken captive to Christ.

But put on the Lord Jesus Christ,
and make no provision for the flesh in regard to its lusts.
Romans 13:14, NASB

Why do we frequently end up with food in our mouths when our best intention was not to overeat? How is it that day after day we can start out feeling committed to following the leading of the Spirit with 0 to 5 eating in the morning and yet flounder by midday? Making provision for the flesh starts in the mind when we entertain these thoughts as if they were harmless. We think it is not a "big deal." "I can handle it on my own," we tell ourselves, "so I don't bother to confess my need to Christ and depend on Him for the strength to resist temptation." Take thoughts of food captive when they first enter your mind, and they will not take you captive. As soon as you recognize them, submit them to the test: "Lord, am I hungry?" If the answer is "no" but you find yourself rationalizing, give that thought to the Lord, see it crucified at the cross, and then bring your mind back under the authority of the Spirit as you meditate on that which is pure and right. James shows us where temptation comes from:

...but each one is tempted when he is carried away
and enticed by his own lust.
Then when lust has conceived, it gives birth to sin;
and when sin is accomplished, it brings forth death.
James 1:14–15, NASB

So we must observe and correct as Paul demonstrated in our study of Romans 7 last week. He observed himself with a fleshly mind, declared it for what it was, and put in the correction by refocusing on the Lord. He set his mind on the things of the Spirit.

When our mindset is changed, our behavior *will* change. With our minds set on the Spirit, we can by the Spirit put to death those frustrating and ungodly misdeeds of the body (Romans 8:13). The Stop, Look, Listen, and Obey tool found in the appendix may provide the help you need to accomplish this.

Let's assume that you proactively begin to fight the battle of the mind. You renounce thoughts that have been holding you captive. You refuse to lust for food or to allow your mind to become preoccupied with such thoughts when you aren't hungry. You no longer accept thoughts of self-deprecation when looking in the mirror. You don't allow the enemy to deceive and have his way with you. This is terrific! Celebrate as you take these steps, knowing with confidence that you are being conformed by the Holy Spirit to the image of Christ.

However, this is only part of the battle. We are called to be alert to what our mind is set on

...Life that moves steadily forward on the path of God's provision is a life of choices—costly choices.

© 2003, Thin Within, All Rights Reserved

LESSON

and where our thoughts are taking us, and replace destructive, fleshly thoughts with godly, edifying thoughts. We must know and dwell on that which is from the Spirit. We are called to live in the present moment, trusting in the life of Christ within us to meet every need and to enable us to do all things.

What does a mind set on the Spirit look like? It is focused on the path of God's provision, living and enjoying life purposefully in the present. It is set on the things of God, the truth of His Word, and your identity in Christ. It dwells on the affirmations of God's Word that declare your ability to do all things through Christ who lives in you. Your focus will become His will, His agenda, and His enabling grace as you look to Him to plan your day. You will rest and rejoice in your dependence on Him as you experience the abundant blessing of a Spirit-filled life of profound peace.

For the mind set on the flesh is death, but the mind set on the Spirit is life and peace.
Romans 8:6, NASB

As you foster the habit of taking captive thoughts of food and eating that aren't associated with legitimate hunger or of appropriate meal planning, you will begin to find that you are not lusting after food. Your mind is focused on what God has for you rather than what your flesh desires. You begin to trust Him to enable you to melt down to your natural God-given size, and you will have peace about your body in the process. You compare yourself less and less with others. Your validation and identity is in Him and His life is in you—*now*! You then rise to the call of the King to take responsibility for your mind, to take authority over your thoughts, and become a good steward of your body—His temple.

This new way of thinking and behaving flows out of our new identity in Christ. It is our heritage as sons and daughters to be led by the Spirit of God (Romans 8:14). We have the Spirit of adoption that draws us closer to God and bears witness with our spirit that we are His beloved children as we cry, "Abba, Father!" (Romans 8:15–16). Verse 17 tells us that if we are children, we are also heirs—heirs with Christ. We are also told that if we suffer with Him, we will also be glorified with Him.

Though we can't yet identify with our Savior in His glorification or perfection, we can identify with Him in His suffering. We are called by faith to share with Him in His death—to be crucified with Christ (Galatians 2:20). If we die with Him, we shall also live with Him and therefore experience resurrected life (John 12:24–25). When we choose to say "no" to the flesh and focus our minds on the Spirit, we will experience a kind of suffering. We are to embrace by faith our death with Christ and pick up our cross to follow Him. Letting go of our old man or old ways isn't natural. It hurts. If it weren't painful, we would do it with ease. Yet we are called by God to do so, and He will meet us with His provision of grace in our place of need and pain, enabling us to walk not by sight, but by faith.

He uses our pain and suffering to enable us by His grace not only to persevere in His refining process, but also to live in freedom from the shackles of our obsession to food. This is the resurrected life! It is a process well worth it.

God allows this struggle for His higher purposes and your ultimate good. He wants you to see and experience that His grace is a *constant* provision, power, and presence that enables you to make life's difficult choices. Choosing to put to death the flesh in order to bring glory to the Lord demonstrates your sacrificial love for Him. Like Paul, we hope that your cry to God is:

I want to know Christ and the power of his resurrection and the fellowship of sharing in his sufferings. . . .
Philippians 3:10a

Each time you sacrifice your own will, you identify with Christ in the Garden of Gethsemane when He begged the Father to remove the cup of suffering and death from him. However, by the power of the Spirit, Christ underwent much suffering. To forsake the expedient for what would be best, Jesus surrendered, "Not my will, but yours be done" (Luke 22:42).

It is painful to put the flesh to death. It is a costly choice that requires a new mindset that lives according to the Spirit, but as we identify with Christ in His death, we can also experience His resurrected life.

When our mindset is changed, our behavior will change.

© 2003, Thin Within, All Rights Reserved

Therefore, since Christ suffered in his body, arm yourselves
also with the same attitude, because he who has suffered in
his body is done with sin. As a result, he does not live the
rest of his earthly life for evil human desires,
but rather for the will of God.
1 Peter 4:1–2

We learn from these verses that we must first arm ourselves with the right attitude or mindset, so fixed on living purposefully in the will of God that we choose to suffer rather than sin. To say "no" to self and "yes" to God is painful—some times much more than others. Each time you choose suffering over your fleshy desires, sin will not be your master in that moment. You have made your choice by the power and provision of the Holy Spirit within. Bound to the will of God, you will be strengthened by Him through that suffering.

And the God of all grace, who called you to his eternal glory
in Christ, after you have suffered a little while, will himself
restore you and make you strong, firm, and steadfast.
1 Peter 5:10

Through this challenging choice, our actions will line up with God's will. We say "no" to sin and "yes" to God. "No" to gluttony and overindulgence and "yes" to eating for the purpose of meeting nutritional needs. "No" to emotional overeating and "yes" to God who alone can satisfy the hungry heart.

I want to know Christ and the power of his resurrection
and the fellowship of sharing in his sufferings, becoming like
him in his death, and so, somehow, to attain to the
resurrection from the dead.
Philippians 3:10–11

How does experiencing the power of Jesus' resurrection and sharing in His sufferings work out practically in the area of food and eating? If chips and salsa suddenly appear before me and I am not at a 0, I can choose to suffer and affirm by faith that I am dead to the sin of eating when I'm not hungry. I can then turn down the chips and salsa. You may scoff at referring to giving up chips and salsa as suffering, but clearly our selfish desires require ruthless determination and dependency on the Lord, as well as prayerful follow-through. We have to choose to die daily to the desire to eat outside of 0 to 5, which may mean a sacrifice while waiting to reach a 0.

Romans 8 has much to say about putting to death the deeds of the flesh. It leads to glory! These costly choices lead to the resurrected life, which comes only out of death (Romans 8:13). What is to be our motivation for making costly choices? Psalm 139:24 says that we must allow God to search our hearts to reveal our motivation and then avail ourselves of the power source of God. If I grit my teeth and press on with an attitude of, "I have to do this," "I should do this," "I ought to do this . . ." etc., then I am motivated by law, reverting back to the flesh yet again, as we saw last week. In doing this, I put myself under a legalistic system empowered by self-effort, rather than under God's grace empowered by the Holy Spirit.

The motivation that Paul calls us to is one of love: "And we know that God causes all things to work together for good to those who love God" (Romans 8:28, NASB). It is a call to trust, as we cling to God in the midst of the pain and choose to suffer rather than sin. Know that He *can* and *will* bring good out of the situation. Verse 29 reminds us that He is conforming us to the image of Christ. What greater good could there be?

As if to tell us "Wait, there's more," Paul focuses on the infinite, limitless reality of God's everlasting, unfailing love. "If God be for us, who can be against us?" (verse 31). "We are more than conquerors through him who loved us" (verse 37).

In summary, we are told that nothing "in all creation will be able to separate us from the love of God that is in Christ Jesus our Lord" (verse 39), not even when we "blow it" by eating outside of 0 to 5 parameters.

These are wonderful reasons to make the costly choices and to honor the Lord with our lives. Let us gladly trade a fleshly mindset for a mind set on the things of the Spirit.

Physiological Information

When you make the choice of waiting for a 0, a degree of discomfort or suffering may occur. Yet there is peace that surpasses all understanding and joy as well.

This week you will continue to establish more accountability for the choices you make. As you begin to take fleshly thoughts captive unto the Lord, you will see that your behavior falls in line with 0 to 5 eating and flesh machinery will become less and less of an issue.

In the last few weeks, you have kept track of your hunger numbers throughout the day. If this is helpful, continue to use the chart daily during the week. Additionally, we want to introduce to you another tool that will facilitate greater accountability for when and how much you eat.

© 2003, Thin Within, All Rights Reserved

LESSON

Hunger Graph

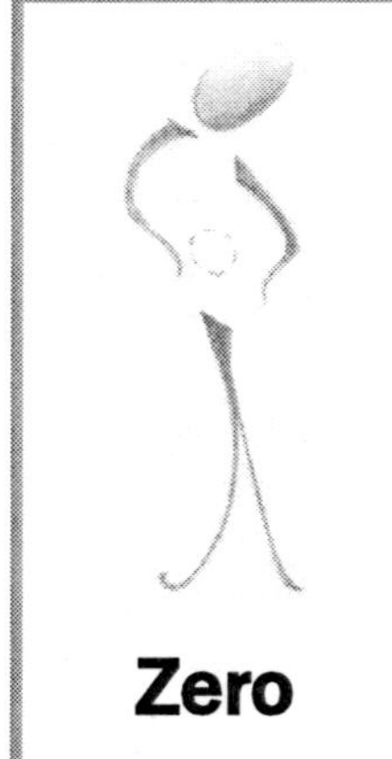

This is a very effective tool to help you become even more familiar with your hunger levels and eating patterns.

To use the Hunger Graph, record the time of day and your hunger numbers before and after eating. The example shows how the graph would look if you ate from a 1 to a 6 at 11 A.M., from a 0 to a 5 at 5 P.M., and from a 2 to a 5 at midnight. Each time you choose to eat or drink anything other than water during the twenty-four-hour period, record the time along with your "before" and "after" hunger numbers.

If the Spirit directs you, use this graph for the next few weeks to apply some of the principles that you have learned so far. If you have no difficulty eating within 0 to 5 parameters at breakfast, but find that around 3 P.M. you eat no matter what your hunger number may be, perhaps this can be an opportunity for you to turn to the Lord for clarity as to what drives you toward food at that time. You may want to pray for discernment and insight from the Lord for options other than eating. For instance, if you notice that anxiety or boredom seem to lure you to eat, ask the Lord what He would have you do—perhaps a walk (or some other activity) just before the "trouble time." People often find that in addition to enjoying the benefits of increased activity, their interest in eating subsides—they lose their "appetite." Having an additional time of fellowship with the Lord prior to the "trouble times" will also help to change inappropriate eating. Living purposefully in the present is the key to living in the Spirit.

Integration

If you set your mind on things of the Spirit, refusing to make provision for your flesh, (lusting for pepperoni pizza when you are not hungry), you will find that the battle of waiting for a 0 is won. Each time you choose not to eat when you are not at a 0, or to stop when you have reached 5, you are putting to death the deeds of the flesh, enabling you to release weight and melt down to your natural God-given size. It is one of the many blessings of making costly choices: one choice at a time, one thought at a time, and one moment at a time.

This week consider using the Hunger Graph as a visible way of seeing if you are giving ground to the flesh or making headway by taking ground for the Spirit by His power. Every time you choose 0 to 5 eating, you are replacing a fleshly mindset with a mind set on the Spirit. The result is that your behavior will reflect more and more godly desires inspired by the Holy Spirit.

A word of caution: Please avoid allowing a Thin Within tool to become a snare of the enemy. These tools don't make you righteous. Only God's grace does that, and only God's grace can work in you to will and to do according to His good pleasure (Philippians 2:13). If He leads you to use these tools, trust in Him and He will teach you through them.

As you remain vigilant against the wiles of the enemy to try to enslave you, foster a mind that is diligent, awake, and aware of any runaway thoughts. Take these captive to obedience of Christ through prayer. Declare them for what they are. "Lord, these thoughts are fleshly and I choose to live according to the Spirit." As you do this, focus your mind and thoughts on things above—on your Savior and His matchless, boundless love and His mercies that are new every morning. Replace fleshly thoughts with thoughts that glorify the Lord.

As you spend time with the Lord, you will discover that thoughts that glorify the Lord bubble up from within, out of the resources of a heart spent sitting at the feet of Jesus.

Rejoice in the Lord always! Again I say, rejoice!

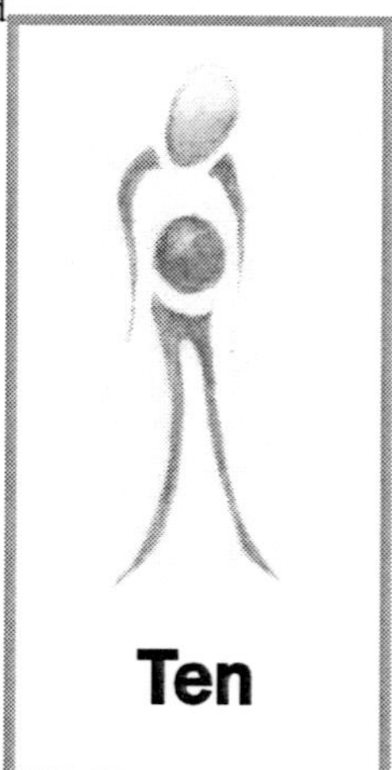

© 2003, Thin Within, All Rights Reserved

<u>My Notes</u>

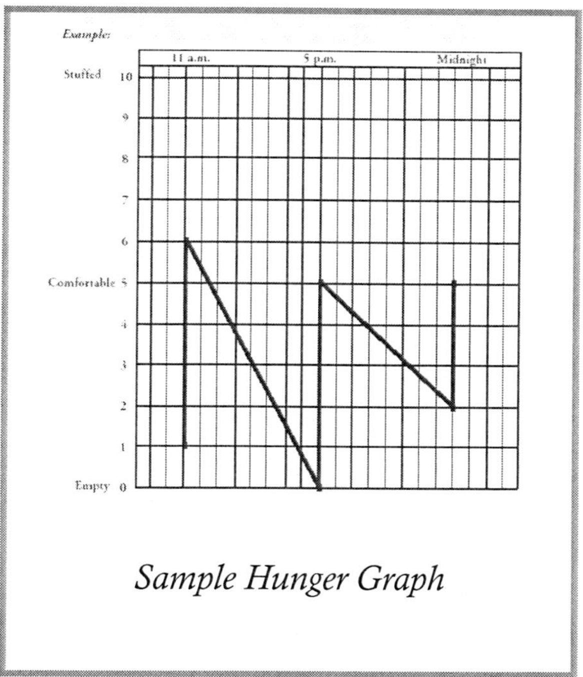

Sample Hunger Graph

© 2003, Thin Within, All Rights Reserved

EXERCISES

Day One

Going Deeper

Continue to spend time studying the Word and in prayer. Foster your relationship with the Lord daily, hourly, even moment by moment. Each time you study the Scriptures, ask God what He wants to teach you. Make a commitment to deepen your relationship with God right now.

____

____

____

Bible Study

Read 2 Peter 1:3–4. Journal your thoughts on the completeness of God's provision for walking in the Spirit.

____

____

____

Knowing God by Heart: Self-Existent

I want to know Christ and the power of his resurrection and the fellowship of sharing in his sufferings, becoming like him in his death, and so, somehow, to attain to the resurrection from the dead.
Philippians 3:10–11

Look up the word "self-existent" in the dictionary and write down a definition that you believe is consistent with God being self-existent. Read John 1:1–4 and relate your definition to these Scriptures.

____

____

____

Getting Practical

We would like you to take one step further into accountability, and prayerfully use the Hunger Graph starting today. (Keep in mind that these Thin Within tools do not make you righteous—only God's grace does that. And only God's grace can empower and strengthen you in His good works. If God leads you to use these tools, allow Him to bring His customized message to you through them.) Copies of the Hunger Graph can be found in the Temple Tool Kit.

____

____

____

Memory Challenge

Start memorizing 1 Peter 4:1–2. Take time to see the message proclaimed in this Scripture. Read the verses out loud several times, then look away and say them from memory.

Therefore, since Christ suffered in his body, arm yourselves also with the same attitude, because he who has suffered in his body is done with sin. As a result, he does not live the rest of his earthly life for evil human desires, but rather for the will of God.
1 Peter 4:1–2

© 2003, Thin Within, All Rights Reserved

Day Two

Going Deeper

What do you think a mind set on the Spirit looks like? Refer to Romans 8:6.

Bible Study

Now that we are certain that God has provided everything we need, let's see what action can be taken. According to 2 Corinthians 10:3–5, what demolishes strongholds? What role do we have in this war? Verse 5 says that we are to take every thought captive and make it obedient to Christ. Notice there are two parts to this process:

- Determine that you will NOT fix your mind on fleshly, selfish things.
- Replace these thoughts with godly, edifying ones from the Spirit.

Journal your thoughts on this process and how it might practically become a part of your day.

Knowing God by Heart

Look up John 5:26 and Exodus 3:14 and note the self-existence of God.

Getting Practical

When filling out your Hunger Graph today, prayerfully consider activities you could do when you are tempted to eat outside of 0 and 5. (Examples: fellowship with the Lord in prayer and/or Bible study, walk around the block, call a friend, go to the Thin Within website for encouragement through testimonies, etc.) Keep this list close at hand. When you are tempted with the thought of eating when you are not truly hungry, first replace the thought with Scripture, then consider doing one of the activities on your list.

Memory Challenge

Continue memorizing 1 Peter 4:1–2 by saying or writing it several times. After some repetition, try repeating it from memory. Take the memory verse card with you and refer to it throughout the day.

Thin Within Tip

If you are not releasing weight, reevaluate your "5." You may require less food to reach a 5 than you did when you started.

© 2003, Thin Within, All Rights Reserved

EXERCISES

Day Three

Going Deeper

Can you relate to this scenario?

You start your day out really well. You have some quiet time with the Lord and commit to Him all you do in this new day. However, by midday you are floundering in the same traps you've fallen into day after day.

Considering what we have studied this week, why do you think that this happens?

____

____

____

____

Bible Study

Read James 1:14–15 and journal about why it is important that we take an ungodly thought captive as soon as it enters our mind. (Refer to the Stop, Look, Listen, and Obey tool in the appendix for help in taking thoughts captive.) Look up the word "captive" in the dictionary. With that definition in mind, what does it mean to take an ungodly thought captive?

____

____

____

____

Knowing God by Heart

Find synonyms for the word "self-existent" in a thesaurus or dictionary. How do these words give you a deeper understanding of God as self-existent? Read Isaiah 43:10. What does this verse say about God's existence?

____

____

____

____

Getting Practical

As you use the Hunger Graph throughout the day, pray for God to help you set your mind on things of the Spirit. Ask God to reveal fleshly thoughts and to help you relinquish such thoughts to Him.

____

____

____

____

Memory Challenge

Review 1 Peter 4:1–2 until you can repeat it from memory.

Thin Within Tip

If you want to be hungry for a dinner out or for a special occasion, consider skipping a meal or eating a very small lunch in order to be at a 0 so you can enjoy the food.

© 2003, Thin Within, All Rights Reserved

Day Four

Going Deeper

Begin to make a list of Scriptures that you can use to take a fleshly thought captive and bring it in line with the Spirit. (You can use some of the verses from today's Bible study exercises.) Try printing these verses on index cards and have them ready for the battle of your thoughts. Add to this Scripture list in the days ahead. Write out a "battle plan."

____

____

____

____

Bible Study

In order to experience the Spirit-led life that Christ offers, what choice must we make (Romans 8:5; Ephesians 4:22–24; Colossians 3:2)?

____

____

____

____

Knowing God by Heart: Omnipotent

Look up the word "omnipotent" in the dictionary and write down a definition that you believe is consistent with God being omnipotent. Read Jeremiah 32:17 and 1 Chronicles 29:11–12 and relate your definition to these Scriptures.

____

____

____

____

Getting Practical

If you haven't released any weight, you may not be eating 0 to 5 even if you think you are. The Hunger Graph can be a useful tool to see how easily you can be deceived.

____

____

____

Memory Challenge

Repeat 1 Peter 4:1–2 from memory. Turn these verses into a prayer for yourself or someone you know.

© 2003, Thin Within, All Rights Reserved

EXERCISES

Day Five

Going Deeper

The Hunger Graph is a great visual aid to show where you struggle with 0 to 5 eating. List ways you can continue to replace a fleshly mindset with a mind set on the Spirit. Remember, the more you do this, the more your behavior will reflect desires inspired by the Spirit.

____

____

____

Bible Study

Read Romans 8:17 and Philippians 3:10. According to these verses, what will we share in? Making a choice to say "no" to our desires and "yes" to God is often painful. God has a purpose in this suffering. What do you think it is? First Peter 4:1–2 says that as you suffer in letting go of your own desires, you will be done with sin in the moment. You are making a conscious choice to suffer for the cause and purposes of Christ by the power and provision of the Holy Spirit. Journal your thoughts on this process.

____

____

____

____

Knowing God by Heart

What do Psalm 66:1–7 and Job 42:2 say about God's omnipotence?

____

____

____

____

Getting Practical

Continue to graph your hunger numbers and observe any times or situations within the day that seem more difficult. Take these to God, asking for His grace, wisdom, and strength to correct them.

____

____

____

Memory Challenge

Meditate on 1 Peter 4:1–2 throughout the day and allow it to draw you closer to God. Ask Him to help you truly believe this Scripture so that it can set you free from all the deceptive lies of the world.

Thin Within Tip

Remind yourself that you are a delicate eater and that you prefer small portions of foods. Tell yourself that you will be very uncomfortable and too full to enjoy anything more if you eat past 5. Rehearse success. In time, these small, positive actions become true habits and preferences. Practice, practice, practice!

  © 2003, Thin Within, All Rights Reserved

Day Six – Optional Exercises

Going Deeper

For every little victory give praise and thanks to God! Ask Him to alert you when your thoughts are drifting away from Him and to help you recognize those thoughts for what they really are. "Lord, these thoughts are fleshly and I choose to live according to the Spirit." Ask Him to help you meditate on the truth of His Word instead of on your own selfish desires so that you can live the resurrected life.

____
____
____
____

Bible Study

Read Romans 8:13. What are we doing to the deeds of the flesh when we live according to the Spirit? Resurrected life comes only out of death. Philippians 3:10–11 reveals how we can know Christ through this suffering and death. Look up the word "know" in the dictionary. What do you think it means to "know" Christ?

____
____
____
____

Knowing God by Heart

Find synonyms for the word "omnipotent" in a thesaurus or dictionary. How do these words give you a deeper understanding of God as omnipotent? Read Jeremiah 27:5 and Romans 1:20. What do these verses tell you about God?

____
____
____
____

Getting Practical

Look over your hunger charts from this week. Do you see any trends? Have you noticed any progress in staying within the godly boundary of 0 to 5?

____
____
____
____

Memory Challenge

Repeat 1 Peter 4:1–2 out loud and ask God to make these verses real in your life. What might God be leading you to "be" or to "do" in response to this passage?

© 2003, Thin Within, All Rights Reserved

EXERCISES

Day Seven – Optional Exercises

Going Deeper

May God himself, the God of peace, sanctify you through and through.
May your whole spirit, soul, and body be kept blameless at the coming of
our Lord Jesus Christ. The one who calls you is faithful and he will do it.
1 Thessalonians 5:23–24

Thank God for what he is accomplishing in your heart this week. How can you show your gratitude to God for his specific message to you?

Bible Study

What compels us to do as God asks? (2 Corinthians 5:14a; Romans 12:1; 1 John 3:2–3) Record your thoughts on these verses in your journal.

Getting Practical

Continue to graph your hunger numbers throughout the day.

Memory Challenge

Share your memory verse with a friend or family member, telling him or her how it relates to your Thin Within journey.

Thin Within Tip

Avoid reverting to dieting "tricks" or "quick-fix" thinking. If you have purchased low-fat foods and don't truly enjoy them, toss them out. If you do enjoy them, by all means continue to eat them in moderation.

     © 2003, Thin Within, All Rights Reserved

Review of the Week

Take time at the end of each week to review what God has taught you and how it is impacting your life. This will give you a great overview to take to your Thin Within Support Group Meeting.

The most significant thing God taught me this week:

My memory verse calls me to have the same attitude as Christ, who suffered in His body. When we make costly choices, we often have to suffer through the moment (or hour). In the past six weeks of this study as I have set my mind on the things of the Spirit rather than things of the flesh, I have suffered in my body:

In the six weeks of this study I have become aware that I eat outside of 0-5 when:

I have seen eating 0-5 as a beneficial choice when:

The most significant thing that God helped me to observe this week that I will focus on correcting next week:

What I have learned about the character of God as self-existent and omnipotent , and how I have come to know and be drawn closer to him:

My prayer requests and praises:

© 2003, Thin Within, All Rights Reserved

LESSON

The Fight of Faith

Introduction

We have an awesome privilege and responsibility as we avail ourselves of the Spirit of God. He works on us from the inside out to renew our minds and remodel our belief systems. The foundation that is laid within is expressed outwardly one step of faith at a time. We are made *new* in Christ. Fathom this thought. Whether you have been His for twenty seconds or twenty years, you are *new* in Christ. Your identity—who you are from *within*—is changed the moment you committed your heart and life to him! Are you walking in faith that He who began a good work in you will complete it from within and without?

Spiritual Foundation

Let's turn to God's Word to see what faith is.

Now faith is being sure of what we hope for and certain of what we do not see.
Hebrews 11:1

Faith is the unwavering confidence in God and the conviction that He will perform what he has promised.

There is but one thing that moves the heart of God—faith. Hebrew 11:6 says, "Without faith it is impossible to please God." If our faith pleases God, what does our performance do? Does God want us to muster up every ounce of our self-effort and "Just Do It"? Not according to Philippians 2:13:

For it is God who works in you to will and to act according to his good purpose.

Many of us hear of "walking in faith" on Sunday mornings or at our midweek Bible studies. But what does it really mean to "walk in faith" or "walk by faith?"

There is a story told of a man who promised a crowd of people that he would push a wheelbarrow on a tightrope strung high across Niagara Falls. He asked his audience if they believed he could do it, and they scoffed and laughed saying it was ridiculous and impossible. They had no confidence or faith that he could do such a feat and were there merely to witness his sure failure. The suspense slowly built as the man did indeed push the wheelbarrow on the tightrope from one side of the thundering falls to the other.

Upon his return, those who witnessed the amazing demonstration applauded with great enthusiasm. The man asked the audience again, "Do you *now* believe I can push the wheelbarrow on the tightrope across the falls?" They all heralded his ability and assured him they believed and had faith that he could do it.

With a twinkle in his eye, the man asked, "Who among you will *get in* the wheelbarrow while I push it to the other side?" The crowd was silent.

The question remains, did anyone in the crowd have faith that the man could push the wheelbarrow to the other side? They certainly said they did! But did they manifest their faith? In other words, were they willing to walk (or ride as in this case) out that faith?

Mark gives us an account of Jesus healing a paralyzed man.

"But that you may know that the Son of Man has authority on earth to forgive sins. . . ." He said to the paralytic, "I tell you, get up, take your mat and go home." He got up, took his mat and walked out in full view of them all.
Mark 2:10–12a

So what does it mean to walk in faith? Is it to say you believe like those at Niagara Falls? Or is it the kind of faith we see in the paralytic man? How does this man walk in faith? He stands up and steps out, literally walking. He does it without visual confirmation. Staying on his mat while insisting he believes that Jesus can heal him wouldn't be walking by faith.

Moving forward or "walking" in faith exemplifies one's faith in an entirely new way. It requires trust and risk that may be frightening. So with fear and trepidation we can turn to God and ask Him to enable us to take one step forward. But it is the Lord who brings us to that place. It is He who puts in our heart a willingness to risk and trust. It is He who enables and strengthens us to step forth into the wheelbarrow. This is walking by faith. It is walking as if it *is* done. Let's be willing to get in the wheelbarrow. Let's take up our mats and walk! God has promised us that He has set us free from strongholds, including overweight and overeating.

Like a tender loving parent, the Lord reaches out and teaches us to walk in faith.

It was I who taught Ephraim to walk, taking them by the arms; but they did not realize it was I who healed them. I led them with cords of human kindness, with ties of love; I lifted the yoke from their neck and bent down to feed them.
Hosea 11:3–4

The Lord faces us. His arms extended, He beckons to us. As the fearful child, we can in that moment choose to lift our foot and step out,

 © 2003, Thin Within, All Rights Reserved

trusting that our Heavenly Father will not forsake us. Rejoicing with even the most faltering of steps, we are walking. Let's be those . . .

. . . who also walk in the footsteps of the faith . . .
Romans 4:12b

As we walk in faith, there is also a very real spiritual battle that rages to keep us from doing so. We will investigate this fight and the victory that awaits those who rise up to this high calling.

It is important to note that if you have given your life to Christ, you have been made new whether or not you see it reflected on the outside. Our actions alone are not the proof that we are new in Christ but rather the infallible Word of God. The fact that we walk in the Spirit is only because He has made us new. If you backslide into old habits and behaviors, you may question if God has really changed you. This place of doubt is an opportunity for you to obediently step out in faith as you grab hold of your Savior and focus on Him who wants to help you mature. Observe and correct in the present moment. Refocus on Him and take another baby step forward. Remember, the Thin Within journey is sometimes described as two steps forward and one back. But it always heads in the right direction, steadfastly into the Father's arms.

Most of us can identify with the attack that comes when we feel tempted to give up and quit—to stop walking. The enemy wants to capitalize on our doubts, our hesitations, and our weaknesses. He tries to convince us to give up or become complacent in or abusive of our freedom. He wants us to forget that in our weakness, our Lord is made strong.

Having identified the pull of the world and of the flesh in previous lessons, we now look to expose the attacks and schemes of Satan. As we prayerfully prepare ourselves, we can take a proactive stance and not be swept away by the enemy's schemes.

Faith is the very basis on which our relationship with God has been established. By faith we accept the gift of salvation. By faith we grow and mature in Christ. As we walk in faith, we are able to stand upon the promises of God and see them lived out daily in a very real way. Our faith stands directly opposed to Satan. This makes Satan mad. He won't take this sitting down.

The Apostle Peter spoke of the devil's attack on those of us with faith:

Be self-controlled and alert. Your enemy the devil prowls around like a roaring lion
looking for someone to devour. Resist him, standing firm in the faith. . . .
1 Peter 5:8–9a

Let's consider some strategies for standing firm in the faith. Paul tells us in Ephesians 6 that we wrestle against powers and rulers of darkness, against spiritual wickedness in heavenly places. There is indeed a war going on! Paul spoke to Timothy on several occasions about the fight of faith (1 Timothy 1:18–19; 1 Timothy 6:12).

At the end of his life, Paul recounted having fought the good fight of faith for which a reward awaited him (2 Timothy 4:7–8). This is a truth that is available to all believers who keep the faith.

The world, the flesh, and the devil are all pulling us in opposition to our faith. The world tells us that "seeing is believing," but God calls the things that are not as though they are (Romans 4:17). There is a popular saying "God helps those who help themselves." Many mistakenly think it is found in the Bible, but we are told in 2 Corinthians 12:9–10 that in our weakness, he is made strong. God calls us to walk in faith even in our weakness, recognizing our impotence and drawing on his strength. He is glorified when we trust in him and lean not on our own understanding (Proverbs 3:5).

It is blessedly liberating when we begin to understand that God doesn't call us to be strong on our own. He knows we will never "get it all together." In fact, he is glorified in our weakness. So throw open your arms to him confessing your needs, so that God can whisper, "My child, now you are ready to see and receive my love, my power, and My purpose for your life. Watch Me work." Your weakness isn't intended to deter you

Faith is the unwavering confidence in God and the conviction that he will perform what he has promised.

© 2003, Thin Within, All Rights Reserved

from "keeping the faith." Instead, allow it to be an "indicator light" that "Ah! God is on the move." Be watchful and wait as you walk in obedience to his leading.

Colossians 3:2 says to set your mind or keep your focus on things above and not on things of earth. Instead of a fleshly mindset, we are called to have a heart of faith with our focus based solely on the truth of God's Word and on His infinite faithfulness to accomplish that which He promises.

Our enemies—the world, the flesh, and the devil—seek to have us trust in our own understanding. When we rely on our own self-effort and stay focused on our circumstances or on comparing ourselves to others, we walk by sight. The way of the world leads to a life of self-condemnation or a life of pride in our own strength and accomplishments. But God resists the proud and gives grace to the humble. A life of faith is a life of humility, always trusting and always being dependant upon the life and strength of our awesome God!

Satan is a liar, a deceiver, and a thief. He has a plan for each person (2 Timothy 2:26). In referring to him as "the thief," Jesus tells us:

. . . the thief comes only to steal and kill and destroy. . . .
John 10:10a

What is it he wants to take from us and how does he seek to destroy or devour us?

First, be assured of this: Satan is powerless to take away from you that which Christ has already done. Christ's work was finished on the cross. He purchased your salvation by exchanging his life for yours. He paid the price, died, and rose again that he might live that resurrected life in you. He sent his Holy Spirit to conform you to his likeness. It is a work that he has begun and which he will complete. Second Corinthians 3:18 says that we are being transformed into the very image of God by the Spirit of the Lord. You can never be robbed of your salvation or the work of the Holy Spirit within you.

That being the case, what can the enemy try to kill and destroy? The answer is simply your faith. If the enemy can keep us in a place of unbelief, we will never appropriate all that is ours in Christ. He can steal our faith and confidence in our new identity and our belief in the transforming power of the grace of God. If he can do this, he can keep us on the sidelines of life, refusing to step out in faith and walk into that which God has planned for us. He can keep us, as a young child, always clinging to the things of this world and demanding our way, our food, and our rights, never confident enough to let go. Therefore, we would miss the experience of the resurrected life.

We are told to put on the whole armor of God (Ephesians 6:11) so that we can stand against the wiles or the schemes of the devil. He has been using some predictable tactics on God's children for thousands of years! The only reason the Israelites wandered in the desert for forty years, unable to go in and possess the land God had promised them, was because of their unbelief. They refused to go forth, walking in faith and confidence that God would do what He promised He would do (Hebrews 3:16–19).

God pledged to give them cities that they did not build and crops that they did not plant—a land flowing with milk and honey. It seemed to them that He had promised the impossible, but because he is God and he is faithful, this wasn't impossible. Instead of walking forward in faith, the Israelites sent spies into the land. The spies returned with a report of giants. They were consumed with fear and terrified to walk forward and possess the land, even though that is exactly what God had promised them. His arms remained outstretched and they clung to other things. They were convinced that they could not be victorious and their fear overshadowed their faith.

Since we know that God does not give us the spirit of fear (2 Timothy 1:7), this was an obvious attack of the enemy. We too, have an inheritance, a legacy left us by our Lord. We can walk in faith into that which God has promised us—victory in Christ—or we can fearfully cling to the things of this world. We have been given everything we need to live a godly life in Christ Jesus (2 Peter 1:3). However, this new life is available to us by *faith* alone! Regarding Abraham,

> [The enemy] tries to convince us to give up or become complacent in or abusive of our freedom.

© 2003, Thin Within, All Rights Reserved

the Scriptures say:

Yet he did not waver through unbelief regarding the promise of God, but was strengthened in his faith and gave glory to God, being fully persuaded that God had power to do what he had promised. This is why "it was credited to him as righteousness." The words "it was credited to him" were written not for him alone, but also for us, to whom God will credit righteousness—for us who believe in him who raised Jesus our Lord from the dead.

Romans 4:20–24

Abraham was credited with righteousness based on his belief—his faith from which he did not waver. Even in the days of the old covenant, we see that God is a God of grace who looks upon the hearts of his people to see their belief that he is able, that he is good, and that he is sufficient.

We are told in Hebrew 4:2 that the Israelites had the gospel preached to them in the wilderness, but it did not profit them because of their lack of faith. We have examined the gospel of grace during these last six weeks, but as with the Israelites, the enemy would love to keep you in a place of unbelief where the Word of God does not profit you.

So how do we resist the enemy, stand strong, and walk in faith? Listen again to Paul as he wrote to the church at Corinth:

For though we live in the world, we do not wage war as the world does. The weapons we fight with are not the weapons of the world. On the contrary, they have divine power to demolish strongholds. We demolish arguments and every pretension that sets itself up against the knowledge of God, and we take captive every thought to make it obedient to Christ.

2 Corinthians 10:3–5

This is not a fleshly battle, but one that takes place in our mind and our heart. Our defense is to expose every thought to the truth and light of God's Word in order to pull down and demolish any stronghold of doubt or disbelief. We have the power to bring every thought captive to the obedience of Christ as the Holy Spirit works in us to transform us through the renewing of our minds. Through our unwavering faith, we walk in confidence in the faithfulness of God, refusing every lie of the enemy as we experience victory in God.

Physiological Information

The walk of faith requires discernment. While we have learned that all things are permissible in Phase One, in Phase Two we recognize that not all things are beneficial. We have the responsibility of exercising care in the choices we make. Each step of faith matters. We want to be sure that each step of faith falls where God intends. Consider the following reminders:

1. God will lead you personally.

As we walk by faith, God will lead one person to eat differently from another (Romans 14:2). God knows how your body will function most efficiently. If He wants you to release to Him a specific food for a season, then that is what you must do as a step of faith in the present moment (Romans 14:14). There are no rules or laws except to do that which the Lord leads you to do, as you are personally directed by his Holy Spirit. He will lead you in a way that will bring you blessing upon blessing.

2. Prayerfully evaluate what foods generally make you feel better or worse.

You will want to become more sensitive to how your body reacts to various foods. Mike, a participant in the program, noticed that eating certain Chinese entrées, even in moderation, made him feel bloated and uncomfortable. He was led by the Lord to abstain from Chinese food. His wife, Patricia, however enjoys Chinese food without any negative consequences. Both are learning to listen to the signals that their God-given bodies send them.

Notice how *your* body responds to 0 to 5 eating. The Lord calls some to increase their intake of fiber by eating fresh fruits and vegetables within 0 to 5. Others may feel led to abstain from artificial sweeteners or coffee because of concerns about the effect they may have on *their* body. In order to best care for your body, God's temple, you will want to stay attuned first and foremost to the Spirit and the reliable signals your body sends to you as you walk by faith.

3. Begin to consider broadening your food horizons to include those foods you haven't previously preferred.

If you experience the nudging of the Holy Spirit that you need to eat a wider variety of foods, then by all means do so. Some people get stuck in certain food ruts that are limited and repetitious. Likewise, if you experience any discomfort with certain foods, even ones you enjoy, consider releasing them to the Lord. The choices are endless: ethnic foods, regional foods, and

LESSON

vegetarian foods, even foods made from scratch. Delight in God's provision, always mindful of how your body responds to the foods you eat.

4. Prayerfully consider what foods you are being called to eat when you are hungry.

Your body is trustworthy for valid feedback, but your body has *not* been redeemed. As a believer in Jesus Christ, your spirit *has* been redeemed. God has given you the Holy Spirit as the *final* authority in order to guide and direct the choices that best meet your physical needs for a healthy body. What worked best for you at 8 A.M. yesterday when you were at a 0 may not be what you need tonight when you are hungry. Ask the Holy Spirit and He will give you divine information.

Prayerfully submit your food choices to the Lord. He may prompt you to reduce the quantity of sweets or deep-fried foods you have coveted for years. Or he may give you permission to enjoy foods you have always stayed away from because you thought they were "fattening." Whatever it may be, seek His wisdom, and step out in faith as he calls you. He will not take away your freedom because all things are permissible. However, all things are not beneficial. Remember, he has your physical and spiritual health at heart. God will lead you specifically and personally as you are yielded to Him

Some of the choices the Holy Spirit will lead you to make may be costly. However, in surrendering to his leading you can look forward to a life of vitality, energy, and peace. Walk in faith, knowing that God will give you information regarding your body that will allow you to function at your best.

Above all, keep in mind what Romans 14:17 says so well:

> For the kingdom of God is not a matter of eating and drinking, but of righteousness, peace and joy in the Holy Spirit. . .

Stand in faith. Trust the leading of the Holy Spirit and the way God designed your body. There are a myriad of food choices available to you. As you remain attentive to the Holy Spirit, you will begin to step forward and experience the adventure of your faith. Enjoy and relish all that your life in Christ has to offer. Obedience in eating 0 to 5 comes from faith. Only by faith can we make choices that honor and glorify our precious Savior and Lord. Whatever is not of faith is sin (Romans 14:23). The basis for our choices becomes, "Lord, what are You calling me to do? Holy Spirit, what are You confirming in my heart? Take my body, which is Your temple, Lord, and use it as You see fit. How can I best glorify You, God, and delight in You in this present moment?" The result of your walk of faith and obedient choices is a deep and abundant joy.

He will guide and direct you every step of the way in becoming all he has promised that you will be in Him.

God encourages us that in quietness and trust we will find strength (Isaiah 30:15). We can, indeed, resist the enemy prowling around seeking to destroy us. We can indeed stand strong and walk in faith.

> . . . For everyone born of God overcomes the world. This is the victory that has overcome the world, even our faith.
>
> *1 John 5:4*

Satan is powerless to take away from you that which Christ has already done.

Hallelujah!

Integration

     © 2003, Thin Within, All Rights Reserved

My Notes ______________________________

© 2003, Thin Within, All Rights Reserved

EXERCISES

Day One

Going Deeper

As you spend time in the Word, ask the Lord what he wants to teach you, making you more sensitive to His will throughout the day. Ask Him to give you a willing spirit to surrender unto him. Today do a study on the word "faith" by looking up its definition and journaling what you find.

Bible Study

How does the Bible define faith? Read portions of Hebrews 11 as you feel led and journal what you learn from reading about God's faithful people.

Knowing God by Heart: Omnipresent

For God, who said, "Let light shine out of darkness," *made his light shine in our hearts to give us the light of the knowledge of the glory of God in the face of Christ.*
2 Corinthians 4:6

Look up the word "omnipresent" in the dictionary and write down a definition that you believe is consistent with God being omnipresent. Read Jeremiah 23:23–24 and relate your definition to these Scriptures.

Getting Practical

Take a step of faith today and trust that all the food that God has made is good.* He has a reason for putting such a variety of choices before you. Throughout this week and the next several weeks, try some foods that you have never tried before as you eat 0 to 5. Then jot down your impressions of them with regards to taste, texture, and enjoyment. Delight in God's incredible creativity in making an abundant variety of foods from which to choose.
First be sure you have no food allergies or medical conditions where certain foods would be inadvisable.

Memory Challenge

Start memorizing Hebrews 11:6. Take time to see the message proclaimed in this Scripture. Read the verse out loud several times, then look away and say it from memory.
And without faith it is impossible to please God, because anyone who comes to him must believe that he exists and that he rewards those who earnestly seek him.
Hebrews 11:6

    © 2003, Thin Within, All Rights Reserved

Day Two

Going Deeper

Do you ever get discouraged wondering if you will ever reach your godly weight goal? Remember that the body gives great feedback, but it is not redeemed as is your spirit. We can get so focused on wanting tangible results that we forget that the Holy Spirit is the higher authority. As we pray and seek the divine leading of the Spirit, we know He is totally trustworthy and will keep our focus properly placed as we are yielded to Him. Journal about allowing the Spirit to be the final authority and observe what he is revealing to you today.

____

____

____

____

Bible Study

According to Hebrews 11:6, what pleases God? Does the author of Hebrews mention anything about how much you need to "get it right?" What do Philippians 2:13 and Proverbs 3:5–6 say about acting according to God's purpose or path? Why do you think God places so much importance on your faith in Him alone?

____

____

____

____

Knowing God by Heart

Continue to grow in your knowledge of God by reading Proverbs 15:3. What does this verse say to you about God's omnipresence?

____

____

____

____

Getting Practical

Continue tracking your numbers on the Hunger Graph and be aware of ways the Holy Spirit may be nudging you to adjust to his plan. Also, enjoy his creativity by experimenting with the rich variety of foods he offers. Try to avoid any legalistic practices from the past.

____

____

____

____

Memory Challenge

Continue memorizing Hebrews 11:6 by saying or writing it several times. After some repetition, try repeating it from memory. Take the memory verse card with you and refer to it throughout the day.

Thin Within Tip

"Dress" for dinner. Put on a belt and don't wear baggy clothes.

EXERCISES

Day Three

Going Deeper

How can we know what is the truth and what is a lie without immersing ourselves in God's Word? The transformation within us comes from the renewing of our minds as we study His Word (Romans 12:1–2). Look up the word "meditate" in the dictionary and then take some time to meditate daily on God's Word. Pray about developing the discipline of regular meditation and memorization of any Scripture that God impresses on your heart. The more we know the Word in our mind, the more it can affect our hearts and our actions.

____

____

____

____

Bible Study

One of the enemy's common tactics is to move us away from God's truth, especially the fact that God has the power to do what He says. According to Romans 4:20–24, what caused Abraham not to waver in his belief of God's faithfulness to his promises? How can we be assured that God will carry out His promises (Hebrews 10:19–23)?

____

____

____

____

Knowing God by Heart

Find synonyms for the word "omnipresent" in a thesaurus or dictionary. How do these words give you a deeper understanding of God as omnipresent? Read Psalm 139:7–10. What does it say about how God is omnipresent, and how is this a comfort to you?

____

____

____

____

Getting Practical

Begin to keep a casual record (or mental note) of how you feel after you eat. Prayerfully evaluate what foods make you feel better or worse.

____

____

____

____

Memory Challenge

Review Hebrews 11:6 until you can repeat it from memory.

Thin Within Tip

Use a knife and fork for foods that you normally eat with your hands, such as pizza, hamburgers, or sandwiches. This helps you take smaller bites as well as eat more slowly and consciously.

© 2003, Thin Within, All Rights Reserved

Day Four

Going Deeper

Obedience in eating 0 to 5 comes from faith in the One who created your body. He fashioned you, and you can trust that he knows what you need. By faith you can eat between 0 and 5 knowing that God will direct you to the proper food at the proper time. You can be completely satisfied in His provision (Psalm 145:15–19). Journal on these thoughts.

____

____

____

____

Bible Study

Our defense against the enemy is found in 2 Corinthians 10:3–5. We must demolish all those things that pull us away from the knowledge of (and *faith* in) God. When we embrace his Word of Truth, we have the power through his Spirit to take every thought captive in obedience to Christ, dispelling any lack of belief or doubt. Develop a personal battle plan based on these Scriptures.

____

____

____

____

Knowing God by Heart: Long Suffering

Look up the word "long-suffering" in the dictionary and write down a definition that you believe is consistent with God being long-suffering. (Note: The New American Standard Bible translates long-suffering as "slow to anger" and "patient.") Read Exodus 34:6–7 and Nehemiah 9:16–17 and relate your definition to these Scriptures.

____

____

____

____

Getting Practical

Those who are accustomed to overeating will discover that eating 0 to 5 requires a lot less food. The idea of smaller portions can be looked upon with resentment or with contentment. It is a choice we each have to make. According Philippians 4:11–13, what gave Paul the ability to be content? Commit to God the amount of food he has allotted for you, believing by faith that He has a plan to prosper you and not to harm you (Jeremiah 29:11).

____

____

____

____

Memory Challenge

Repeat Hebrews 11:6 from memory. Turn this verse into a prayer for yourself or someone you know.

© 2003, Thin Within, All Rights Reserved

EXERCISES

Day Five

Going Deeper

Journal about the necessity and function of the different parts of God's battle armor found in Ephesians 6:10–18. Pray about making a habit of arming yourself against the enemy every day with His full protection.

____

____

____

____

Bible Study

The Bible is very clear that we are in a battle against the devil and his schemes. We *will* face evil—not *if*, but *when* (Ephesians 6:10–18). We need to be prepared for this ahead of time. The enemy does not want us to trust and believe in God's provision and promises. He would love to see us mired in unbelief over whether or not God's Word will profit us. He wants us to believe that 0 to 5 eating is too restrictive and burdensome. We need the full armor of God to keep us standing firm in our faith no matter what we see or hear to the contrary. Journal your thoughts.

____

____

____

____

Knowing God by Heart

What do Psalm 103:8, Joel 2:13, and 1 Timothy 1:15–17 say about God's long-suffering?

____

____

____

____

Getting Practical

Have you observed any positive changes in your eating as you look over your last two weeks of Hunger Graphs? Praise God for every step toward more consistent obedience! Psalm 37:5 says "Commit your way to the LORD; trust in him and he will do this." Whether or not you feel that progress has been made, commit this day and the days ahead to Him and allow Him to continue to renew your mind and call you into obedience regarding your eating.

____

____

____

____

Memory Challenge

Meditate on Hebrews 11:6 throughout the day and allow it to draw you closer to God. Ask Him to help you truly believe this Scripture so that it can set you free from all the deceptive lies of the world.

Thin Within Tip

Put a coin in a jar for each 0 to 5 eating occasion. When the jar is full, give yourself a non-food reward, such as a night out at the movies or sports event, a massage, a pedicure, or even a soak in the tub with some special bath salts.

© 2003, Thin Within, All Rights Reserved

Day Six – Optional Exercises

Going Deeper

What does Isaiah 30:15 say is our strength? How do we overcome the world and find the victory that is spoken of in 1 John 5:4?

Bible Study

Read Ephesians 1:18–21. What is available to us when we believe? Reflect on the wonder of having access to the same mighty power by which God raised Christ from the dead! Notice that the divine power He provides gives us *everything* we need for life and godliness (2 Peter 1:3–4).

Knowing God by Heart

Find synonyms for the word "long-suffering" in a thesaurus or dictionary. How do these words give you a deeper understanding of God as long-suffering? Read 2 Peter 3:9 and Colossians 1:13–14. What do these Scriptures tell you about God?

Getting Practical

Continue to track your hunger numbers throughout the day.

Memory Challenge

Repeat Hebrews 11:6 out loud and ask God to make this verse real in your life. What might God be leading you to "be" or to "do" in response to this passage?

© 2003, Thin Within, All Rights Reserved

EXERCISES

Day Seven – Optional Exercises

Going Deeper

Have you found a blessing in obedience? List recent occasions where God richly blessed you as you obeyed Him.

____

____

____

____

Bible Study

God loves you so much that he has already planned a way of obedience for you (Deuteronomy 30:11–14; 1 Corinthians 10:13). As you obey what He has called you to do, what will be the reward (John 15:10–11)?

____

____

____

____

Getting Practical

Have you begun to experience God's bountiful variety of foods this week, breaking out of the old habits and routines and finding freedom in choices? God offers an abundant, full life (John 10:10) as we embrace Him and his incredible provision. Savor and enjoy Him!

____

____

____

____

Memory Challenge

Share your memory verse with a friend or family member, telling him or her how it relates to your Thin Within journey.

Thin Within Tip

Instead of entering the drive-thru of your favorite fast-food restaurant when you're not at a 0, just drive by!

 © 2003, Thin Within, All Rights Reserved

Review of the Week

Take time at the end of each week to review what God has taught you and how it is impacting your life. This will give you a great overview to take to your Thin Within Support Group Meeting.

The most significant thing God taught me this week:

My memory verse (Hebrews 11:6) tells me that it is impossible to please God without faith. During this Thin Within journey I have pleased God because in faith I have:

In the physiological section of this week's lesson I was encouraged to broaden my horizons and eat foods that my body needs to feel it's best. This week I have come to understand that my body will feel it's best when I eat:

The most significant thing that God helped me to observe this week that I will focus on correcting next week:

What I have learned about the character of God as omnipresent and long-suffering , and how I have come to know and be drawn closer to him:

My prayer requests and praises:

© 2003, Thin Within, All Rights Reserved

LESSON

Celebration of God's Grace, Part Two

Introduction

Have you experienced the abundant provision and power of living the life of faith during the past week? Walking in faith is a glorious adventure.

The abundant life stretches before us as our gracious Lord meets us and invites us to draw near to Him at every turn. This week, as we celebrate His unfathomable and matchless grace, we will look into the life of Gideon, a man that God transformed from within by faith.

Spiritual Foundation

In the book of Judges, we see that God's people were refusing to heed the words of the Lord to turn from their idolatrous and rebellious ways. As a result, God allowed the Midianites, a warring people from the east to attack, pillage, and plunder their land for seven consecutive years.

Speaking of these Midianites, God's Word says:

They came up with their livestock and their tents like swarms of locusts. It was impossible to count the men and their camels; they invaded the land to ravage it. Midian so impoverished the Israelites that they cried out to the LORD for help.
Judges 6:5–6

The land appeared desolate and the fearful people struggled, not knowing when the enemy would march through, raiding and destroying that which the Israelites had worked so hard to acquire. Imagine the despondence and discouragement that must have plagued them day and night as they lived in fear.

Judges 6:11 introduces us to Gideon, hiding in an old winepress where he was threshing wheat. He, too, was afraid that the Midianites would take all his grain and deprive him of his livelihood, if not his life.

Can you identify with Gideon's fear? Do you find yourself hiding at times behind romance novels, TV shows, movies, soap operas, the computer, or in the kitchen pantry? We may also hide behind a mask of whom we want to appear to be, never really letting people see who we really are.

The angel of the LORD came and revealed himself to Gideon as he thrashed wheat.

God reached out to Gideon in his fear and shame right there in that winepress. So, too, does he reach out to us wherever we may find ourselves—alone, fearful, ashamed, guilty, or entrenched in sin—God reaches out to touch us right where we are. As we examine His interaction with Gideon, we will see how He draws us closer to Himself into a relationship of dependency and intimacy.

1. God determined that Gideon was His mighty warrior.

The angel greets fearful Gideon with a declaration:

"The LORD is with you, mighty warrior"
Judges 6:12

We might wonder at the irony of God greeting one cowering and hiding as a "mighty warrior." But God sees beyond the obvious and calls things that are not as though they are (Romans 4:17). Out of the abundance of His grace, God calls Gideon out of his place of fear and out of living life enslaved by very bleak circumstances. He calls Gideon to live by faith above his circumstances, to rise up to something new and wonderful, a supernatural equipping and empowering that He will give him.

▶ **Personalize It: God has declared you as His mighty warrior.** Do you see that God has done this very thing and so much more for you? You are more than a conqueror in him (Romans 8:37). God has given you a new identity. He has changed you from the inside out. Gideon was declared a warrior; however living like one would be a product of his actions by faith as God enabled him. You, dear child of God, have not just been declared new, you have been *made* new. You have been given a new nature, the nature of a mighty warrior, "more than a conqueror" by the power of a holy God resident within you. By the equipping of the Holy Spirit, you are to rise up and walk in that which God not only declares you to be but also has made you to be. By faith avail yourself of this grace, this unmerited blessing of God.

2. God allows Gideon to argue and even blame Him.

Have you ever argued with God, saying, "If I am a new creation, why don't I act like it? If You indwell me, why am I so defeated?" Gideon did. He minimizes the fact that an angel is speaking with

© 2003, Thin Within, All Rights Reserved

him and immediately argues that God is not with him.

"But sir," Gideon replied, "if the LORD is with us, why has all this happened to us? Where are all his wonders that our fathers told us about when they said, `Did not the LORD bring us up out of Egypt?' But now the LORD has abandoned us and put us into the hand of Midian." Judges 6:13

Instead of taking any responsibility for what happened, Gideon blamed God. We know from later verses that Gideon's family, like most, was entrenched in idolatry. For that very reason, God allowed the people from the east to have their way with Israel, which was God's righteous judgment. Gideon denied that he shared in the responsibility for this judgment because it was easier to blame God.

▶ **Personalize It: God can handle your arguments and complaints**. God met Gideon's arguments again and again, offering him what he needed in order to lead him from fear to faith, from doubting to daring, and finally to fully trusting in God. He will meet you as well and respond to your arguments. He is a just God in all of his ways. His response will always be to point you to his truth, to challenge you to walk by faith. God is patient and loving toward you, and he will never give up on you.

Do you ever see your trials as a result of God abandoning you? Gideon certainly did. The fact is God is always with you (Matthew 28:20b). In his marvelous grace, God has imparted his Spirit to you as a deposit guaranteeing what is to come (Ephesians 1:13–14). He will never leave you or forsake you (Hebrews 13:5). You can choose to believe the Lord or you can believe a lie. Which will you choose?

3. God gives strength to Gideon to walk in faith.

Even though God allows Gideon to argue with Him, the Lord didn't argue with Gideon. Instead, He cut to the core of why He had called Gideon.

The LORD turned to him and said, "Go in the strength you have and save Israel out of Midian's hand. Am I not sending you?" "But Lord," Gideon asked, "how can I save Israel? My clan is the weakest in Manasseh, and I

am the least in my family." The LORD answered, "I will be with you, and you will strike down all the Midianites together." Judges 6:14–16

Talk about grace! The incredible power and provision of God's amazing grace called Gideon out of a place of hiding, shame, disgrace, and self-condemnation. Grace called Gideon to participate in something miraculous that God was going to do.

Do you condemn yourself? Do you feel like the "least of the least?" You may think that guilt, disgrace, and shame are your identity. But remember, you are a child of God. Take hold of this by faith. Arguing with God, "But I don't *act* new!" doesn't disprove it. God has done it. Not only are you no longer the least of the least, you are also more precious than gold and silver to Him who gave his only Son for you.

Rest in what He has made you.

How? What makes the difference? How can you move forward out of your winepress or pantry into the calling of God? How can you experience all He has planned for you? How can you be what He says you already are?

Let's look at what happened to Gideon. He was to go in the strength he had. But what strength did Gideon have? Since the Lord was with Gideon, it stands to reason that the strength was to be the Lord's. In fact, God tells Gideon not to focus on what seems obvious—his heritage—but instead to focus on who commissions and empowers him. The calling was high, above and beyond what Gideon could accomplish in his own strength. But God wasn't calling him to do it alone. He would do it for, in, and through Gideon.

In our case, God is not only with us but also *in* us! What an amazing fact.

▶ **Personalize It: God gives you strength**. Have you ever felt as if you didn't have the strength to make the sacrificial choices to which God was calling you? Does 0 to 5 eating sometimes seem impossible, or does releasing your excess weight seem beyond the scope of your capability? Well, you are right. It is, and you are in good company. God has called you not to go in your strength apart from Him, but in the strength that He gives

> Grace called Gideon to participate in something miraculous that God was going to do.

© 2003, Thin Within, All Rights Reserved

LESSON

as He goes before you. Choose by faith and by the power of the Holy Spirit to come out of your winepress so that you can walk in obedience to God's call upon your life. Respond to the grace that God has poured out upon you, to strengthen, provide, empower, equip, and enable you to defeat this foe. Acknowledge your impotence—admit that you are at the end of yourself—and throw up your hands to God who will pour out bountifully all the things you need for life and godliness (2 Peter 1:3–4).

4. God waited for Gideon.

When Gideon argued with Him, God in His grace provided reassurance. But Gideon was still not sure what he should believe, so in his doubt he gives God a "test." He tells God he has to go, and runs off to slaughter a goat and bake some bread to prepare as an offering for the Lord. Such amazing presumption, and still God responds yet again and meets Gideon at this place of doubt, hesitation, and wavering faith. God does not turn away. He turns toward Gideon, accepting him fully. He says . . .

"I will wait until you return."
Judges 6:18b

After presenting his offering, Gideon is rewarded by the "proof" he seeks. God lovingly yet powerfully builds his faith as he consumes the meat and the bread with fire. Gideon comes to his senses and realizes he truly has seen the angel of the Lord (Judges 6:22). He now knows he is in the company of those who inhabit heaven.

Do you see it? The Creator of the universe says, "You are my man and I will wait for you." Amazing Grace.

▶ **Personalize It: God waits for you.** Our Lord is the same yesterday, today, and forever. He waited for Gideon and he waits for you as you scurry after that which you think is so important or that which you think will meet your own needs. He waits as you question, as you doubt, as you struggle, or as you try to perform. He waits because *you* are who he wants and loves.

Have you been making the Lord wait for you? What do you think you need to do, be, or say in order to end the wait? Don't make Him wait any longer. Step out in faith.

5. God alone is worthy of Gideon's worship.

God's grace pours out on Gideon as he condescends to reach out to this fearful, self-conscious man lacking in faith. And as Gideon tastes the reality of what has transpired, it moves him to reverent fear.

▶ **Personalize It: God alone is worthy of your worship.**

By His grace, God calls us to know Him and to approach Him, and to be in relationship with Him daily. He promises that if we seek Him, we will find Him. He is faithfully indwelling us with his precious Spirit. Our response is to be one of reverence and adoration that so mighty a One should offer Himself for us because He wants a relationship with each and every one of us. Will we bow down in worship and surrender all unto him? While our sacrifices may seem costly, He enables us to make them and they pale in comparison to that which He has sacrificed for us.

6. The Lord gave Gideon peace.

Gideon's reaction momentarily moves him in a direction the enemy wants us to go—away from *reverent* fear into *paralyzing* fear. God desires that we revere Him and be moved to worship and live sacrificially for him. The enemy seeks to kill and destroy that which God desires. He wants us to remain impotent—to turn reverent "fear of God" into being "afraid of God." Gideon is caught for a moment in paralyzing fear, but God's mercy and grace pour forth once again.

But the LORD said to him, "Peace! Do not be afraid.
You are not going to die." So Gideon built an altar
to the LORD there and called it The LORD is Peace.
Judges 6:23–24a

When circumstances and the calling of God were so clearly above and beyond the ability or power of Gideon, he rejected paralyzing fear and declared that God was not only to be worshiped but that He was the source of peace that calms a quaking heart.

▶ **Personalize It: The Lord will give you peace.** Can you comprehend the Lord as your peace? Peace isn't the absence of conflict, as we will see in a minute. God's peace is walking in the confidence that He will provide in the midst of any conflict. His ways are good and right even when they are costly. In faith we see that good things happen as a result of his amazing grace.

Is God your peace? In what ways do you

© 2003, Thin Within, All Rights Reserved

need God to be your peace? Will you choose to allow His grace to flow over you and grant you the goodness that comes from resting in God's provision?

What follows Gideon's declaration that God is peace is truly remarkable. Gideon moves from being the "least of the least" in his place of fear, trembling, and hiding, and begins to walk as the "mighty warrior" that God declared him to be. He sets his mind on the things of the Spirit and steps out in faith to that which God calls him. He chooses not only to believe God, but also to put his trust and confidence in Him alone, consciously resisting the pull of his flesh, the world, and the enemy. He reveres God, knowing that the Almighty God calls him, empowers, and equips him. His life from that moment on begins to reflect this reverence with a peace that surpasses understanding (Philippians 4:7).

7. God called Gideon to walk in faith.

A specific commission now comes as God makes it clear how Gideon is to begin. Because he lived in a family of idol worshipers, Gideon is called to apply what he had learned in his "close encounter" with God in the winepress. He is called to destroy his father's altar to a pagan God, which was a stronghold of flesh machinery (Judges 6:25).

Gideon was called by God to take a stand against the influence of his family and their choice to worship idols. He was given the opportunity to be a conduit of God's grace into the lives of those he loved by his willingness to make some costly choices.

▶ **Personalize It: God calls you to walk in faith.** Can you relate to Gideon? Do you have spiritual or food-related challenges in your family? Have mealtimes in the past been chaotic and stressful, or peaceful and enjoyable? You may have been raised in a home with an altar to a false god. Have you received a call from God to tear down some tributes to pagan idols and erect a proper altar to him for his glory? To do so may involve taking some risks and it may be costly, yet tremendous rewards await you as well.

Gideon, still struggling with his faith,

knows God's will but lacks the courage and assurance that God will actually use and empower him. Haven't we all been there? Still questioning the will of God, Gideon tests him two more times to make "extra sure." Graciously, God meets Gideon where he is on each occasion, making an extra provision for Gideon's fear:

"If you are afraid to attack, go down to the camp with your servant Purah and listen to what they are saying.
Afterward, you will be encouraged to attack the camp." So he and Purah his servant went down to the outposts of the camp.
Judges 7:10–11

As God's grace has been freely poured out into your life, you have the opportunity to be a conduit for that same grace into the lives of those around you. As believers in Christ we are called to exalt and imitate Him (Ephesians 5:1). As we follow Him closely, watch Him carefully, and obey Him willingly, we will become godly role models for others. All of this is possible because, by virtue of our faith in Him, our righteous Lord dwells in our hearts. Will you take the risk today knowing that by faith God will bless your costly choice to bring glory and honor to him?

It is amazing to see the grace of God continue to pour out upon Gideon as he takes baby steps of faith. From hiding in the winepress to tearing down and burning his father's altars, he has grown by leaps and bounds. Trembling, he walks in obedience to the truth of who God says he is. He was so fearful, yet he obeyed, and God graciously met him in his fear.

So Gideon took ten of his servants and did as the LORD told him. But because he was afraid of his family and the men of the town, he did it at night rather than in the daytime.
Judges 6:27

Gideon stepped out in faith and obeyed God's call. The people in the town did not respond favorably to what they saw the following morning. They wanted to kill Gideon, but the Lord protected him. As God's born-again children, we have His Spirit continually indwelling us, and as we walk in obedience, each step of faith gives us a greater sense of His presence and power.

God is patient and loving toward you, and He will never give up on you.

© 2003, Thin Within, All Rights Reserved

LESSON

As you read on in Judges, you will see that Gideon continues, indeed, to walk in faith. He clings to God's grace, embracing his new identity as a "mighty warrior." It is through Gideon that God will save Israel from the conquerors of the east. This one who thought of himself as the "least of the least" rises to the call of leadership and recruits an army of Israelites to join him to fight against Midian and their allies.

8. God won the victory.

You are probably familiar with the rest of the story of how Gideon and only 300 men defeated an army "as thick as locusts." The battle was the Lord's. After all was said and done, the Lord had dealt a mighty blow to the masses and 120,000 of the enemy had fallen (Judges 8:10).

God meets us in our place of need as well, and has given us a far greater provision for our fear and our sense of inadequacy. We have been blessed with the continual indwelling presence and power of God's Holy Spirit. We have no need to "test" God or ask for signs, because we have the privilege of experiencing his magnificent power and grace each time we take a step of faith.

As Gideon rose up to his call and cooperated with God, he had the blessing of participating in God's work in a big way. He saw idolatry fall and he saw an amazing victory. So much was accomplished as he rejected the lies of the enemy and set his mind on that which was from God. Through his faith, God won the victory that had already been planned.

▶ **Personalize It: God has won the victory for you**. He has done it, dear beloved! You can go in whatever strength you have because His strength is working powerfully within you. You can renounce the lies and any idolatry in your life and choose to walk in faith. Allow God's grace to fall afresh upon you as you do. Nothing in your life is too big for God. With only 300 Israelites, God defeated a massive foe. So, too, can he defeat the massive "foe" of overweight, food addiction, bulimia, anorexia, or any other stronghold. What a mighty God we have!

Physiological Information

Take whatever strength or resolve you have and God will multiply it, just as he did for Gideon. God's plan is to transform you from the inside out, making you into that naturally thin person He designed you to be. He is doing that even now, beginning from within your heart, your mind, and your beliefs. God has ordained that as these things are brought in conformity with Him, your outside will conform, reflecting that naturally thin person that He has called you to be. Just like Gideon, you can step out in faith. When you do, you will find each and every time that you are empowered to walk in obedience by God's indwelling Spirit.

In week three, we pointed out that we act in accordance with our beliefs. The marathon runner and the couch potato each "succeeded" according to the way they viewed themselves.

If you believe that God is making you into the naturally thin person He created you to be and you begin to think of yourself as being conformed into that person, it will affect your behavior. This isn't about "the power of positive thinking." It is about renewing your mind in the area of your self-perception. It is about believing that God is powerfully at work in you moment by moment by His Spirit and His grace because of His great love and plan for your life. Remember, He has a hope and a future for you, and what He has begun in you He is faithful to complete!

Let's evaluate the habits of naturally thin people. We're not thinking of someone who eats only salads in order to remain thin or an exercise fanatic who fears getting fat, but someone who is thin from within. Perhaps it is someone you know. What does he or she eat? When? How much? Are they obsessed with food and eating? How do they eat? Do they compulsively jump on and off scales? Do they exercise? If so, how much? What are the habits of this naturally thin person? If you can identify what those habits are and emulate them, you will cooperate with the work that God is doing within you even now.

Keys to Conscious Eating

1. Eat only when my body is hungry.
2. Reduce the number of distractions in order to eat in a calm environment.
3. Eat when sitting down.
4. Eat when my body and mind are relaxed.
5. Eat and drink the food and beverages my body enjoys.
6. Pay attention to my food while eating.
7. Eat slowly and savor each bite.
8. Stop *before* my body is "full."

© 2003, Thin Within, All Rights Reserved

In 1975, after a study of naturally thin people, Thin Within began sharing the Keys to Conscious Eating, which reflected the eating patterns of these people. If many of the "keys" seem like common sense to you now, rejoice and celebrate that God has already been at work in you.

If you have already been doing some of these things, it means you are becoming a naturally thin eater. God is doing a work in you now, even though you may not feel like it. However, it is important to praise Him for each step of faith you have taken and praise Him for all that He has done.

He calls you to go in the strength you have to fight against that which may seem impossible. But it isn't impossible, because He is able to do immeasurably more than all you ask or imagine, according to His power that is at work within you (Ephesians 3:20).

Integration

By the grace of God you have the Holy Spirit resident within you as your constant source of power. You have been born of the Spirit and you have strength beyond imagining. You are now called to rise up and walk as you continue on this exciting journey.

If you experience feelings of fear, apprehension, anxiety, shame, or guilt, remain mindful of God's call to Gideon in his place of impotence. He calls to you to allow Him to provide. He will do all that is required.

Are you relying on your own self-effort in order to become a thin person? Continue to walk forward in what He has done and experience success in Him moment –by moment.

God's grace is poured out upon us each and every moment. We can allow ourselves to experience it when we don't dwell on our "mistakes" or "failures." You may have "blown it" a moment ago, but *this* moment is new. Observe. Were you hungry when you ate? Were you sitting down when you ate? Were you eating foods that were simply available instead of satisfying? Did you let down your guard and eat when you were feeling emotional? Then avail yourself of God's grace and correct. Confess to God that you "blew it" and that you need His help and His cleansing. This is confession or observation. Then ask Him to strengthen you as you turn and follow Him. This is repentance or correction. With His power you can do this. Come out of the winepress, out of fear, out of shame, guilt, and despair. Step into that which God has for you—to live and enjoy all that He has made you to be.

Observations and Corrections Chart

This week you may choose to use the Observations and Corrections Chart. (It can be found in your Temple Tool Kit starting on Day 51).

THIN WITHIN OBSERVATIONS AND CORRECTIONS CHART

Observation	Thoughts / Needed Corrections
1. I ate when my body was hungry.	
2. I ate in a calm environment by reducing	
3. I ate when I was sitting.	
4. I ate when my body and mind were relaxed.	
5. I ate and drank only the things my body loved.	
6. I paid attention only to my food while eating.	
7. I ate slowly, savoring every bite.	
8. I stopped before my body was full.	

Use it as often as you like to observe which Thin Within Keys to Conscious Eating you're using or not using. Whenever you eat or drink, place a check mark or star beside the key that you used. Empty boxes at the end of the day are an indication for you to pay more attention to that particular key. In this way, you can observe and correct by making appropriate adjustments.

Have fun with this and don't become too tied down to it. Prayerfully ask the Lord to show you what he wants you to see. Rejoice, again I say rejoice!

Armed with the Spirit of the living God, we encourage you to go in his strength. God is with you, mighty warrior!

My Notes

© 2003, Thin Within, All Rights Reserved

EXERCISES

Day One

Going Deeper

This week we are going to study the experience of Gideon, finding golden nuggets along the way that will bring us to a celebration of God's grace and provision. Begin by reading Judges 6:1–5 and then describe the condition the Israelites were in at that time. According to verse 1, what brought on this huge problem for Israel? Can you make any connection between what they were experiencing and what we experience when we stay in sin and ignore God? Journal about any correlation you might see in your own life.

____

____

____

____

Bible Study

Judges 6:6 shows the first step in finding freedom. Journal what you see as the process of restoration when we are in a miserable state of oppression. When we cry out for help, God _will_ answer us (Jeremiah 29:12–13; 33:3). How did God answer the Israelites in Judges 6:7–10?

____

____

____

____

Knowing God by Heart: Infinite

"And so I will show my greatness and my holiness, and <u>I will make myself known</u> in the sight of many nations. <u>Then they will know that I am the LORD.</u>"
Ezekiel 38:23

Look up the word "infinite" in the dictionary and write down a definition that you believe is consistent with God being infinite. Read Psalm 90:2 and relate your definition to this Scripture.

____

____

____

____

Getting Practical

Review the Keys to Conscious Eating. Ask God to show you how to incorporate these keys into your daily eating habits so they might be of the most benefit to you.

____

____

____

____

Memory Challenge

Start memorizing Philippians 1:6. Take time to see the message proclaimed in this Scripture. Read the verse out loud several times, then look away and say it from memory.

Being confident of this, that he who began a good work in you
will carry it on to completion until the day of Christ Jesus.
Philippians 1:6

  © 2003, Thin Within, All Rights Reserved

Day Two

Going Deeper

Evaluate the habits of a naturally thin person that you know. What and how does he or she eat? When? How much? Do they read labels? Are they obsessed with food and eating? Do they jump on and off scales? Do they exercise? How do they eat? If we can identify and emulate the habits of a naturally thin person and begin to think of ourselves as a "thin person in process," our behavior will change as we cooperate with the work that God is doing within us. Journal your thoughts.

____
____
____
____

Bible Study

Just as Gideon did not appear to be a mighty warrior for God, we may not appear to be living out of our identity in Christ. As we allow God to enable us, He will transform us from within to do mighty things in Him. Read Romans 8:37 and other verses that God has impressed on your heart these last few weeks, verses that reinforce who you are in Him and how He is completing a good work in you (Philippians 1:6).

____
____
____
____

Knowing God by Heart

Continue to grow in your knowledge of how God is infinite by reading Psalm 145:3, 13 and 1 Kings 8:27. Write your thoughts.

____
____
____
____

Getting Practical

Review the Keys to Conscious Eating. Pick one that you feel is significant for you and then commit to making it a habit in your life. Tell someone else about this new habit so they can help you.

____
____
____
____

Memory Challenge

Continue memorizing Philippians 1:6 by saying or writing it several times. After some repetition, try repeating it from memory. Take the memory verse card with you and refer to it throughout the day.

Thin Within Tip

Flee when you feel an overwhelming temptation to eat past 5. Excuse yourself and go to another room for a "time out" to regroup and pray.

© 2003, Thin Within, All Rights Reserved

EXERCISES

Day Three

Going Deeper

Read Judges 6:11–12. How did Gideon's location conflict with God's declaration to Him? God looked at Gideon through eyes of grace and love and saw a mighty warrior. Are you "hiding out in a winepress," living in fear based on your external circumstances? You may be hiding in all kinds of places: behind romance novels, TV shows, movies, the computer, or the kitchen pantry. Wherever you may find yourself—alone, fearful, ashamed, guilty, or entrenched in sin—God will reach out to touch you and form you into His image right where you are. Journal about His action of drawing you closer and developing a deeper relationship with you.

____

____

____

____

Bible Study

Journal about how God showed Gideon his grace and provision in Judges 6:13–16. From where was Gideon's strength to come? How was Gideon tempted to respond? Reflect on your own powerlessness and helplessness in the area of eating and losing weight. But don't stay there! Lay this down before the Lord so that you will experience all he has given you for life and godliness (2 Peter 1:3–4).

____

____

____

____

Knowing God by Heart

Find synonyms for the word "infinite" in a thesaurus or dictionary. How do these words give you a deeper understanding of God as infinite? Read Isaiah 40:28. What does this verse tell you about God?

____

____

____

____

Getting Practical

We would like to introduce a new Thin Within tool today called the Observations and Corrections Chart. It is designed to show you which of the Keys to Conscious Eating you are using and which you may be neglecting. (Remember: This is only a tool to help you eat from 0 to 5. Allow the Spirit to lead you as to whether or not you should use this chart to guide your obedience in Him.) Whenever you eat or drink, place a mark next to all the keys you use. At the end of the day, *observe* which keys have few or no marks next to them and make an effort to *correct* by using those keys.

____

____

____

____

Memory Challenge

Review Philippians 1:6 until you can repeat it from memory.

   © 2003, Thin Within, All Rights Reserved

Day Four

Going Deeper

Review the Keys to Conscious Eating once again, and note how many of them relate to Psalm 46:10, "Be still and know that I am God." Journal your thoughts on this. Before you eat each meal, take time to be still and allow God to help you eat in a way that is honoring him.

____

____

____

____

Bible Study

Do you see God's loving-kindness and grace in this picture? How does Gideon receive God's "proof" (Judges 6:23–24)? Is God your peace? In what ways do you need him to be your peace? Will you allow God's grace to flow over you and grant you his peace that passes all understanding (Philippians 4:7)?

____

____

____

____

Knowing God by Heart: Transcendent

Look up the word "transcendent" in the dictionary and write down a definition that you believe is consistent with God being transcendent. Read Isaiah 55:8–9 and relate your definition to these Scriptures.

____

____

____

____

Getting Practical

Continue to use the Observations and Corrections Chart as the Spirit leads you.

____

____

____

Memory Challenge

Repeat Philippians 1:6 from memory. Turn this verse into a prayer for yourself or someone you know.

Thin Within Tip

Thank God for the shelter He provides for you as you walk around your house or yard. You'll be amazed as your heart overflows with thanksgiving and praise! As you look at your surroundings, continue to thank God for all of His provisions.

© 2003, Thin Within, All Rights Reserved

EXERCISES

Day Five

Going Deeper

Take some time to pray, asking God to bring you into a total trust relationship with Him. If you are fearful or uncertain about some aspect of this struggle with food (for example, 0 to 5 eating, the overwhelming amount of weight you need to lose, or the painful sacrifice of giving up the amount of food that you have grown accustomed to), take this to the Lord. He is faithful and will strengthen you just as He did Gideon. Write a renewed prayer of commitment to Him, expressing your faith that He can and *will* do this in you.

____

____

____

____

Bible Study

What had God declared to Israel as the reason for their oppression (Judges 6:10)? What action does God ask of Gideon first (Judges 6:25–26)? Are there any altars, idols, or Asherah poles in your life that God may be calling you to tear down? What are they? (These could include people or things you value more than God or that have more influence on your behavior than God does.)

____

____

____

____

Knowing God by Heart

What do Exodus 3:14, Psalm 150:2, and 2 Corinthians 4:7; 9:14–15 tell you about how God is transcendent?

____

____

____

____

Getting Practical

Is there anything you have found that helps you slow down and eat consciously? Make a note of it and prayerfully incorporate it into your mealtimes.

____

____

____

Memory Challenge

Meditate on Philippians 1:6 throughout the day and allow it to draw you closer to God. Ask him to help you truly believe this Scripture so that it can set you free from all the deceptive lies of the world.

Thin Within Tip

"Resist the devil and he will flee from you. Come near to God and he will come near to you" (James 4:7b–8a). Tell the enemy to get lost. Tell the Lord how much you enjoy drawing near to Him!

© 2003, Thin Within, All Rights Reserved

Day Six ~ Optional Exercises

Going Deeper

We can experience the fullness of God's grace when we don't store up our "mistakes" or "failures." You may have "blown it" a moment ago, but *this* moment is new. Avail yourself of God's grace and His correction. Confess and then ask Him to strengthen you for change. Repentance is the correction as we turn away from sin. Journal how you can observe and correct in this moment.

____
____
____
____
____

Bible Study

Notice Gideon's obedience in carrying out God's command (Judges 6:27–32). Were there any difficulties as a result of his obedience (in other words, was it easy to obey)? Later, we'll see that God richly rewarded Gideon and gave him an incredible victory. However, his obedience was somewhat uncomfortable at first. What does this say to you?

____
____
____
____
____

Knowing God by Heart

Find synonyms for the word "transcendent" in a thesaurus or dictionary. How do these words give you a deeper understanding of God as transcendent? Read Isaiah 43:10 and Romans 1:20. What do these verses say about God?

____
____
____
____
____

Getting Practical

Use the Observations and Corrections Chart today as God leads you.

____
____
____
____

Memory Challenge

Repeat Philippians 1:6 out loud and ask God to make this verse real in your life. What might God be leading you to "be" or to "do" in response to this passage?

© 2003, Thin Within, All Rights Reserved

EXERCISES

Day Seven – Optional Exercises

Going Deeper

In some ways, it is frightening to believe God and to step out in faith to do what he asks us to do. But God knows our weaknesses and insecurities and as we seek Him, He will bring us to a place of total trust in him. Read Judges 6:36–40 and 7:9–15. Reflect on the way God poured out his grace on Gideon in his time of fear and uncertainty. How can you apply this to your life? Record your thoughts.

____

____

____

Bible Study

Read Judges 7:1–8; 15–23, and 8:10. As he held onto God's grace, Gideon continued to walk in faith and live in the identity given him by God. What was the result? Only God could accomplish such an incredible victory by working through Gideon and his small army. What does that say about the victory you desire in your own life? Is there anything too big for God?

____

____

____

Getting Practical

What have you learned from using the Observations and Corrections Chart these last four days? Are there any keys that you feel the Spirit nudging you to use more frequently in order to eat from 0 to 5 more consistently? Take these observations to God in prayer and ask him to give you the strength to rest in his Spirit as you make godly corrections.

____

____

____

Memory Challenge

Share your memory verse with a friend or family member, telling him or her how it relates to your Thin Within journey.

Thin Within Tip

Replace "bad habits" with "godly behavior." For example, if you always eat a bowl of cereal or ice cream before bed regardless of hunger, replace it with a cup of hot herbal tea. If you eat popcorn while watching TV, consider an activity using your hands, such as needlework or lifting small dumbbells, to avoid mindless munching.

    © 2003, Thin Within, All Rights Reserved

Review of the Week

Take time at the end of each week to review what God has taught you and how it is impacting your life. This will give you a great overview to take to your Thin Within Support Group Meeting.

The most significant thing God taught me this week:

Philippians 1:6 tells me that God has begun a new work in me. I can best describe this new work as:

It is a struggle to be confident in this new work when:

The most significant thing that God helped me to observe this week that I will focus on correcting next week:

What I have learned about the character of God as infinite and transcendent, and how I have come to know and be drawn closer to him:

My prayer requests and praises:

© 2003, Thin Within, All Rights Reserved

C-58

© 2003, Thin Within, All Rights Reserved

Month Three

Lessons &

Exercises

© 2003, Thin Within, All Rights Reserved

You are now entering Phase III of your Thin Within journey. Consider the description of Phase III below as you seek to renew your mind.

Phase III - Mastery Phase "I will not be mastered by anything"

Our Thin Within journey points us to the only one who is to have mastery over our lives and our every choice….the Lord God himself. It's so easy to turn to food for comfort or escape from whatever troubles us, but God is our only refuge! He is our way of escape.

Oreos or cheese enchiladas are not to have mastery over us! We are to enjoy food yet we are called to discern when we are hungry and by the power of the Holy Spirit, make wise food choices. God knows what our energy requirements are, since He designed us, and it's exciting to learn to ask Him, to obey His lead, and to depend on Him to direct our choices.

This is the most exciting journey of your life because it really isn't simply about the food, eating or weight. It's about a life that is surrendered to an all-powerful, all-loving God who desires nothing but the best for you in all things….His beloved! Freedom with responsibility produces a life of deep abiding joy!

© 2003, Thin Within, All Rights Reserved

Building Godly Boundaries

Introduction

We have enjoyed the privilege of sitting at Jesus' feet these many weeks. We have listened to His Spirit teach us through His Word regarding our food, eating, and our lives in Christ as He has drawn us even closer to His heart.

The riches of God's amazing grace are seen in the new life He has purchased for us. We are walking more fully by faith and exercising discernment within the bountiful freedom He has given us.

"Everything is permissible for me" — but not everything is beneficial. "Everything is permissible for me" — but I will not be mastered by anything.
1 Corinthians 6:12

While we are free to enjoy all foods, we recognize that not all things are beneficial. During Phase One, we relished the freedom we have been given from the law, diet rules, and food plans. In Phase Two, we began to take responsibility for exercising discernment and making more beneficial choices, which come from a heart of love for all that the Lord has done and is doing in us and through us.

As we prayerfully establish godly boundaries by the power of His Holy Spirit, we become authentic people.

In Phase Three, we continue our walk of faith as we take a stand that we will not be in bondage to anything of this world. We stand knowing we have been made new in Christ and have been given everything we need to live a life of godliness. As you continue to depend on the Lord, He will guide and direct you as to what He wants to bring home to your heart. He has a personal plan, a hope, a desire, and a future for your life that is reflected in Jeremiah 29:11.

Spiritual Foundation

As you spend time with the Lord in fellowship through prayer and the reading of His Word, as you set your mind on things of the Spirit rather than things of the flesh, and as you walk in faith that God has made you new, you begin to take responsibility for your life and your behavior. You cherish what God has created and entrusted to your care—your body, your behavior, your choices, your mind-set, your beliefs, your emotions, and your will.

Keeping a godly guard over that which He has so graciously given you is a vital part of continuing to grow and mature in Christ. We do this through establishing and maintaining godly boundaries.

What are godly boundaries and why do we need them?

Boundaries are those demarcations that you establish and maintain in order to protect that which God has entrusted to you. To guard these gifts, you must have a plan in place that will protect them from the attack of the world, the flesh, and the devil. This safeguard occurs through establishing godly boundaries.

In order to understand what a boundary is and what it is supposed to do, we must first look at how the term is used in Scripture. In the following verses, we can see that the Lord set boundaries that served a specific function during creation.

You set a boundary they cannot cross; never again will they cover the earth.
Psalm 104:9

. . . when he gave the sea its boundary so that the waters would not overstep his command, and when he marked out the foundations of the earth.
Proverbs 8:29

A boundary is a line that is not to be crossed. It is designed to guard what is behind it from being infiltrated by outside forces. Paul spoke of boundaries to Timothy:

Timothy, guard what has been entrusted to your care.
1 Timothy 6:20a

Guard the good deposit that was entrusted to you— guard it with the help of the Holy Spirit who lives in us.
2 Timothy 1:14

Additionally, boundaries are to keep out of our lives that which must be purged. For instance, with our food and eating we want to release our selfishness and our greed as they give room for the flesh, the world, and the devil and hinder our maturity in Christ.

Godly boundaries will protect that which God has entrusted to us while never hindering our becoming more conformed to His image. If at any point a boundary obstructs our walk of faith, then

© 2003, Thin Within, All Rights Reserved

it has become fleshly rather than godly in nature. To avoid this, we depend on the Lord daily through prayer and the reading of His Word.

To set godly boundaries, we resist the natural tendency to revert to the flesh. The flesh wants to protect itself from making sacrifices to which the Lord calls. It wants to hang on to its self-centered demands, a stance that is not consistent with godly boundaries. Our boundary setting must line up with the Word of God, be based on faith, and heed the leading of the Holy Spirit through prayer.

Godly boundaries do not say, "You had better not mess with me." This is an inappropriate attitude for one of God's servants. While we may be called to "shake the dust" off our feet and move on in some instances, we are to do so with grace and kindness. To be certain that your boundaries are, in fact, godly, submit your situation to God through prayer.

Why is this an important concept in your Thin Within journey? One of the things we have discovered over the many years of working with people who battle with food, eating, and weight-related issues is that many have never developed a proper perspective of what should be guarded. Their boundary lines have become vague. There is often a lack of understanding as to why and how to set boundaries from a biblical perspective. For instance, you may have grown up in a family where you were abused in some way, thus violating appropriate boundaries. You may have thought as a young man or woman that such abuse was normal, not realizing that life wasn't meant to be that way.

This disregard for your boundaries may have carried over into other aspects of your life. Many who have been abused physically, emotionally or sexually, have food, eating, and weight-related issues. They may have difficulty recognizing that their body is fearfully and wonderfully made and is to be protected by establishing and maintaining godly boundaries.

This is a biblical concept that Paul spoke of (Acts 20:31; 1 Corinthians 16:13) and that Jesus taught when He spoke about guarding ourselves (Luke 12:1). Let's look at ways in which the holy Son of God demonstrates godly boundaries.

1. Jesus maintained a godly boundary when faced with endless opportunities to do more.

Jesus gave them this answer: "I tell you the truth, the Son can do nothing by himself; he can do only what he sees his Father doing, because whatever the Father does the Son also does.
John 5:19

One of the hardest things for many who struggle to establish and maintain godly boundaries is to set limits on what they do and don't do in life. Do you feel as if your life is out of control? Do you feel as if everyone places demands and expectations on you? The good news is the Lord doesn't expect you to do it all! He wants you to establish godly boundaries that will protect your time, energy, emotions, and heart. This doesn't necessarily mean reacting with an absolute "No!" to the next person who calls with a request. However, it does require a willingness to depend on the Lord to show you specifically what you are to do, just as the Father showed Jesus.

2. Jesus maintained a godly boundary when faced with pressure from His family.

Jesus' brothers said to Him, "You ought to leave here and go to Judea, so that your disciples may see the miracles you do. No one who wants to become a public figure acts in secret. Since you are doing these things, show yourself to the world." For even his own brothers did not believe in him. Therefore Jesus told them, "The right time for me has not yet come; for you any time is right."
John 7:3–6

This is perhaps one of the most challenging areas for many. When family members place pressure on us, we may compromise proper godly boundaries. There is a place and time for a godly "yes" and a godly "no." We must prayerfully depend on the Lord to help us to know how to respond in the right way.

To avoid hurting someone's feelings, we may forsake that which we feel strongly about in order to win another's favor. In saying "yes," we

> Boundaries are those demarcations that you establish and maintain in order to protect that which God has entrusted to you.

© 2003, Thin Within, All Rights Reserved

may end up resenting those who we perceive to be "demanding." Instead, we need to be authentic and express in a godly way our need to guard that which He has entrusted to us, speaking the truth in love (Ephesians 4:15).

For instance, the family of a participant pressured her to celebrate holidays by eating heartily of all the food that was brought to the family parties. Because there was such an emphasis on food, she frequently compromised her 0 to 5 eating in the hopes of not offending anyone, and she resented her family for "pressuring" her to overeat. When she failed to be honest with herself and her family, guilt and shame inhabited her heart. By establishing godly boundaries, she could walk in confidence that her 0 to 5 eating was important to God. Always wanting to please her relatives was a flesh pattern that needed to be put to death.

When we have established a godly boundary that will impact our family members, it will be important to prayerfully ask for wisdom and a gentle spirit when speaking the truth at the appropriate time and place.

3. Jesus maintained a godly boundary when faced with pressure from friends.

Very early in the morning, while it was still dark, Jesus got up, left the house and went off to a solitary place, where he prayed. Simon and his companions went to look for him, and when they found him, they exclaimed: "Everyone is looking for you!" Jesus replied, "Let us go somewhere else—to the nearby villages— so that I can preach there also. That is why I have come."
Mark 1:35–38

Do you experience a tugging to help every friend who has a need? What about the lady in charge of the church nursery when she calls you at the last minute to volunteer for the 11 A.M. service? Is it hard to say "no" even when the Lord impresses it on your heart to do so?

First, notice that while the demands of people pressed in on Jesus, He maintained a proper boundary. He took time to pull away from some of those who were in need in order to be alone with His Father. With the pressure always to do more for others, do you feel as if you are being "selfish" to require time alone? God clearly wants you to have time with him. He is a jealous God who knows that your time with Him is essential.

Second, while the crowds wanted more from Jesus, He refused to lose sight of what the Father called Him to do. There still remained many who were blind, crippled, or who had lost hope. Many remained in their graves despite Jesus' miracle of raising Lazarus from the dead. In fact, even with so much more He "might" have done, at the end of His earthly ministry He was able to pray with confidence that He had completed the work the Father had given Him to do (John 17:4). The Father hadn't called Jesus to do all things for all people. What the Father called Jesus to do, He faithfully did.

Follow Jesus' example and resist pressure from others to "find a need and fill it," unless the Father directs you and it is His will for you. Although many were waiting and wanting more from Jesus, He frequently moved on to minister in another place.

This also demonstrates another principle that we must keep in mind. Many find it easier to "remove the speck" from the eye of another than to deal with the "log" in their own eye. It is part of the natural man to want to fix the other person. We may think that the Lord wants us to do this. "After all," we reason, "if He didn't want me to fix my friend, she certainly wouldn't have asked for my opinion in the first place." However, as we maintain the boundary of time alone with the Father and draw near to Him, He convicts us first to "remove the log" from our own eye. This may be painful, but it is necessary. It is only as He directs us to look inward that He enables us, by His Spirit, to make godly corrections in our own lives. He may, in turn, move us to lend help and wisdom to others, always being aware that respecting the boundaries of others is a part of our maturity in Christ. Let's quickly review the boundaries that Jesus set in His life.

1. Jesus maintained a godly boundary when faced with endless opportunities to do more.

2. Jesus maintained a godly boundary when faced with pressure from family.

3. Jesus maintained a godly boundary when faced with pressure from friends.

These three points are a model for us as we seek to establish and maintain godly boundaries. It is a weakness of our flesh to "people please." Paul speaks to this directly.

Am I now trying to win the approval of men, or of God? Or am I trying to please men? If I were still trying to please men, I would not be a servant of Christ.
Galatians 1:10

© 2003, Thin Within, All Rights Reserved

We aren't walking in the Spirit if we continually seek the approval of others. We may try to please people in the name of "Christian servanthood," but according to Galatians 1:10, we are not being an authentic servant of Christ when we "serve" with an eye to please people. James says it well when he says that no good thing comes to a double-minded man who is unstable in all of his ways (James1:7–8). We must remain ever circumspect in our choices.

If we define a boundary regarding our time, yet our choices indicate a lack of scrutiny over our schedules, then we have compromised that boundary. Our choices indicate our actual boundaries. If we are joyless, overly busy, out of control, and at odds with our family, then we have not maintained godly boundaries even if what fills our time appears godly, like serving at our local church. As you walk in response to the Spirit, the Lord will lead you according to that which He has set before you.

If you try to please everyone, you may not only leave needs unmet (we can never do it all), but you may also end up with resentments and even physical ailments. The Lord never intended for us to live life in such a way that we feel overwhelmed and beaten down. Remember, He says that His yoke is easy and His burden light (Matthew 11:30). It is true that this is another costly choice. However, it is worth it. When you stop trying to please everyone, you will obviously leave some people feeling unhappy. However, as you depend on the Lord to lead and guide you as to what is and what is not from Him, you can rest in confidence that He will say to you, "'Well done, good and faithful servant! . . .Come and share your master's happiness!'" (Matthew 25:21).

4. Jesus maintained a boundary with Himself.

In the Garden of Gethsemane, Jesus' humanity was clearly seen as He battled with His own godly boundary. The only thing to which He would give Himself was the will of God, even at the expense of His own desire.

> *"Father, if you are willing, take this cup from me;*
> *yet not my will, but yours be done."*
> *Luke 22:42*

Many of us struggle with a desire to do things that God does not call us to do. Our boundary must be only what the Lord wants, even when we want otherwise. Have you ever allowed yourself to put something off by procrastinating? This is a clear yet subtle example of how our desire to please self inappropriately can cross a godly boundary. Putting off what we know God has called us to do is clearly disobedience or sin. But by saying we will do it "later," we often deceive ourselves and experience less conviction from the Holy Spirit—we don't feel our outright rebellion quite so strongly. We must do what the Lord says to do when the Lord says to do it: "Not my will, but yours be done, Lord" (Luke 22:42).

Have you ever felt by the middle of the day that you have "failed" in eating 0 to 5? Have you then been tempted to say, "Well, this day is a lost cause, so I might as well just forget it." You won't feel godly conviction as strongly by saying, "I'll begin again tomorrow." Your wall of procrastination muffles the voice of the Holy Spirit. How many of us have, as one participant puts it, "lived a lifetime of Mondays"? We promise to start again on Monday and somehow Monday never comes.

A boundary must be firmly established and then honored. In the moment God calls you to do something, declare: "Not my will but Yours be done, Lord."

5. Jesus maintained a boundary regarding what was allowed in the temple.

> *Jesus entered the temple area and drove out all who were*
> *buying and selling there. He overturned the tables of the*
> *money-changers and the benches of those selling doves.*
> *"It is written," he said to them, "'my house will be called*
> *a house of prayer,' but you are making it a*
> *'den of robbers'."*
> *Matthew 21:12–13*

Throughout the preceding weeks, we have emphasized that God has declared your body to be His temple. His Holy Spirit lives within you. Just as Jesus drove out that which wasn't appropriate to reside in the temple of God, it is also your responsibility now to "drive out" that which shouldn't be within you.

One way to accomplish this may be to come face to face with ways in which your boundaries have been violated either in the past or the present by someone who treated you poorly. You may even think that someone else is to blame for your struggles with food, eating, or weight-related issues. What will you do with these painful or convicting thoughts? The Lord has come to bind up your broken heart, to mend whatever is torn. He wants you to let go of any bitterness or pain that may have blurred or violated your God-given boundaries.

Other things to "drive out of the temple" are selfishness, greed, lust, and envy. Scripture lists

© 2003, Thin Within, All Rights Reserved

those things that war against the Spirit within us. This will be a lifelong process, but as you cling to the Lord and continue to depend on Him, He will convict your heart and direct your path. His "cleansing" isn't merely the removal of dirt and grime, it is the entrance and presence in you of that which is holy and pure, and will bring an overflowing sense of peace and joy.

Sit at the feet of your Savior and Lord who asks you to trust and follow Him. There you will experience His strength to guard that which He has entrusted to your care as you establish and maintain godly boundaries.

Physiological Information

As Jesus guarded what was allowed to enter the physical temple, so too are we called to guard what is allowed into our physical body. Eating 0 to 5 honors a godly boundary. You want your body to be healthy and free of excess weight. This requires guarding, protecting, and maintaining this boundary.

Before eating, we suggest that you stop and prayerfully check in with the final authority, the Holy Spirit, and ask "Am I hungry? Is food the answer to my present need? How much and what kind of food does my body require right now?"

If you establish this as a wall through which you must pass before you eat, it will help you remain within the boundaries of 0 to 5. For instance, the next time you head for the kitchen to get one of your favorite snacks, stop and ask "Am I hungry right now?" If your answer is, "Yes, I am physically hungry. I am at a 0." Great! Bon appétit!

However, suppose that after stopping at 5 you get some sad news from a dear friend. Before you end up on the couch with the Kleenex and a bag full of microwave popcorn, stop and ask the Lord, "What am I looking to get from food right now? What need do I want met?" In this case, maybe it is a need for comfort. Be determined. Stand fast with your godly boundary of 0 to 5

eating and turn to the Lord instead of the popcorn to meet your emotional needs.

Another way to set godly eating boundaries is to establish a place where you can have conscious meals. Our culture would have us believe that sitting in front of the TV is as good a place as any. However, starting today, begin to enjoy your meals in the kitchen or at the dining-room table, if you do not do this already. Perhaps you haven't seen the top of your dining-room table in months, as it is the "catch all" place for homework, newspapers, car keys, and various other sundries! Ask the Lord to help you set a godly boundary for conscious eating, a place that is calm and free from chaos. If you establish this as a boundary, you will find yourself less prone to being distracted when you eat. Chaotic environments often produce chaotic eating. Establish a special place for your meals and keep that area free from clutter.

Social eating can be a testing ground for boundary setting. First, define your purpose in attending the social gathering. It isn't likely that your goal will be to overindulge. You may decide it is to make a work connection, to socialize with friends, to meet new people, or some other purpose. Establishing your purpose in attending the event will help you avoid crossing over your godly boundary of 0 to 5 eating. If your main purpose is not the food, then you may want to attend the function after you have eaten so your attention will be on making that business acquaintance or to socialize with friends.

One way of handling church potlucks or eating out is allowing yourself to stay at a 0 longer or to only eat 0 to 2 earlier in the day, so you will be certain to be at a 0 for the occasion. When attending a potluck, survey all the choices first. From all that is offered, select only the excellent choices, knowing you can always return for more later. If you start at one end of the table without planning ahead, most likely you will end up with more on your plate than you need and be tempted to eat beyond 5.

> The Lord never intended for us to live life in such a way that we feel overwhelmed and beaten down.

© 2003, Thin Within, All Rights Reserved

LESSON

When eating at a restaurant, you don't need to eat all the food that is served to you. Some participants ask for a carryout container before their meal arrives. Then when the waiter brings the food, they put a large portion into the carryout container so they won't be tempted to overeat. Also, sharing the meal with a willing friend is a great way of maintaining your godly boundary of eating from 0 to 5.

Integration

Godly boundaries are a vital part of caring for that which God entrusts to you. He cares about your body, your health, your choices, your emotions, will, beliefs, actions, and thoughts. He knows that years of not maintaining appropriate boundaries can result in frustration and pain. He knows your heartache. He wants to heal your suffering spirit, bind up your broken heart, and call you into an obedient walk where you make godly choices and experience the abundant life.

As we prayerfully establish godly boundaries by the power of His Holy Spirit, we become authentic people. When we feel uneasy or uncomfortable in a particular situation, we take that situation to the Lord in prayer. When we are concerned, we will lovingly and honestly verbalize our concern. When we delight in the joy of the Lord, we outwardly reflect who we truly are within. We step out of the darkness of denial and rebellion into the light of authenticity.

As you continue to grow and mature in the Lord, ask yourself if you have moved beyond Phase One, where all things are permissible. Have you developed discernment by selecting that which is excellent and appropriate for God's temple? Prayerfully ask the Lord if you are bowing down to anything other than Him. As you set boundaries, it is a good time to confess to the Lord anything inappropriate that remains. Does your need to please people drive you to do more than what the Lord would have you do? Are you mastered by your love for chocolate or pizza? Can you say "no" to some of your favorite foods? All things are permissible and sometimes even beneficial, but can you turn them down? Even though it is permissible, are you free not to have some of your favorite foods? Ask the Lord if there yet remains anything that masters you. Refuse to bow to anything other than to our living God.

Pressures come from family, friends, your flesh, and the enemy to eat outside of 0 to 5. As you pray for the grace of God to equip you to maintain godly boundaries, you will experience more victory in your life. Remember that the temple of God—your body—is intended to reflect His glory.

Our Lord cherishes and values us. He wants us to guard our life, our choices, emotions, wills, and bodies—all these things are precious. He has given them to us to enjoy and use for His glory. As we seek to do as He directs, we will discover an outpouring of His blessing.

LORD, you have assigned me my portion and my cup; you have made my lot secure. The boundary lines have fallen for me in pleasant places; surely I have a delightful inheritance.
Psalm 16:5–6

To set godly boundaries, we resist the natural tendency to revert to the flesh.

© 2003, Thin Within, All Rights Reserved

<u>My Notes</u>

© 2003, Thin Within, All Rights Reserved

EXERCISES

Day One

Going Deeper

Read 1 Corinthians 6:12. How does this speak to you in light of all that God has taught you in Thin Within? Pray that He would show you those things in your life that are not beneficial. Ask Him to reveal to you ways in which you need to take a better stand to honor the temple of the Holy Spirit and not be mastered by anything but Him.

____

____

____

____

Bible Study

From the reading of the lesson, how would you define a godly boundary? What is its purpose? (See Psalm 104:9, Proverbs 8:29, 1 Corinthians 16:13, 1 Timothy 6:20a, and 2 Timothy 1:14.)

____

____

____

____

Knowing God by Heart: Immutable

"You are my witnesses," declares the LORD, "and my servant whom I have chosen, so that you may know and believe me and understand that I am he. Before me no god was formed, nor will there be one after me."
Isaiah 43:10

Look up the word "immutable" in the dictionary and write down a definition that you believe is consistent with God being immutable. Read Psalm 102:25–27 and relate your definition to these Scriptures.

____

____

____

____

Getting Practical

As we enter Phase Three of the foundational material, prayerfully let God lead you in using a combination of the tools and suggestions. No two participants are alike and everyone's experience will differ. At times you may choose to use the tools, while at other times you will lay them aside. However, feel free as the Spirit directs to utilize any or all of them in the Temple Tool Kit.

____

____

____

____

Memory Challenge

Start memorizing 1 Corinthians 6:12. Take time to see the message proclaimed in this Scripture. Read the verse out loud several times, then look away and say it from memory.

"Everything is permissible for me" — but not everything is beneficial.
"Everything is permissible for me" — but I will not be mastered by anything.
1 Corinthians 6:12

     © 2003, Thin Within, All Rights Reserved

Day Two

Going Deeper

By eating 0 to 5 these last eight weeks, you have established a boundary for good health to prevent excess weight. To maintain that boundary, try a little experiment this week. Before eating, stop and prayerfully ask God, "What do I want from food right now? What need am I trying to meet by eating?" When you find that your need is not hunger, don't eat! Turn to the One that can and will meet all your needs (Philippians 4:19, Hebrews 4:16, 2 Peter 1:3). Journal what you discover.

____
____
____
____

Bible Study

Read about Jesus' own boundary in John 5:19. There are so many things that fill our time and draw on our energy and emotions. What was Jesus' standard for how He spent His day? Take some time to journal about how you spend your time and how it lines up with God's plan.

____
____
____
____

Knowing God by Heart

Continue to grow in your knowledge of God by reading Malachi 3:6 and 1 Samuel 15:29. What do these verses say to you about God being immutable?

____
____
____
____

Getting Practical

Utilize those parts of the Temple Tool Kit that are most helpful to you.

____
____
____
____

Memory Challenge

Continue memorizing 1 Corinthians 6:12 by saying or writing it several times. After some repetition, try repeating it from memory. Take the memory verse card with you and refer to it throughout the day.

Thin Within Tip

When you want to eat but are not at 0, pull out a Memory Challenge card and repeat the Bible verse out loud as you proclaim the truth.

© 2003, Thin Within, All Rights Reserved

EXERCISES

Day Three

Going Deeper

As you look at your past boundaries, you may see how they were violated and you may be tempted to blame people and situations for your struggles with food, eating, or overweight issues. What will you do with these painful or convicting thoughts? The Lord has come to bind up your broken heart, to mend whatever is torn. He wants you to let go of any bitterness or pain that you may have allowed to enter your soul. How will you respond to this?

____
____
____
____

Bible Study

What do Proverbs 3:5–6, Proverbs 16:9, Jeremiah 10:23, and Matthew 6:33 say about God's plan for your daily time and energy? Do you feel pressured to do and be more every day? Examine your current boundaries in this area and pray about what corrections God wants you to make.

____
____
____
____

Knowing God by Heart

Find synonyms for the word "immutable" in a thesaurus or dictionary. How do these words give you a deeper understanding of God? Read Hebrews 13:8 and Hebrews 6:17–20. What do these Scriptures tell you about God?

____
____
____
____

Getting Practical

There are special challenges in staying within godly eating boundaries at social occasions. First, preparation is the key in avoiding overeating as you define your purpose for going to a social event. As you practice foresight, write down your plan for an upcoming social eating occasion and identify your goals. Ask God for the desire and ability to honor Him in all your eating.

____
____
____
____

Memory Challenge

Review 1 Corinthians 6:12 until you can repeat it from memory.

Thin Within Tip

Play with your food! Why not? Who says you can't make a smiley face out of your peas and corn? It might slow you down a bit and help you eat less.

© 2003, Thin Within, All Rights Reserved

Day Four

Going Deeper

Ask the Lord if you have moved beyond the point of indulging in all that is permissible (1 Corinthians 6:12). Have you been selecting that which is excellent? Ask Him to reveal to you if there yet remains anything to which you bow down. In the area of eating, I am mastered by___________? (Fill in the blank with any food or drink that you find difficult to refuse or that may control you in some way.) Take this issue to God and submit yourself to Him. Pray for His power to equip you to stand firm. Journal about what He reveals to you.

Bible Study

A key to Jesus being able to establish His boundaries according to what His Father wanted is found in Mark 1:35. As we spend some solitary time with God each day, we can know Him and His will more clearly. The more we are established in Him from morning until night, the more we can maintain our boundaries—even against pressure from family and friends. (See Psalm 25:5, Psalm 88:13, and Psalm 143:8.)

Knowing God by Heart: Wise

Look up the word "wise" in the dictionary and write down a definition that you believe is consistent with God being wise. Read Daniel 2:20–22 and relate your definition to these Scriptures.

Getting Practical

In certain eating occasions, it is easy to completely disregard the 0 to 5 hunger numbers. After some time in prayer, list ways that you can stay within your boundaries when you go to a potluck, an all-you-can-eat restaurant, your favorite restaurant on someone else's tab, or any other situation that is especially difficult for you.

Memory Challenge

Repeat 1 Corinthians 6:12 from memory. Turn this verse into a prayer for yourself or someone you know.

© 2003, Thin Within, All Rights Reserved

EXERCISES

Day Five

Going Deeper

Journal about pressure you feel from family or friends that tempts you to compromise your boundaries. After reading Galatians 1:10, submit this pressure to the Lord and ask Him to help you establish godly boundaries that please Him above all else. Pray for strength to remain within these boundaries through the power of the Holy Spirit.

____
____
____
____

Bible Study

The battle against "self" remains one of the toughest. What was Jesus' boundary in Luke 22:42? What is His advice to us in Matthew 16:24?

____
____
____
____

Knowing God by Heart

What do Job 12:12–13 and Psalm 104:24 tell about God being wise?

____
____
____
____

Getting Practical

Which word would you use to describe the environment where you eat most of your meals-calm or chaotic? If your answer was chaotic, then prayerfully consider what measures you could take to lessen the distractions and establish a new godly boundary.

____
____
____
____

Memory Challenge

Meditate on 1 Corinthians 6:12 throughout the day and allow it to draw you closer to God. Ask Him to help you truly believe this Scripture so that it can set you free from all the deceptive lies of the world.

Thin Within Tip

If you are interrupted during your meal by the doorbell, the phone, or some other distraction, consider that this might be God's "way out" of temptation to overeat (1 Corinthians 10:13).

© 2003, Thin Within, All Rights Reserved

Day Six – Optional Exercises

Going Deeper

Has God called you to do something today/this week/this month that you have either not done or have put off until later? Have you disobeyed God by procrastinating? Jesus said, "Not my will, but yours be done" (Luke 22:42). May this be your prayer as you follow the leading of the Spirit rather than the desires of the flesh.

____
____
____
____

Bible Study

According to Matthew 21:12–13 and 1 Corinthians 6:19–20, is there anything inappropriate that needs to be driven out of His temple? Are there any past wounds, painful thoughts, or bitterness that God wants to wipe away so that He can fill those places? Prayerfully ask Him to show you any sin that may be crowding out the fruit of the Spirit (Isaiah 44:21–22).

____
____
____
____

Knowing God by Heart

Find synonyms for the word "wise" in a thesaurus or dictionary. How do these words give you a deeper understanding of God as wise? Read Proverbs 3:19–20 and Colossians 2:2–3. What do these Scriptures tell you about God?

____
____
____
____

Getting Practical

Allow the Spirit to lead you in your boundary setting of 0 to 5 eating as you reach and maintain your natural God-given size.

____
____
____
____

Memory Challenge

Repeat 1 Corinthians 6:12 out loud and ask God to make this verse real in your life. What might God be leading you to "be" or to "do" in response to this passage?

© 2003, Thin Within, All Rights Reserved

EXERCISES

Day Seven – Optional Exercises

Going Deeper

Thank God for what He is accomplishing in your heart this week. Express your gratitude for His specific message to you.

Bible Study

Have you made any progress this week in letting go of something that has mastered you? Pray that the boundaries God has brought to your attention will become even more firm in your life through the Spirit's strength in you. Ask Him to help you turn to Him whenever you're tempted to go beyond these boundaries. (See also Psalm 119:117, Isaiah 41:10, and Ephesians 6:10.)

Getting Practical

Take the observations you make from this week's Temple Tool Kit and look for possible corrections that can lead to consistent 0 to 5 eating.

Memory Challenge

Share your memory verse with a friend or family member, telling him or her how it relates to your Thin Within journey.

Thin Within Tip

Eat with a naturally thin eater. (Children and the elderly are often great examples.) Take note of his or her behavior and mirror it.

  © 2003, Thin Within, All Rights Reserved

Review of the Week

Take time at the end of each week to review what God has taught you and how it is impacting your life. This will give you a great overview to take to your Thin Within Support Group Meeting.

The most significant thing God taught me this week:

____
____
____
____

With respect to waiting for hunger and stopping when my body was satisfied, I would describe my progress as:

____
____
____
____

As I seek to make beneficial choices, I want to be sure, as the memory verse stated, not to be mastered by anything. The foods or restaurants that can tend to master me are:

____
____
____
____

The most significant thing that God helped me to observe this week that I will focus on correcting next week:

____
____
____
____

What I have learned about the character of God as immutable and wise, and how I have come to know and be drawn closer to Him:

____
____
____
____

My prayer requests and praises:

____
____
____
____

© 2003, Thin Within, All Rights Reserved

LESSON

Forgiveness

Introduction

Over the past nine weeks, the Lord has drawn us closer to His heart. We have experienced the touch of His grace upon our lives, our hearts, and our bodies. He continues His work within us, forming and shaping us into His image. Much restoration has occurred and yet there still remains some rubble to clear away. As we rest in His hands and submit our will to Him, the remaining rubble will be removed and we will experience the abundant life of peace and joy. He is doing a new thing!

In Phases One and Two, we saw that above all else, the Lord desires intimacy with us. He longs to be our all in all. He knows the end from the beginning. He knows our pain, sorrows, joys, dreams, and hopes. He has a plan for us—to give us a hope and a future as we walk by faith one step at a time. In Him we live and move and have our being (Acts 17:28).

Last week we discovered that God has entrusted some very precious things into our care and protection. As valued stewards, we are given the responsibility of establishing godly boundaries. We are called to walk in our new identity in Christ and guard our thoughts, choices, and our bodies as God-given gifts. We are called to stand firm against the world, the flesh, and the devil, remembering that we are fully equipped by the power of the Holy Spirit to walk in obedience as we seek to please God and honor His temple.

Spiritual Foundation

In Week Three, we identified and investigated flesh machinery. Today we will discover the key to unlocking the mystery behind much of our emotional eating. This key, which opens the door for us to lay bare our hearts and souls before God, isn't a secret, but it can be elusive because many of us lack the courage to use it.

For years people run from the pain of past hurts in an effort to protect themselves or avoid some harsh realities they have sought to escape. Often their refuge is that of food. People think, perhaps unconsciously, that food will anesthetize their pain, their worries, and their reality. When we medicate pain with misused pleasure, the predictable result is addictive behavior. This means of escape may have been established early in childhood, or it may have come much later, following a traumatic event or perhaps a situation experienced in adult life. Even if we have suffered as a victim of someone else's sin, as so many of God's precious people have, it does not justify or excuse present time, sinful behavior. We must not look for places to lay blame because blaming means that we are not taking responsibility for our choices or our behavior today.

One thing is certain—we have all experienced pain. This is not to minimize your experiences, but only to share with you, dear beloved, that even our Savior experienced pain, as have all of His people since the beginning of time.

Allow the Holy Spirit to lead you gently and stand with you as you look squarely at those things from which you want to run away. It is our prayer that you will come to see, through God's amazing grace, that He intends for the pain and wounds of your life to result in something good far beyond your imagination. As unbelievably difficult as this may seem, the Lord who pours out grace upon all things, will meet you in your place of need, providing you with the strength to endure (Romans 5:3–5).

He longs for your healing. Jesus Himself suffered and was wounded so that we might be healed.

But he was pierced for our transgressions,
he was crushed for our iniquities;
the punishment that brought us peace was upon him,
and by his wounds we are healed.
Isaiah 53:5

The very reason that Christ set aside His kingly glory in Heaven and took on the flesh and limitations of a human was so that He could experience the challenges of everyday life and provide all that was needed for our freedom and our healing. When Jesus began His earthly ministry, He referred to Himself (Luke 4:17–21) when quoting Isaiah 61:1:

The Spirit of the Sovereign LORD is on me,
because the LORD has anointed me to preach good news
to the poor. He has sent me to bind up the brokenhearted,
to proclaim freedom for the captives
and release from darkness for the prisoners,
Isaiah 61:1

At heart, the purpose of Jesus' coming to earth—suffering, dying on the cross, being buried, and rising from the dead—was to enable us to face and admit our wounds. When we allow our true brokenness to surface, we can trust God to

© 2003, Thin Within, All Rights Reserved

use those very things to help us live the resurrected life.

Let's begin to examine those things the enemy would like to use to confuse or paralyze us. He desires to manipulate our past and plant lies in our hearts and minds so we will question our worth and value as well as our future (John 8:44). We can only overcome these deceptive lies through the truth of God's Word.

Be self-controlled and alert. Your enemy the devil prowls around like a roaring lion looking for someone to devour.
1 Peter 5:8

I have given you authority to trample on snakes and scorpions and to overcome all the power of the enemy; nothing will harm you.
Luke 10:19

Another tactic the enemy employs is the idea that we can achieve perfection by doing enough good things. Paul dealt a deathblow to the idea that one could attain perfection either by observing the Jewish law or through gaining knowledge. He recognized that he had not achieved it, but kept pressing on "to take hold of that for which Christ Jesus took hold of [him]" (Phil. 3:12). Paul was not willing for his human failings to have the last word, so we read such words as "straining," "pressing on," and "taking hold." The one thing he emphasized was "forgetting what is behind." He meant forgetting not only the failures and sins but also the successes and spiritual achievements that can lead to a prideful spirit.

So how are we to deal with the difficult and painful things in our past? This week we will garner the courage to allow God to turn the master key. What is this key? Perhaps you have guessed. It is God's grace, which is extended to all God's beloved through the power of the Holy Spirit at work within us. It is also His forgiveness, which was freely given on the cross at Calvary. It is through forgiveness that our temple is cleansed and the remaining rubble cleared away.

Let's pause for a moment and define "forgiveness." Webster says it is ceasing to feel resentment for an offense, renouncing anger, granting pardon, and harboring no resentment. In a very real way, it is releasing the one who offended. When we truly forgive, we let the offender off our hook saying, "Lord, this person belongs to You. He [or she] hasn't met my needs or expectations, but I entrust this person to You." In this challenging yet powerful process, the one who is ultimately released is the one most enslaved—ourselves! So our goal is to be released from the bondage of unforgiveness as we walk in freedom through the cleansing power of forgiveness.

During this radical "heart surgery," there must be a rooting out of the old, and perhaps some probing and severing of that which is diseased. The Master Surgeon will gently stitch, expertly bind, and then heal. The entire process may be lengthy, and there is no denying that it can be painful. However, as we allow the healing to take place, we emerge as restored people—the reason for Christ coming to earth is accomplished in us and through us. The key to walking fully in this freedom is receiving the forgiveness that was provided at the cross. This forgiveness extends to us and also to those who have wronged us. Apart from God's marvelous grace, there is no forgiveness.

In an inexplicable way, admitting our true feelings is crucial in establishing our freedom (John 8:32). If we don't face the truth, we can't really acknowledge what needs to be forgiven, and therefore, we can't adequately forgive. There is no sadder, more desperate captive than one held in bonds formed by one's own bitterness and refusal to release another person through forgiveness.

Even when we deny the hurt or pain in our life, something within us retains the knowledge of that pain. We can't entirely forget or run from it. The pain hangs on as a predator with a taste of its prey within its talons of steel. As a slight infection can subtly work its way through and ultimately

> **If we don't face the truth, we can't really acknowledge what needs to be forgiven, and therefore, we can't adequately forgive.**

© 2003, Thin Within, All Rights Reserved

LESSON

consume the entire body, so, too, does a root of bitterness that comes from denying our need to forgive.

Forgiveness can be very difficult because it goes against the flesh, which, if we are completely honest, seeks revenge. We tend to keep a record of wrongs and come up with all sorts of excuses not to forgive. The flesh seeks to defend itself and place blame elsewhere. This began in the garden when Eve blamed the serpent and Adam blamed Eve. He even blamed God for giving him Eve! Jesus knows that in our humanity we will continue to wound and be wounded, so in His mercy, He has given us the opportunity for ongoing forgiveness as He calls us to forgive seventy times seven (Matthew 18:21–22).

If you have not begun your personal journal, we encourage you to do so during this week of discovery. As you sit before the Lord, expect Him to meet you as you open your heart to Him. Talk with Him and ask Him to search your heart to see if there is anything that needs to be exposed to the light of the glory of the cross. As you confess to Him, allow your heart to be cleansed by the blood of Christ so that you can walk in the confidence that you are indeed forgiven and cleansed as white as snow (Isaiah 1:18).

> ## Self-condemnation is a lie that keeps us from hearing the godly voice of conviction.

Before we continue, it is important to highlight what forgiveness is not. Forgiveness is not forgetting. Only the Lord forgives and forgets.

"I, even I, am he who blots out your transgressions,
for my own sake, and remembers your sins no more."
Isaiah 43:25

In fact, first we need to acknowledge fully the transgression, forgive, and then perhaps never forget. Stacy, upon facing sexual abuse she experienced as a child by a family member, realized twenty years later that it might not be prudent to leave her children alone with that same person. She finally faced the pain of her own abuse, choosing purposefully to forgive the one who wronged her. However, she did not forget.

Forgiveness is not condoning something that is morally wrong. It is also not denial, saying, "It doesn't really bother me," or "I am sure she didn't mean it that way, so I will bury it rather than face it," or "He always abuses those closest to him, because that's just the way he is."

Another form of denial is minimizing the gravity of a wrong that was done: "At least she wasn't my dearest friend" or "Don't all families cut you out of their lives when you don't measure up to their expectations?"

There is also what is called "sanctified denial." This involves simply going through the motions, saying "I forgive (name) for what he/she did. Amen." While the intention may be somewhat sincere, this is actually applying a Band-aid where open-heart surgery is needed. Facing the pain, allowing yourself to speak the truth about it (perhaps only to God), and even grieving over it may be necessary. In order to properly process our pain, we need to deal with our grief over whatever has died. Inwardly your spirit knows when it is wounded and it will continue to cry out for healing. A wounded heart grabs onto all sorts of counterfeits if it hasn't undergone corrective surgery by the Master Surgeon's hand. Remember that pain plus misused pleasure is a perfect formula for addictive behavior, which is why many people turn to overeating. However, by facing these challenging issues and submitting them to the Lord, you can experience total healing and go forth responsibly.

Forgiveness is also not a feeling. You cannot wait until you feel all warm and fuzzy toward the person who has overstepped your boundary or who has wronged you. Forgiveness is something God has empowered you to do, in faith, by His grace. It is an act of obedience and mercy motivated by the Spirit. It is a choice we make to obey God and trust Him to bring healing.

How on earth can we forgive? We would never claim that it is easy—not at all. Let's first look at the example we are to follow.

Therefore, as God's chosen people, holy and dearly loved,
clothe yourselves with compassion, kindness, humility,
gentleness, and patience. Bear with each other and forgive
whatever grievances you may have against one another.
Forgive as the Lord forgave you.
Colossians 3:12–13

 © 2003, Thin Within, All Rights Reserved

When you came to the cross and acknowledged your own sin, you received the blessing of forgiveness. Now the Lord beseeches you to forgive as the Lord forgave you.

The Lord looked at each sin, mistake, and wrong act, and forgave each and every one completely from His place of perfect holiness. He bowed His head and declared, "It is finished," forgiving all sin—past, present, and future—forevermore. He didn't wait to forgive until we admitted our wrong. It was done on the cross two thousand years ago.

He forgives not just your sin, the sin of your children, your best friend, or your pastor. He also forgives the sin of the child molester, the wife beater, the rapist, the gossip, the thief, the self-righteous legalist, the backbiter, the abusive parent, the manipulator, and the food addict. On the cross, Jesus took on the shame of the one abused as well as the abuser. He knew the pain of the tormented and the tormentor, the pain of the broken heart and the heart breaker. He knew the loss of innocence and the one who took it. He knew the darkness of suicide and the guilt of the murderer—all of it, every bit of it. It is an amazing thing, but Jesus forgave it all.

A man who knew his own sin and shame very well was crucified next to Jesus, yet in the hours before he died, he knew in whom he must trust:

Then he said, "Jesus, remember me when you come into your kingdom." Jesus answered him, "I tell you the truth, today you will be with me in paradise."
Luke 23:42–43

Grace, grace, God's grace. Grace that is so complete and limitless that it can pardon and cleanse us from any and all sin.

And this is the way in which we are to forgive? How are we to do that which seems impossible? First and foremost, we are to rest and walk in forgiveness that has been freely given to each of us. One of the most difficult things for many people who struggle with food, eating, and body issues is the resentment they feel toward themselves. There may be a measure of self-loathing or a sense of worthlessness, which often manifests itself in approval seeking or, surprisingly enough, as a prideful spirit. Sometimes this results in abusing one's body in any number of ways, including anorexia, purging, overeating, or other excessive or destructive behaviors. This can then result in a cycle of yet more self-loathing or a hardened heart that keeps others at a distance.

The Value of Daily Exercise

In addition to helping control your weight, research shows that regular physical activity can reduce your risk for several diseases and conditions and improve your overall quality of life. Regular physical activity can help protect you from the following health problems: lowering your blood pressure, raising your high-density lipoprotein (HDL) levels (good cholesterol) and lowering low-density lipoprotein (LDL) levels (bad cholesterol), improving blood flow, and increasing your heart's working capacity.

- Heart Disease and Stroke. Daily physical activity can help prevent heart disease and stroke by strengthening your heart muscle,
- High Blood Pressure. Regular physical activity can reduce blood pressure in those with high blood pressure levels. Physical activity also reduces body fatness, which is associated with high blood pressure.
- Noninsulin-Dependent Diabetes. By reducing body fatness, physical activity can help to prevent and control this type of diabetes.
- Obesity. Physical activity helps to reduce body fat by building or preserving muscle mass and improving the body's ability to use calories. When physical activity is combined with proper nutrition, it can help control weight and prevent obesity, a major risk factor for many diseases.
- Back Pain. By increasing muscle strength and endurance and improving flexibility and posture, regular exercise helps to prevent back pain.
- Osteoporosis. Regular weight-bearing exercise promotes bone formation and may prevent many forms of bone loss associated with aging.
- Studies on the psychological effects of exercise have found that regular physical activity can improve your mood and the way you feel about yourself. Researchers also have found that exercise is likely to reduce depression and anxiety and help you to better manage stress.
- Keep these health benefits in mind when deciding whether or not to exercise. And remember, any amount of physical activity you do is better than none at all.

(NIH Publication No. 96–4031)

© 2003, Thin Within, All Rights Reserved

LESSON

This cycle continues—until it is broken.

How do we break this cycle? Think back in your life to when you first became aware of a negative view of yourself. Some may never have felt negatively about themselves, and for that we praise God. However, others may have believed messages—such as "you are a loser"—sent by classmates, parents, relatives, or other influential figures. Perhaps you felt a sense of shame when the boy next door "went too far" with you, or maybe it was when you were placed on your first diet at age twelve and you felt unacceptable.

Regardless of whenever or wherever it began, allow the Holy Spirit to root it out. Expose it, submit it to God, and ask Him to help you sort out what you or someone else did that needs forgiveness. Is the enemy trying to get you to believe the lie that what happened to you or what you did is unforgivable—that you are an exception to the cross of Christ? Allow the Holy Spirit to do what is necessary in order for you to be healthy and whole. We suggest that you do this whenever something hurtful or painful surfaces. Journal your prayers throughout this experience.

Is there anything for which you need to rest in God's forgiveness? What about the condition of your body or your relationships with family members or friends? Beloved, you must receive God's grace for yourself. He died for the shame you feel when you look in the mirror or a storefront window or when the airplane seat doesn't quite fit comfortably or when children (or adults) stare. He died for all that shame. Ask the Lord to make His forgiveness fresh and real for you. From that vantage point, choose to receive cleansing so that you can stand on a firm foundation of forgiveness and walk with confidence in obedience to Christ.

Bringing each situation to the foot of the cross may take some time, but the time is worth taking. Whenever you entertain a self-deprecating thought, take that thought captive and choose in that moment to allow the Word of God to renew your thinking. Remember Paul's voice: "There is now no condemnation for those who are in Christ Jesus" (Romans 8:1). Self-condemnation is a lie that keeps us from hearing the godly voice of conviction. It is the enemy's strategy to keep us focusing on ourselves rather than walking in the freedom of forgiveness as we accept responsibility for our own actions. There is such freedom when the master key is turned and we step through the door of forgiveness. As our hearts receive true cleansing and healing, we are equipped to act with godly accountability. We can then walk in the truth of God's Word and in the light of His love, extending that love to others.

Ask the Lord to reveal to you those whom you need to forgive. Pray and ask God to lead the way. He may surprise you and take you to an incident early in your life, or a recent experience on which He wants to shed His light. Go wherever the Lord directs. If you think it would be wise, seek godly professional counsel as you walk this path of healing and wholeness.

Most importantly, do not attempt to cover your feelings with food. The Lord made us with deep feelings for a reason and we are not to negate or short-circuit them. We are to manage our feelings in a godly way. This is part of being made in His image, and He wants us to express our feelings authentically yet without sinning (Ephesians 4:26).

David is a good example of an emotional man after God's own heart. Denying what we feel is denying the way the Lord made us. Shout out to God about who did what to you and how you feel about it. As author and Bible teacher Beth Moore suggests, we challenge you to "tell" on the one who wronged you. Tell on them to God. He can take it. The Holy Spirit will enable and equip you to deal with this pain in a godly way.

Sandra couldn't understand why reaching a 0 frightened her, that is, why she feared feeling physiological hunger. Over the course of time, as she faced some childhood issues, she realized that much of the abuse she had experienced was at meal times regarding what she did or didn't eat. She was called a "picky" eater, threatened, and physically abused. She coped with these pressures by sneaking food and continued this practice as an adult. She began to realize that she felt unsafe, vulnerable, and out of control when hungry, and that she could gain control by never allowing herself to feel empty. Food became her comforter and her best friend.

Sandra said that working through the pain, rage, and other emotions that surfaced during this time was one of the most challenging experiences of her life. But she allowed herself to face the feelings she had been running from and she gave them one by one to her compassionate,

© 2003, Thin Within, All Rights Reserved

loving Lord. It was only then that she was able to forgive the ones who had wronged her.

Through prayer, the use of her journal, and a deeper understanding of God as her comforter, hunger ceased to have the negative connotation that she associated with abuse. She was no longer fearful and was able, once and for all, to be at peace while experiencing a 0. She allowed physical hunger to be a cue for conscious eating and actually began to enjoy that "empty" feeling. As a result, she was set free to joyfully release her excess weight.

Physiological Information

Do you run to food when you are sad, lonely, happy, confused, or when experiencing heightened emotions? As you begin to release others from wrongs they have committed, like Sandra you will find that you can say "no" to food when you are not hungry. As you recognize that only God is your sufficiency, the impetus for emotional eating will dwindle and you will release the excess weight. He and He alone is able to meet all of your needs for love, approval, and significance!

One of the practical ways to apply this week's material is to notice the emotions and feelings that surface while waiting for your 0 and take them to a compassionate and loving God. Rather than "trying" to solve the problem with food, solve it with the Lord. In His great wisdom, He will offer you wholeness and healing and bind up your broken heart, as well as call you into an obedient walk of faith.

Some people have never enjoyed exercise and may blame being overweight on "I'm just not coordinated" or "I never could do sports, so how can I be thin or fit?" You will want to step out of excuse making and start taking some risks. This will include forgiving yourself for past disappointments or exercise "failures," and starting to move your body in ways that support health and vitality. Do not become obsessed with exercise as a way to lose weight. It is a medical fact that it is very difficult to lose weight by exercise alone. However, we encourage you to acknowledge the benefits

Forgiveness paves the way for a multitude of changes relative to your eating.

that movement offers your body, God's temple.

After asking your doctor for permission to exercise, we challenge those who are in reasonable condition to think of an enjoyable activity that could add an additional fifteen to twenty minutes beyond your usual schedule of activity (more if you feel so lead). If you like dancing, then dance. If you like cycling, get out your bike. If you enjoy walking, put on those shoes and walk around the block or the mall. Some people spend five minutes each on several different activities: five minutes of bicycling, five minutes of dancing in the living room, five minutes of a brisk walk, and five minutes on a cross-country ski machine strategically placed in their family room. Adding variety to your exercise time can make it more enjoyable.

If you have a health condition that precludes vigorous activity, perhaps you can participate in some water aerobics moving to your favorite music. People in their sixties, seventies, or even eighties who have rarely exercised in the past can discover the benefits and enjoyment of movement.

Consider listening to praise music on tape as you walk around the neighborhood, or use walking as a time to praise God or pray for your neighbors. Many people are now opting to try inline skating, as it is reminiscent of the fun of their youth. Join a gym if you think it is something that would motivate you or something you would enjoy. It is a great way of meeting people and of learning new ways of moving your body.

If you have always disliked physical activity, remember that God created your body to be active six days a week and to rest on the seventh. He wants you to experience your body functioning at its best. Will you choose to cooperate with Him? As with eating 0 to 5, pay attention to your body as you exercise. If your knee aches, stop. If you are out of breath, slow down. Most of all, praise God for the good gift of the body He has given you.

In addition to forgiving yourself for poor health or an overweight condition, you may need to forgive yourself for forsaking physical activity or for the inconsistency of eating 0 to 5. If you

© 2003, Thin Within, All Rights Reserved

LESSON

feel you have blown it, that you really hate the way you look, or that you have gained so much weight that your pants won't fit, then forgiving yourself is in order. Let's stop this destructive thinking dead in its tracks and deny the enemy ammunition to steal and destroy that which belongs to God. Start taking responsibility for the role you have played, and as you do, you will step out of the trap of self-blame and into the blessing of godly conviction.

For we do not have a high priest who is unable to sympathize with our weaknesses, but we have one who has been tempted in every way,
just as we are —yet was without sin. Let us then approach the throne of grace with confidence, so that we may receive mercy and find grace to help us in our time of need.
Hebrews 4:15–16

Don't put off starting again because you think you need to pay some sort of "penance." God is right there waiting for you to turn to Him. Begin now. If you are not at 0, don't eat. When you reach your comfortable 5, stop eating. Observe and correct. Confess and repent. God forgives you. Receive His forgiveness and allow the Holy Spirit to lead you in ways of righteousness and truth.

As you walk in the freedom of forgiveness and obey that small still voice within, you will more likely eat 0 to 5 and put in the appropriate correction when you have gotten off track. You may also find yourself more willing to try various ways of moving your body. Before you know it, you will experience many health benefits and be feeling much better than you ever imagined.

Integration

Forgiveness paves the way for a multitude of changes relative to your eating. You may have some past issues to bring before the Lord before experiencing the full benefit of a "clean slate." However, as you work through these issues, cling to the Lord each and every step of the way. He will see to it that you will emerge victorious.

Walk forward in faith, believing God will take care of those who have offended you. He is a just God, so you can confidently extend forgiveness to them knowing that what He says is true:

Do not take revenge, my friends, but leave room for God's wrath, for it is written: "It is mine to avenge; I will repay," says the Lord.
Romans 12:19

Forgiving others helps to free us from emotional eating, flesh machinery that draws us to food when we aren't hungry. As we release those who have offended us and no longer look to those around us to meet our needs for love, affirmation, and significance, we are set free to look to the one true God who can meet all of our needs. Step forward into the freedom of forgiveness and experience all that God has for you.

Forgiving ourselves will affect our willingness to move our bodies. Not everyone, especially those who have lived a sedentary lifestyle, has a perfectly coordinated body. We are no longer stuck with the image of ourselves as that clumsy junior high student. We are now set free to experiment with ways of moving our body. Walking in forgiveness gives us courage to begin anew by virtue of the Spirit who empowers and enables us.

As we walk in the freedom of forgiveness, our world opens up. We are no longer living in the darkness of bitterness and resentment of which we may not have been fully aware. A load is lifted from our shoulders as we cast off the burden of self-condemnation and vengeance onto the powerful shoulders of our Savior who sacrificed it all for His beloved!

But for you who revere my name, the sun of righteousness will rise with healing in its wings. And you will go out and leap like calves released from the stall.
Malachi 4:2

> We encourage you to acknowledge the benefits that movement offers your body, God's temple.

© 2003, Thin Within, All Rights Reserved

My Notes

© 2003, Thin Within, All Rights Reserved

EXERCISES

Day One

Going Deeper

As you sit at the feet of Jesus, ask His Spirit to fall fresh on you. Thank Him for His forgiveness of your sins at the cross of Calvary. Ask Him to help you this week to identify those He desires you to forgive.

Bible Study

Journal about what Psalm 86:5, Colossians 1:13–14, and 1 John 1:9 say about God and His forgiveness. Can you think of any sin for which you have not yet asked to receive God's forgiveness? Journal a prayer of confession to the Lord.

Knowing God by Heart: Merciful

Then you will know the truth, and the truth will set you free.
John 8:32

Look up the word "merciful" in the dictionary and write down a definition that you believe is consistent with God being merciful Read Psalm 116:5 and Romans 9:14–16 and relate your definition to these Scriptures.

Getting Practical

From your reading, what connection does forgiveness have to emotional eating?   Prayerfully evaluate your eating. Do you battle with eating when you feel emotional? Describe it in your journal

Memory Challenge

Start memorizing Colossians 3:12–13. Take time to see the message proclaimed in this Scripture. Read the verses out loud several times, then look away and say them from memory.

Therefore, as God's chosen people, holy and dearly loved, clothe yourselves with compassion, kindness, humility, gentleness and patience. Bear with each other and forgive whatever grievances you may have against one another.
Forgive as the Lord forgave you.
Colossians 3:12–13

   © 2003, Thin Within, All Rights Reserved

Day Two

Going Deeper

As we mature in our relationship with the Lord and begin to draw near to Him, we develop a greater sense of our own need for His cleansing and forgiveness. Read Luke 7:37–48. Describe the motivation of the woman. What did she do? Why? What relationship is there between forgiveness and love? Journal about any ways in which you can identify with this woman.

____

____

____

____

Bible Study

Read Psalm 32:1–2. How are you like the person mentioned in these verses? Humans cling tenaciously to memories and regrets. God, on the other hand, promises to remove our sins far from us and remember them no more (Isaiah 43:25). Read Daniel 9:9 and Psalm 130:3–4. Describe the nature of our sin and the nature of God's forgiveness.

____

____

____

____

Knowing God by Heart

Continue to grow in knowledge of how God is merciful by reading Nehemiah 9:30–31 and Psalm 106:43–45. Write your thoughts.

____

____

____

____

Getting Practical

The next time you get "off track," immediately—without wasting any time—(observe) confess and (correct) repent. Receive God's forgiveness. Don't let another moment go by before returning to the boundary of 0 to 5 eating.

____

____

____

Memory Challenge

Continue memorizing Colossians 3:12–13 by saying or writing it several times. After some repetition, try repeating it from memory. Take the memory verse card with you and refer to it throughout the day.

Thin Within Tip

When wrestling with the "do-I-eat-that-or-don't-I" question, declare that God is bigger than the stronghold of food and allow Him to enable you to resist temptation and walk away from the food.

© 2003, Thin Within, All Rights Reserved

EXERCISES

Day Three

Going Deeper

Read Matthew 26:27–28 and Ephesians 1:7–8. Journal what these verses say to you. Close your eyes and picture the blood of the Holy Son of God poured out for you, so that you might experience His forgiveness. Write a prayer thanking God for His mercy, grace, and forgiveness.

____
____
____
____

Bible Study

Read Colossians 3:12–17. In your journal, describe the ways in which the Lord has forgiven you. What does it mean to you personally to "forgive as the Lord has forgiven you?" Is there anyone that you consider personally responsible for your struggles with issues related to food, eating, and your weight? Will you choose to forgive them today as the Lord forgave you?

____
____
____
____

Knowing God by Heart

Find synonyms for the word "merciful" in a thesaurus or dictionary. How do these words give you a deeper understanding of God as merciful? Read Ephesians 2:4–5 and Titus 3:3–7. What do these verses tell you about God?

____
____
____
____

Getting Practical

Continue to ask yourself before eating "What need am I turning to food to meet?" If it isn't legitimate physiological hunger (you are not at a 0), then ask the Lord to reveal to you if there is anything you need to release to Him. Then ask His strength in doing so.

____
____
____
____

Memory Challenge

Review Colossians 3:12–13 until you can repeat it from memory.

Thin Within Tip

Remember that if you do not eat 0 to 5, you will remain overweight or increase in size. But each time you obediently wait for hunger and stop at 5, it makes each future choice a little easier. Obedience begets obedience. Through the power of the Holy Spirit at work in you, 0 to 5 eating will become your consistent response.

© 2003, Thin Within, All Rights Reserved

Day Four

Going Deeper

The issue of forgiveness may stir deep emotions and feelings within you. Pray that the Lord will make you sensitive to the leadings of His Spirit and that you will have the courage to follow His leading. When you wait for 0 today, be especially sensitive to any emotions that are stirred up inside of you. Make a point of journaling your thoughts before you eat to see if this helps with curbing emotional eating.

____
____
____
____

Bible Study

In Luke 23:34, Jesus gives us an example of forgiving even when the offender is unaware or unwilling to acknowledge the wrong done. In Acts 7:59–60, Stephen demonstrates forgiveness toward those who were brutally stoning him to death. Ask God to show you who you need to forgive for wrongs done to you, including those who have willingly or unknowingly wounded you. If you ask, the Lord will also grant you a heart that is able to forgive these people. Keep the list you make, as we will use it on Day Five of this week.

____
____
____
____

Knowing God by Heart: Incomprehensible

Look up the word "incomprehensible" in the dictionary and write down a definition that you believe is consistent with God being incomprehensible. Read Job 11:7 and 36:26–29 and relate your definition to these Scriptures.

____
____
____
____

Getting Practical

Select three ways that you are able and willing to move your body. Contact your doctor for exercise recommendations and for permission to begin exercising, if you are not doing so now. Then do at least one of the things recommended three times this week. Enjoy!

____
____
____
____

Memory Challenge

Repeat Colossians 3:12–13 from memory. Turn these verses into a prayer for yourself or someone you know.

© 2003, Thin Within, All Rights Reserved

EXERCISES

Day Five

Going Deeper

Refer to the list of people you need to forgive from Day Four. Journal about each and every person and the offense experienced at their hands. If you struggle with wanting to forgive them, ask the Lord to help you to be able and willing, so that you will not grieve the Holy Spirit. Make note of each person and for what you forgive them. For example: "I, _____________________, out of obedience to God forgive _____________, for the pain I experienced from critical and hurtful comments. I take back ground given to the enemy through my bitterness and yield that ground to the control of the Lord Jesus Christ."

____
____
____
____

Bible Study

Ponder what Peter did in his denial of Jesus (John 18:25–27). Consider the restoration that Jesus initiated on the beach after His resurrection when He called Peter into ministry to "feed [his] sheep" (John 21:15–17). Describe in your journal the depth and breadth of this kind of forgiveness. In what way does this incident reflect just how incomprehensible God is? How does this relate to forgiveness?

____
____
____
____

Knowing God by Heart

What do Job 38:4–5 and Ecclesiastes 3:11 and 8:16–18 say about how God is incomprehensible?

____
____
____
____

Getting Practical

Journal on your experience in finding enjoyable ways to move your body.

____
____
____
____

Memory Challenge

Meditate on Colossians 3:12–13 throughout the day and allow it to draw you closer to God. Ask Him to help you truly believe this Scripture so that it can set you free from all the deceptive lies of the world.

Thin Within Tip

Make a list of all the ways you have improved in your eating. Ask God to help you see and remember all of the changes He has made in you. Place the list where you can see it.

   © 2003, Thin Within, All Rights Reserved

Day Six – Optional Exercises

Going Deeper

We suggest that in order to avoid the trap of "sanctified denial," you journal the pain and wrong you feel you have suffered by the one you need to forgive. But then choose specifically and directly to submit and release it to the Lord, and to forgive the one who wronged you. This may take some time to complete, so we encourage you to make this a regular part of your quiet time with the Lord.

____

____

____

____

Bible Study

Read Matthew 6:14–15, Mark 11:25, and Luke 6:37. Why is it important for you to forgive others? Journal about this, including anything you may have learned through the lesson or the exercises this week.

____

____

____

____

Knowing God by Heart

Find synonyms for the word "incomprehensible" in a thesaurus or dictionary. How do these words give you a deeper understanding of God as incomprehensible? Read Romans 11:33 and Psalm 145:3. What do these verses tell you about God?

____

____

____

____

Getting Practical

Have you found yourself turning to food to meet a need other than physiological hunger? Journal what you have found.

____

____

____

____

Memory Challenge

Repeat Colossians 3:12–13 out loud and ask God to make these verses real in your life. What might God be leading you to "be" or to "do" in response to this passage?

© 2003, Thin Within, All Rights Reserved

EXERCISES

Day Seven – Optional Exercises

Going Deeper

Continue to journal on the subject of forgiveness and how God is speaking to you. If there is anyone for whom you need to journal notes of forgiveness, please continue to prayerfully do so today.

____
____
____
____

Bible Study

Romans 12:17,19 gives us assurance that forgiveness isn't about letting another "off the hook." What comfort do you draw from these verses? What exhortation?   Often those who wrong us may not stop. In fact, we may live with the very people who wound us the most. Consider anyone in your life that God has called you to forgive for ongoing wounds they inflict. What encouragement do you receive from Matthew 18:21–22?

____
____
____
____

Getting Practical

Pray about making observation and correction an automatic desire and action when you eat outside of 0 to 5.

____
____
____
____

Memory Challenge

Share your memory verse with a friend or family member, telling him or her how it relates to your Thin Within journey.

Thin Within Tip

When you're away from food for an extended period of time, carry a small baggy holding a balanced snack. Food choices containing fiber, protein, and fat (such as roasted nuts) will sustain you to the next sit-down meal.

  © 2003, Thin Within, All Rights Reserved

Review of the Week

Take time at the end of each week to review what God has taught you and how it is impacting your life. This will give you a great overview to take to your Thin Within Support Group Meeting.

The most significant thing God taught me this week:

This week's memory verse stated that I am holy and dearly loved. Do I believe that statement? As one who is dearly loved, I am asked to clothe myself with compassion, kindness, humility, gentleness, and patience. In order to "bear" with each other and forgive one another's grievances I most need Him to help me clothe myself with:

With respect to beneficial choices, I would describe my progress as:

The most significant thing that God helped me to observe this week that I will focus on correcting next week:

What I have learned about the character of God as merciful and incomprehensible, and how I have come to know and be drawn closer to Him:

My prayer requests and praises:

© 2003, Thin Within, All Rights Reserved

LESSON

Prayer

Introduction

These last ten weeks have been both exciting and liberating as you've sought to restore God's temple by making healthier food choices and melting down to your natural God-given size. Last week was a crucial time of cleansing as we applied the blood of Christ through the powerful and freeing work of forgiveness. Walking in faith as you forgive yourself and others is an ongoing process of extending grace. Remain steadfast as you continue working through this powerful process, and don't give up until you are able to surrender the situation as well as the offender to God.

This week we'll focus on the most sacred part of God's temple, the holy of holies, which is miraculously made available to us at the time of our salvation. With the establishing of our bodies and lives as the temple of God, we became the holy of holies, the dwelling place of God! It is in conscious awareness of our Lord that we want to abide and search out the depth of the riches that are available to us.

Spiritual Foundation

The design of the temple in the Old Testament had three distinct parts: the outer court, the inner court or holy place, and the holy of holies.

The outer court was accessible to everyone who could enter and worship there.

The inner court was the privileged place of ministry for the Levites, God's chosen priests. Only those assigned and called on a rotation basis had the right to enter.

The innermost part of the temple, the holy of holies, was the most sacred place, where the glory of God dwelt. Separated from the rest of the temple by a thick curtain, the holy of holies was closed to all except the high priest, who was allowed to enter only once a year to offer sacrifice for the sins of the nation. So awesome was this privilege that a rope was tied around the high priest's ankle so he could be pulled out if he died in the presence of Almighty God. This would avoid the unlawful entrance of anyone into the terrifying presence of God, knowing that to do so would be to incur the penalty of death.

When Jesus died on the cross of Calvary, the thick curtain that separated the holy of holies from the inner court was literally torn in two. Christ acted not only as our great high priest, but also as our crucified Savior, the Lamb of God. He carried into the holy of holies His own blood for the permanent sacrifice of our sins. By doing this, He opened the way so that all would have access to and fellowship with God.

What an unbelievably awesome privilege to have access to the holy of holies forever opened to us, the very place where God dwells! Though He never leaves us, we can choose to visit with Him only occasionally or we can linger in His presence. However, if we fail to delve deeper into that most holy place, it's almost as if that curtain had never been rent.

Are you content to stay in the inner court and fail to experience the awesome presence of God that comes from entering the holy of holies? You can choose not to appropriate all that is yours, but the desire of God's heart is for you to experience His constant presence and provision. Here you can abide with an attitude of humble dependence, deep love, and devotion as you bask in the awareness of His love.

In this secret place, we are to pray without ceasing and "cast all [our] anxiety on Him because He cares for [us]" (1 Peter 5:7). He cares for the deepest places, hurts, and struggles of our hearts, none of which is hidden from Him. He knows us intimately as no one else ever will, even the things that we desire to keep hidden from others and perhaps even ourselves.

But if we walk in the light, as he is in the light,
we have fellowship with one another,
and the blood of Jesus, his Son, purifies us from all sin.
If we confess our sins, he is faithful and just and will forgive
us our sins and purify us from all unrighteousness.
1 John 1:7, 9

In this place of abiding we have constant fellowship, forgiveness for the sins we confess, and cleansing from all unrighteousness. He purifies us and makes us new each time we humbly turn to Him in faith. In this secret place, we are secure in the provision of His love and grace. We can cry out to Him:

Search me, O God, and know my heart;
test me and know my anxious thoughts.
Psalm 139:23

As we open our hearts to Him and invite His instruction, correction, and cleansing, He gives us insight into our struggles. He will reveal those things that we need to release to Him in order to find healing, even those things of which we are unaware.

© 2003, Thin Within, All Rights Reserved

In the secret place, we can gaze upon His beauty knowing that our sufficiency is to be found in Him alone. Food cannot fill those empty places within our hearts. What may have been only head knowledge of the truth of God's Word now becomes a deep, inner knowing—a heart knowledge.

And we, who with unveiled faces all reflect the Lord's glory, are being transformed into his likeness with ever-increasing glory, which comes from the Lord, who is the Spirit.
2 Corinthians 3:18

This is where we can experience the power of His transforming grace! As we behold His glory, we are taken from the temporal to the eternal. It is easy to get so focused on the process and the work that needs to be done, that we can lose sight of who is doing that transforming work.

Much has already taken place in the outer man as you have learned to take responsibility for your body and listen to the leading of the Holy Spirit as you attend to the signals of hunger and fullness. You have learned to make wiser food choices, which are both satisfying and beneficial to your health, as you have risen to the call of the King. The outer walls, of course, are what everyone sees. If you still desire to release excess weight, perhaps you have yet to look full into His wonderful face and fully trust Him to change you from glory to glory.

How about the work that has been done in your inner being? Have you recognized that you are transformed by the renewing of your mind? Have you sought to align your thinking with the truth of God's Word? Have you made costly choices with your will as you realize that the resurrection life comes only out of death to your flesh? Have you taken responsibility for your emotions and thoughts by taking captive anything that exalts itself above the knowledge and truth of God? Have you counted the cost and considered those areas that still need work? Regardless of your feelings, have you learned to stand on truth and walk in faith according to the Word of God?

In this process, you may become weary. However, Jesus said, "Come to me, all you who are weary and burdened, and I will give you rest" (Matthew 11:28). In Hebrews 4:11, we are told that we should "make every effort to enter [God's] rest." In Isaiah 30:15, we are encouraged to remember that "[i]n repentance and rest is your salvation, in quietness and trust is your strength."

When we see a problem, we often charge ahead in our own strength rather than waiting on God. It is easy to become very active and focused on our own efforts and lose sight of the fact that God has everything under His control. Therefore we can confidently trust and enter into His rest.

It is in the secret place, trusting in His faithfulness, that we behold His beauty. We can then cast our cares on Him and wait expectantly for Him to complete the work He has begun in us. The paradox is that as we rest in Him, we become strengthened in our inner being. This was Paul's prayer for believers at Ephesus:

I pray that out of his glorious riches he may strengthen you with power through his Spirit in your inner being, so that Christ may dwell in your hearts through faith. And I pray that you, being rooted and established in love, may have power, together with all the saints, to grasp how wide and long and high and deep is the love of Christ, and to know this love that surpasses knowledge— that you may be filled to the measure of all the fullness of God. Now to him who is able to do immeasurably more than all we ask or imagine, according to his power that is at work within us . . .
Ephesians 3:16–20

This is an awesome prayer for strength in the inner being, for comprehension of the depth of Christ's love, which is to be filled with the fullness of God whose power is able to do immeasurably more in us than we can even imagine! Paul encourages the Ephesians (and us) to gaze upon His beauty, so that their expectations would be as magnificent as the omnipotence of God. In comparison, we may realize that our prayers are too small. As we dwell in the secret place, our knowledge of God deepens

> When Jesus died on the cross of Calvary. . . . He opened the way so that all would have access to and fellowship with God.

© 2003, Thin Within, All Rights Reserved

LESSON

and our longings are heightened as our inner being is strengthened so that we are ready to face the foe.

As we discovered in earlier lessons, Satan attacks us through distractions, doubts, and unbelief, but he cannot steal from us what Jesus purchased through His death, burial, and resurrection. We are called to resist Satan, standing firm in faith. We also saw that we have been given spiritual armor for this battle. Instead of being passive, we are called to put on armor daily and stand against the schemes of the devil.

We take up the sword of the Spirit, which is the Word of God, and we wield it, pressing forward, yet on our knees in prayer.

The weapons we fight with are not the weapons of the world.
On the contrary, they have divine power
to demolish strongholds.
2 Corinthians 10:4

We are not in this battle alone.

In the same way, the Spirit helps us in our weakness. We do not know what we ought to pray for, but the Spirit himself intercedes for us with groans that words cannot express. And he who searches our hearts knows the mind of the Spirit, because the Spirit intercedes for the saints in accordance with God's will.
Romans 8:26–27

Jesus also joins us in this battle as our great High Priest. He is now at the right hand of the Father, and we are told in Hebrews 7:25 that He always intercedes for us.

We also are called to be priests and partake in this work of intercession.

. . . you also, like living stones, are being built into a spiritual house to be a holy priesthood, offering spiritual sacrifices acceptable to God through Jesus Christ.
1 Peter 2:5

Unlike the high priests in the Old Testament who approached the holy of holies in fear and trembling and never more than once a year, we are called to

. . . approach the throne of grace with confidence, so that we may receive mercy and find grace to help us in our time of need.
Hebrews 4:16

You, too, can boldly approach the throne of grace and find a present help. Have you done that as you have struggled with heart hunger in these last few weeks? When we want to eat but we are not at a 0, we can boldly and confidently approach Him and ask, by His Spirit, to enable us to put to death the lust of the flesh:

"Lord, You have said I am to walk in the Spirit and not fulfill the desires of the flesh."

"Lord, enable me to walk in the newness of life."

"Lord, when I am in doubt that I can wait until I am hungry, show me what is going on in my heart that I need to deal with or give to You. What is causing this emptiness that I want to fill up with food?"

"Lord, at times I feel rebellious and resistant to walking in obedience to Your call to surrender this food to You. You have said I am dead to sin, so make me willing to release my strong hold on food and take my eyes and mind off of everything except You, Lord."

God is a very present help in time of trouble (Psalm 46:1), and He has promised to give grace and help in time of need (Hebrews 4:16). As we call out to Him, confessing our impotence, we also call forth His strength. Remember, He gives grace to the humble—those who recognize their desperate need of Him. Jesus taught His disciples to pray, "Lead us not into temptation" (Matthew 6:13). So we pray intentionally and preventively, "Lord, keep me from falling."

In Matthew 26:41, Jesus called His disciples to watch and pray so that they wouldn't enter into temptation. We are to pray for wisdom and discernment to be alert to the schemes of the enemy. Prayer and walking in confidence of His calling was clearly Jesus' answer for temptation, and it must be ours as well.

It is easy to get discouraged in this restoration process when the pounds don't melt away as quickly as we would like. The battle may seem unending, but Jesus told His disciples that they were called to pray and not grow weary or give up (Luke 18:1–8). We are to persevere in

As we spend time in that secret place of prayer, He reveals to us what we need to know and He strengthens us to accomplish His will.

© 2003, Thin Within, All Rights Reserved

prayer as we continue to deal deathblows to our fleshly habits in the power of our awesome God.

What untold blessings we enjoy in the secret place of prayer as we rise to the call of our High Priest! Prayer is our primary offensive weapon that enables us to be confident in what God will do as we engage in battle. We can go forth praising, trusting, and knowing our mighty God has won this battle within us. We know that the Holy Spirit and Jesus are constantly praying for us, so we can have great confidence that we are more than conquerors through Him who loved us (Romans 8:37).

If God is for us, who can be against us?
Romans 8:31

Physiological Information

The Lord leads and directs us in our intimate time with Him. He is our primary source of insight regarding how we are to live according to His plan and purpose. As we spend time in that secret place of prayer, He reveals to us what we need to know and He strengthens us to accomplish His will. When you come before the Lord, submit to Him all that you have learned about food, your body, and what works and doesn't work for you. He will expose anything that isn't accurate and will reveal to your spirit any truth that He wants to use to mold you into His very likeness.

Since we started our journey ten weeks ago, our prayer has been that you have begun to walk more fully in faith rather than in the flesh and to recognize that His ways are higher than your ways. As you have come to know that while all things are permissible, not all things are beneficial, you have set boundaries confirming that you won't be mastered by anything.

One boundary you will want to maintain is never to be in bondage to the teachings of man, no matter how convincing, if they do not line up with the Word of God. Yet having said that, we urge you to prayerfully consider becoming informed regarding your health. This is not, however, meant to direct you to return to bondage. We understand that you may have an aversion to reading labels or magazine articles, or surfing Internet websites for information about food and health. However, we encourage you to rely prayerfully on the Holy Spirit to show you the place of proper balance for nutrition and exercise.

As you gather some basic knowledge, you can ask the Lord to show you what He would have you do with this information. One participant who was indulging in copious quantities of Diet Coke, refused to read anything about aspartame, the artificial sweetener in diet soda. She knew about the claims that had been made about aspartame, but refused to investigate this issue for herself. When she felt the Lord prompting her to become more informed about the effect of aspartame and caffeine on her body, she submitted and became convicted that the Lord would have her abstain for a season from her dependency on Diet Coke. This was what the Spirit of God revealed to her. She felt convinced during her time of prayer that she had a responsibility to guard what came in and out of her body, God's temple. She realized she was to submit to the will of the Lord, making another costly choice. She released her desire for Diet Coke into His hands in order not to be mastered by anything.

One participant wondered why eating 0 to 5 required so little food. She was surprised and frustrated that only a few bites, eaten slowly, could take her from a 0 to a 5. As she became informed regarding nutrition, she learned that fat was more filling than fruits and vegetables. She realized that choosing to eat foods that had less fat during her meal allowed her to enjoy a taste of dessert at the end of her meal and feel satisfied in the process. She broadened her boundaries so that her food choices no longer consisted only of very rich food. She became more informed and diversified as she submitted to the leading of the Lord in prayer.

These people, and many more like them, were able to make decisions driven by the Spirit rather than their flesh. The Lord doesn't want us to put our heads in the sand. Doing so is just as much of the flesh as is being obsessed or preoccupied with dietary laws. God wants His people to respect and understand how He made our bodies and which fuel will best support health and vitality. Being informed doesn't mean being obsessed or being a "health-food fanatic." It simply means allowing the Holy Spirit to direct you personally as to what He would have you do with all information. Resist the flesh's attempt to turn what He teaches you into a law for yourself or anyone else!

Many people discount the benefits of exercise. However, we encourage you to review the National Institute of Health material presented in last week's lesson and offer it to the Lord in prayer as you ask for His insight. Then be willing

© 2003, Thin Within, All Rights Reserved

LESSON

to do that which He desires for you as you experience the joy and peace beyond measure that comes from walking in obedience to Him.

Finally, if you have trouble consistently eating 0 to 5, or if you are being mastered by your love of certain foods or something else, pray about that. If you are tempted to overindulge on chocolate ice cream, call out to the Lord and seek Him above all else. He may impress on you to release that particular food for a season in order to break this stronghold. You are free to eat, but remember He says you are to be free "not" to eat as well. Prayer is the place where you learn to discern what God's best is for you.

Integration

It is only in that secret place of intimacy with the Lord as we gaze upon His beauty and majesty that we can experience the fullness of His glory. In that place, we know beyond measure that we are loved no matter how we "perform." And in that place, we can submit to Him all that we feel, learn, experience, and need in order to be refreshed and made battle ready.

We encourage you to rely prayerfully on the Holy Spirit to show you the place of proper balance for nutrition and exercise.

As you allow the Lord to open your life to Him, take all you discover and offer it back to Him in praise. The mystery of life is revealed to us in Christ. He wants to unlock the wonders of all that you treasure and experience in Him. As you surrender fully to Him and allow Him to use the challenges of life to mold your character, you will learn and grow. There may yet be costly choices to make, but the rewards are boundless!

As we make prayer a deeper part of our experience, entering reverently into that holy of holies with God, we discover that He satisfies all of our needs. He answers our questions about food, eating, and weight. He satisfies us emotionally. He helps us to take each step of faith. He helps us to know if boundaries need adjusting. He empowers us to forgive as He washes us clean yet again. We experience true intimacy with Him in this secret place of prayer.

© 2003, Thin Within, All Rights Reserved

My Notes

© 2003, Thin Within, All Rights Reserved

EXERCISES

Day One

Going Deeper

What would you say is the purpose of prayer? Evaluate your own prayer life and how it might be expanded. Ask God to bring you to that secret place where you can experience Him and His presence on an even richer level.

____
____
____
____

Bible Study

Read 1 John 1:7, 9, 1 Peter 5:7, and Psalm 139:23 and journal on God's provision for you through prayer. How does 2 Corinthians 3:16–18 show God's transforming grace in action?

____
____
____
____

Knowing God by Heart: Faithful

I will give you the treasures of darkness, riches stored in secret places,
so that you may know that I am the LORD, the God of Israel, who summons you by name.
Isaiah 45:3

Look up the word "faithful" in the dictionary and write down a definition that you believe is consistent with God being faithful. Read 1 Corinthians 1:9, Psalm 33:4, and Deuteronomy 7:9 and relate your definition to these Scriptures.

____
____
____
____

Getting Practical

Keep a prayer journal this week and ask God to reveal new insights on your obedience in eating 0 to 5.

____
____
____
____

Memory Challenge

Start memorizing Psalm 139:23–24. Take time to see the message proclaimed in this Scripture Read the verses out loud several times, then look away and say them from memory.

Search me, O God, and know my heart; test me and know my anxious thoughts.
See if there is any offensive way in me, and lead me in the way everlasting.
Psalm 139:23–24

Thin Within Tip

If you're offered a special treat but are not at 0, save it and eat it later.

© 2003, Thin Within, All Rights Reserved

Day Two

Going Deeper

Through our time with God, He reveals what we need to know, and He strengthens us to accomplish His will. Submit to Him all that you have learned about food, your body, and what works for you. Let Him expose those things that are false and confirm those that are true so He can use them in your life. Journal about what you discover.

____

____

____

____

Bible Study

As we look at all we've learned, it can sometimes feel as if we have a lot to *do*, and we may become weary in our labor. What does Jesus say in Matthew 11:28–30? What do Hebrews 4:11 and Isaiah 30:15 say about rest? Journal your thoughts about resting in the Lord.

____

____

____

____

Knowing God by Heart

Continue to grow in your knowledge of God by reading Psalm 145:13, Hebrews 2:17–3:6, and Hebrews 10:23. What do these verses say to you about God's faithfulness?

____

____

____

____

Getting Practical

Continue journaling your prayers and share your specific needs with God.

____

____

____

____

Memory Challenge

Continue memorizing Psalm 139:23–24 by saying or writing it several times. After some repetition, try repeating it from memory. Take the memory verse card with you and refer to it throughout the day.

© 2003, Thin Within, All Rights Reserved

EXERCISES

Day Three

Going Deeper

Ask the Lord about that which He wants you to be informed. As He reveals His answer to you, make a point of following His lead. There are a variety of ways that you can become informed: magazines, books, web pages, and television documentaries. You may be reluctant to accept or sort out man's teachings on nutrition and health issues, but the Holy Spirit will show you a place of balance that will benefit you personally. Pray for wisdom and discernment in this area.

____

____

____

Bible Study

Read Ephesians 3:15–20. Where does our strength come from? Pray this prayer to Him as you read it, allowing Him to use the words to empower you with His desire for you.

____

____

____

Knowing God by Heart

Find synonyms for the word "faithful" in a thesaurus or dictionary. How do these words give you a deeper understanding of God as faithful? Read 1 John 1:9, 1 Corinthians 10:13, and 2 Thessalonians 3:3. What do these Scriptures tell you about God?

____

____

____

Getting Practical

Take the benefits of daily activity shared in last week's lesson to the Lord in prayer. Wait on Him as He convicts you of your need to incorporate a new level of activity in your life. Remain tenderhearted to the Lord's leading in this area and resist procrastinating in what He calls you to do.

____

____

____

Memory Challenge

Review Psalm 139:23–24 until you can repeat it from memory.

Thin Within Tip

Chew sugarless gum while preparing meals. It's hard to nibble if you already have something in your mouth.

  © 2003, Thin Within, All Rights Reserved

Day Four

Going Deeper

Romans 8:26–27 and Hebrews 7:24–25 say we are not alone in this battle. Write your thoughts about the roles of the Holy Spirit and Jesus.

____
____
____
____

Bible Study

We have studied God's protection for us in the battle against Satan in Ephesians 6. Read the passage again noticing the role of prayer (Ephesians 6:10–20). Journal about how prayer and God's Word (the sword of the Spirit) are the two offensive weapons we have in this war (2 Corinthians 10:4).

____
____
____
____

Knowing God by Heart: Omniscient

Look up the word "omniscient" in the dictionary and write down a definition that you believe is consistent with God being omniscient. Read 1 Chronicles 28:9 and relate your definition to this Scripture.

____
____
____
____

Getting Practical

Record any answers to prayers that God has shown you this week.

____
____
____
____

Memory Challenge

Repeat Psalm 139:23–24 from memory. Turn these verses into a prayer for yourself or someone you know.

© 2003, Thin Within, All Rights Reserved

EXERCISES

Day Five

Going Deeper

Since all things are permissible but not all things are beneficial, offer all information you read or observe (about eating, food, exercise, health) to God for His scrutiny and allow Him to lead you to that which is beneficial. Be open to new insights, allowing the Spirit to direct where you go with that information.

Bible Study

Recalling thoughts of the Old Testament temple and high priest, read Hebrews 4:14–16. Journal on our access to God through Jesus and the role prayer plays in our daily life.

Knowing God by Heart

What do 1 Samuel 2:3 and Job 37:16 say about how God is omniscient?

Getting Practical

Journal on how prayer has benefited you this week.

Memory Challenge

Meditate on Psalm 139:23–24 throughout the day and allow it to draw you closer to God. Ask Him to help you truly believe this Scripture so that it can set you free from all the deceptive lies of the world.

Thin Within Tip

If you end up eating at an all-you-can-eat restaurant, consider ordering the meal "to go." Once the carryout container is filled, sit with your family/friends and place a small portion of the food on your plate to enjoy right there at the restaurant. Take the rest home to enjoy later.

© 2003, Thin Within, All Rights Reserved

Day Six – Optional Exercises

Going Deeper

As we make prayer a deeper part of our experience and enter reverently into that holy of holies with God, we discover that He satisfies all of our needs. He answers our questions about food, eating, and weight. He satisfies us emotionally. He helps us to take another step of faith and know if our boundaries need adjusting. He empowers us to forgive as He washes us clean yet again. Journal on this true intimacy with God in this secret place of prayer.

____

____

____

____

Bible Study

God promises to help us in our time of need (Psalm 46:1). We can take whatever we are struggling with to Him as He enables us to walk in obedience through His Spirit. We can ask Him why. He may answer yes, no, or wait, but He will answer.

____

____

____

____

Knowing God by Heart

Find synonyms for the word "omniscient" in a thesaurus or dictionary. How do these words give you a deeper understanding of God as omniscient? Read Psalm 139:1–6,13–16. What do these verses tell you about God?

____

____

____

____

Getting Practical

Review your prayer journal from this week and give thanks to God for His provision in those prayers.

____

____

____

____

Memory Challenge

Repeat Psalm 139:23–24 out loud and ask God to make these verses real in your life. What might God be leading you to "be" or to "do" in response to this passage?

© 2003, Thin Within, All Rights Reserved

EXERCISES

Day Seven – Optional Exercises

Going Deeper

God has provided the secret place so that we might live within it each moment of our daily lives. We don't need to leave this inner sanctum. There are many Scriptures that can be used in your prayers to God. Allow prayer to become as natural as breathing. Ask God to expand your prayer life with Him.

____
____
____
____

Bible Study

What was Jesus' answer for temptation in Matthew 6:13 and 26:41? Journal about temptation in your life and how God is leading you to deal with it. Read Luke 18:1. What does this say to you about the power of prayer?

____
____
____
____

Getting Practical

If you continue to struggle with consistency in 0 to 5 eating, or with certain foods/drinks or particular eating occasions, submit your struggle to God in prayer and allow Him to show you what He wants you to do. Ask Him to make you willing and able to release whatever it is that you need to release.

____
____
____
____

Memory Challenge

Share your memory verse with a friend or family member, telling him or her how it relates to your Thin Within journey.

Thin Within Tip

Not sure that you are at 0? Sometimes "hunger" is really thirst. Drink eight ounces of water and wait thirty minutes. True hunger will remain after the "water test."

     © 2003, Thin Within, All Rights Reserved

Review of the Week

Take time at the end of each week to review what God has taught you and how it is impacting your life. This will give you a great overview to take to your Thin Within Support Group Meeting.

The most significant thing God taught me this week:

This week's memory verse asks God to test me and know my anxious thoughts. I tend to have anxious thoughts in the area of:

The passage goes on to ask Him to see if there is any offensive way in me. In these 11 weeks God has shown me that one offensive way in me is:

The passage ends by me asking that God lead me in the way everlasting. Through these 11 weeks, God has led me to:

What I have learned about the character of God as faithful and omniscient, and how I have come to know and be drawn closer to Him:

My prayer requests and praises:

© 2003, Thin Within, All Rights Reserved

LESSON

Celebration of God's Grace, Part Three

Introduction

Twelve weeks ago, we began a life-transforming journey. Isn't it thrilling to see all that God has done and still plans to do in your life? You have not yet arrived at your final destination because this journey will last your entire life, but what an adventure from glory to glory!

We have focused over the past three months on our new identity in Christ, making costly choices, setting godly boundaries, deepening prayer, and accepting the power of forgiveness. You have come to see God's temple, your body, as a place of service, celebration, and worship to our great God. You understand more deeply who He is as you enter into His love that endures forever (Psalm 118). This lesson celebrates God's grace and draws us to worship Him by recounting the great things He has done.

Last week, we talked about the holy of holies, our intimate place of personal worship. In this secret place of abiding, we submit ourselves to the transforming power of God's matchless grace. Our knowledge of God is deepened, our expectations are heightened, and our inner being is strengthened. It is here that we can come to the end of ourselves, utterly dependent on the Lord, and where we can come to rely upon His constant provision, presence, and power. In the secret place, we find the answer to our questions, the satisfaction of our longings, and the motivation that encourages us to press onward.

God's transforming power is available to us throughout our lives. This week we have not come to the end of a journey, but we will celebrate being God's people in process. His work is not finished as He continues to conform us into His likeness. We joyfully give thanks to and worship the King of Kings, rejoicing in the resurrected, abundant life. If you have yet to see all of the changes you had hoped for, delight in the fact that He continues to work in you.

. . . being confident of this, that he who began a good work in you will carry it on to completion until the day of Christ Jesus.
Philippians 1:6
This journey has just begun!

Spiritual Foundation

Remember the discussion about fighting the fight of faith? The world, the flesh, and the devil would love to snatch what has been implanted and move you to a place of unbelief. Be vigilant, on your guard, and wary of his schemes:

- "I haven't lost all of my excess weight. Am I a failure yet again?"
- "I've been in this program for three months and I don't see the radical changes in myself that I see in Rebecca or Peter."
- "I bet God will give up on me, so why should I keep trying?"

While it may be tempting to revert back to that old negative dieting mind-set, we encourage you to put on the full armor of God and renounce those thoughts. Remember who you are in Christ and that you are no longer a slave to those flesh patterns. Look to the Lord as you persevere in faith.

To develop an appreciation for the process that you've been undergoing, be encouraged by one of God's beloved who underwent the transforming work of a mighty God. The Apostle Paul is an example of someone who rejoiced at being in process, as God worked in and through him.

He shares what he was like before Christ abruptly entered his life. Here he explains to some devout Jewish leaders just how much like them he had been:

"I am a Jew, born in Tarsus of Cilicia, but brought up in this city. Under Gamaliel I was thoroughly trained in the law of our fathers and was just as zealous for God as any of you are today.
Acts 22:3

Perhaps, like Paul, you have a testimony that you can offer to the world. Were you an exercise-aholic that has now found sanity and balance? Did you battle with anorexia or bulimia before experiencing God's healing touch? Were you a workaholic who now enjoys setting godly boundaries through the power of the Holy Spirit?

Paul had lived according to an amazing burden imposed by the Law.

If anyone else thinks he has reasons to put confidence in the flesh, I have more: circumcised on the eighth day, of the people of Israel, of the tribe of Benjamin, a Hebrew of Hebrews; in regard to the law, a Pharisee; as for zeal, persecuting the church; as for legalistic righteousness, faultless.
Philippians 3:4–6

© 2003, Thin Within, All Rights Reserved

Many have lived with great pride in adhering to incredibly strict standards set by numerous "experts," most of whom have different opinions regarding diets and "correct" percentages of fat, carbohydrates, and protein. Perhaps you experienced "success" in a rigorous program of daily weighing and measuring. Perhaps, like Paul, God has now called you onto a different path.

Paul (at the time called "Saul) thought he had "arrived" before he knew Christ. He represented everything that was required according to Jewish law. He was a Pharisee, upholding so many laws and rules it would make our heads spin. He had every reason to think he had "made it." Though Saul may have been faultless as far as legalistic righteousness was concerned, God wasn't finished with him—far from it.

A Thin Within participant tells of the year she lost one hundred pounds. People praised her, yet she found that, in spite of having the attractive fit body she had dreamed of, a deep longing and emptiness remained. She yearned for something that being thin and fit didn't satisfy. Outwardly she had "made it." According to the standards of the world, she had arrived, but there was much work yet to be done from within. She knew the truth: something profoundly deep was missing. Other participants in her class asked her why she was attending since she clearly didn't have a weight problem. Her response was "to allow God to have access to my heart, which hasn't been unbound from food."

Each of us has an empty place within, and we will try to fill it with something if we do not return to our first love (Revelation 2:4). In spite of success, praise of people, relationships, money, and power, the emptiness will remain because it needs to be filled with the awesome love of our Lord Jesus Christ. Can you identify with this? Paul could.

As Saul, he abided by the letter of the law and had allowed it to become his god. In the process, he left authentic love behind.

The Lord says: "These people come near to Me with their mouth and honor Me with their lips, but their hearts are far from Me. Their worship of me is made up only of rules taught by men."
Isaiah 29:13

Saul zealously persecuted the early Church, attacking those to whom Christ had entrusted the Gospel message. He sought to squelch the movement of Christianity, having many arrested and imprisoned or put to death (Acts 22:4). He thought in his pharisaic piety that he was doing a great service for God. He was a Pharisee of all Pharisees—what any good aspiring Jewish boy should hope to become. His education and performance were top notch! No doubt he tried to fill the emptiness in his heart with religious fervor of acts done "for God." Yet the emptiness within him deepened even more.

Then one day, as this man who "had it made" marched steadfastly toward Damascus on his way to root out and arrest more of those "rebel" Christians (Acts 9:2), he was stopped dead in his pious tracks and found himself on his knees. Grace came down and humbled this man who was filled with pride, hatred, venom, and self-righteousness.

"About noon as I came near Damascus, suddenly a bright light from heaven flashed around me.
Acts 22:6

The One who lives in Heaven rescued Saul from the dominion of darkness and brought him into the kingdom of the Son (Colossians 1:13). What amazing grace!

The Christian killer would become the soul winner. What amazing grace!

As Saul bent to the ground (Acts 22:7), his proud Pharisee facade shattered. He rose from that place temporarily blind, but spiritually able to "see" more clearly than ever. He saw his self-righteous piety for the sin that it was. He also saw his desperate need for grace and mercy. From that moment on, he was a changed man. He now saw the Lord as eternal *YAHWEH*. Grace met Saul. Grace took him to the ground in reverence and awe of the one true God. Grace raised him to his feet as one transformed. Grace. Amazing grace!

God fanned the flames beneath the crucible of Paul's life. The refinement process was now under way, and Paul would never again be

Press on. Move forward. Fix your eyes on the goal! Jesus is ever before you with arms outstretched. Keep walking, one step at a time, ever onward.

© 2003, Thin Within, All Rights Reserved

smug in his sense of accomplishment. Now he was a man of humility and his eyes were set on a much grander goal.

Not that I have already obtained all this, or have already been made perfect, but I press on to take hold of that for which Christ Jesus took hold of me. Brothers, I do not consider myself yet to have taken hold of it. But one thing I do: Forgetting what is behind and straining toward what is ahead, I press on towards the goal to win the prize for which God has called me heavenward in Christ Jesus.

Philippians 3:12–14

Imagine, if you will, being Paul the apostle. You have a "criminal record." You have murdered not "bad guys" like thieves, crooks, or tax collectors, but Christians. In one instant, you go from thinking you were "the best thing God had going" to being the "worst of sinners."

But for that very reason I was shown mercy so that in me, the worst of sinners, Christ Jesus might display His unlimited patience as an example for those who would believe on Him and receive eternal life.

1 Timothy 1:16

Dear beloved, have you done worse than Saul? Do you feel somehow that you are beyond the reach of God's tender mercies and His amazing bountiful grace? Draw nearer and feel His warm breath upon your face. Listen to His heart beating for you.

The LORD your God is with you, he is mighty to save. he will take great delight in you, he will quiet you with his love, he will rejoice over you with singing."

Zephaniah 3:17

Has grace come down and visited you? He calls you now to rise up and allow any vestige of self to be shattered as you seek total and utter dependence on the Lord who loves you so very much. His amazing grace has called to you from the boundless vastness of Heaven, reaching across eternity to fill you, to move you, and to love you. Remember He is a sovereign God and He will have His way. What amazing grace!

Please don't conclude this part of your journey thinking either that you are a failure or that you have arrived. To believe either would be to buy into the tactics of the enemy. God desires so much more for you. His grace reaches to you here. Now. How did God respond to the one who had killed His people in the name of serving God? With grace, grace, and more grace!

Saul was confronted by God's grace and mercy at the pinnacle of his career. When he recognized his true condition and might have been tempted to beat himself up over mistakes or "failures," he was comforted by God's grace and mercy.

We can learn from Paul during our "successes" as well as our "failures." God reaches out to us and encourages us not to remain in either place, but to "press on" and "take hold." Let's model our behavior after Paul:

Not that I have already obtained all this, or have already been made perfect, but I press on to take hold of that for which Christ Jesus took hold of me.

Philippians 3:12

1. People in process trust God to continue His work.

We can rest in the blessed fact that our Father continues to work in us, fashioning and forming us (Philippians 1:6). Lingering too long over "success" or "failure" prevents us from experiencing the blessing and grace that God has for our continual growth and maturity. When we become complacent with where we are, we fail to avail ourselves of the fullness of what God has for us in Christ.

Perhaps you have been tempted to beat yourself up for not applying yourself more wholeheartedly during this journey. Even if you have melted down to your natural size, guess what? God says you haven't completely arrived. You have not yet taken hold of that for which Christ Jesus took hold of you. Not until you are in Heaven will that day come. Paul expresses this well:

Brothers, I do not consider myself yet to have taken hold of it. But one thing I do: Forgetting what is behind and straining toward what is ahead . . .

Philippians 3:13

> While it may be tempting to revert back to that old negative dieting mind-set, we encourage you to put on the full armor of God and renounce those thoughts.

 © 2003, Thin Within, All Rights Reserved

2. People in process don't dwell on their failures or successes.

Do you dwell on those things about which you have regrets? Dieting failures? Gaining too much weight while you were pregnant? Never learning to ride a bike? Failed relationships? Failed education? Not doing something because you were overweight or out of shape? It could be anything. Can you imagine the enemy preying on Paul as he was alone at night with his thoughts? Satan is the accuser and he had a lot of ammunition to use on Paul, who no doubt could have dwelt on his past failures and sin. Instead, he chose to put behind him those things for which Christ had died. He strained toward what was before Him, using the imagery of a runner in a long-distance race.

I press on towards the goal to win the prize for which God has called me heavenward in Christ Jesus.
Philippians 3:14

3. People in process fix their eyes on Jesus and the hope He gives.

It may be tempting for us to fix our eyes on anything but Jesus: the scale, the clothes that we hope to fit into, people who compliment us when they notice we are thinner, a promotion, a new relationship. On what are your eyes fixed? In what is your hope?

The writer to the Hebrews says it well:
Let us fix our eyes on Jesus, the author and perfecter of our faith, who for the joy set before him endured the cross, scorning its shame, and sat down at the right hand of the throne of God.
Hebrews 12:2

Paul went from being confident in himself to being humbly dependent on the Lord. His faith clearly kept him moving forward to the goal of knowing Christ and being conformed daily into His image. Let us adopt the same attitude and allow our walk of faith to propel us forward, remaining ever and always humbly dependent on our great Lord and Savior. Let us submit to Him and trust that He will continue His work in and through us. Let us throw off the bindings of past failures as well as the successes and press on to that which is yet ahead. Fix your eyes on Jesus. He will perfect your faith!

Physiological Information

In the past three months, have you heard a call from the Lord to a life of health and vitality in mind, body, and spirit? As you submit your will, emotions, expectations, choices, and your body to Him, you will experience fulfillment in all respects.

As you continue to "press on" and "take hold," we encourage you to celebrate every quantum step of faith. Here are some ways in which you can press on, but remember that "doing" is not to take precedence over being with the Lord:

<u>For Spiritual Fitness</u>

- Be part of a local Bible-teaching church.
- Memorize Bible verses.
- Join a Bible study.
- Get involved in a "Read through the Bible" program.
- Commit to praying for or with a friend.
- Let go of something you've needed to surrender to Him.

<u>For Emotional Fitness</u>

- Start a journal if you haven't already.
- Write a note to someone who needs encouragement.
- Call someone you haven't talked to in a while.
- Take some time to "play," to do something fun.
- Take a meal or visit a friend in need.
- Start reading a wonderful book.
- Clean out a closet or a kitchen drawer.

<u>For Physical Fitness</u>

- Take a walk.
- Increase your water consumption and cut back on other beverages.
- Dance with your children, spouse, roommate, or with the Lord.
- Work in the garden.
- Investigate a new park.

Step out in faith in at least one area to get yourself out of a rut. Press on. Move forward. Fix your eyes on the goal! Jesus is ever before you with arms outstretched. Keep walking, one step at a time, ever onward.

Integration

Walking with the Lord, growing in deeper dependence upon Him, and living a life of faith is a lifelong process during which He nudges us by the power of His Holy Spirit and His amazing grace. The grace that pardons us is also a provision, a power, and presence upon which you can

© 2003, Thin Within, All Rights Reserved

LESSON

draw as you set your gaze steadfastly on the goal ahead. His desire is for us to become more and more like Jesus, and that is to be the cry of our hearts.

As we press on, we let go of not only our failures but also our successes. Rather than pointing to those defeats or accomplishments as proof of the type of person you are, dare to focus on Christ. Continue to submit to the Master's touch. You are His masterpiece. The good work He has begun He will complete!

What a wonderful adventure we are on. We have experienced God's amazing touch on our lives and will continue to do so, delighting in His promise that:

> . . . *he who began a good work in you will carry it on to completion until the day of Christ Jesus.*
> *Philippians 1:6*

As we press on, we let go of not only our failures but also our successes. Rather than pointing to those defeats or accomplishments as proof of the type of person you are, dare to focus on Christ.

D-52   © 2003, Thin Within, All Rights Reserved

<u>My Notes</u>

© 2003, Thin Within, All Rights Reserved

EXERCISES

Day One

Going Deeper

Has grace come down and visited you these last three months? Have you experienced God's amazing grace extended to fill you, move you, and love you? What effect has God's grace had on your journey?

____

____

____

____

Bible Study

Read Philippians 1:6 and 3:12–14. What do these verses say to you regarding the changes you hoped for that have not been realized these first twelve weeks of *Thin Within?*

____

____

____

____

Knowing God by Heart: Eternal

> *Be still, and <u>know that I am God; I</u> will be exalted among the nations, I will be exalted in the earth.*
> *Psalm 46:10*

Look up the word "eternal" in the dictionary and write down a definition that you believe is consistent with God being eternal. Read Revelation 1:8 and 22:13 and relate your definition to these Scriptures.

____

____

____

____

Getting Practical

Begin a list of any noticeable changes (even small ones) that have occurred in your eating since starting Thin Within. Thank God for these changes.

____

____

____

____

Memory Challenge

Start memorizing Philippians 3:13–14. Take time to see the message proclaimed in this Scripture. Read the verses out loud several times, then look away and say them from memory.

> *Brothers, I do not consider myself yet to have taken hold of it. But one thing I do: Forgetting what is behind and straining toward what is ahead, I press on toward the goal to win the prize for which God has called me heavenward in Christ Jesus.*
> *Philippians 3:13–14*

Thin Within Tip

Record all your victorious moments in your journal and review them when you feel weak or discouraged. This could be called your "victories" journal.

© 2003, Thin Within, All Rights Reserved

Day Two

Going Deeper

This week start storing up an arsenal of God-given directives that will encourage you to continue to press on in the Lord. Pray about the goals that God would have you make in order to stay spiritually fit. Record these goals and then pray about a date for one or more of them to be realized. How can you restructure your life to reach these goals? (Refer to the Physiological Information section of this week's lessons for some ideas.)

____
____
____
____

Bible Study

How did God respond to Paul (Saul at that time) when he had killed God's people who were serving the Lord (1 Timothy 1:16)? Journal about how God feels about you, whether or not you have lost all your weight or accomplished all your goals (Zephaniah 3:17).

____
____
____
____

Knowing God by Heart

Continue to grow in knowledge of how God is eternal by reading Deuteronomy 32:40, 33:27, and Isaiah 57:15. Write your thoughts.

____
____
____
____

Getting Practical

Continue adding to your list of changes that have occurred in your eating in the first twelve weeks of Thin Within. Give praise to God for His mercy and grace in time of need.

____
____
____
____

Memory Challenge

Continue memorizing Philippians 3:13–14 by saying or writing it several times. After some repetition, try repeating it from memory. Take the memory verse card with you and refer to it throughout the day.

© 2003, Thin Within, All Rights Reserved

EXERCISES

Day Three

Going Deeper

Prayerfully take your emotional fitness needs to God. Allow Him to show you goals and maybe even a date by which to fulfill them. What action can you take to move toward the goal of emotional fitness?

____
____
____
____

Bible Study

We can learn from Paul how to allow God's grace to affect us when we are aware of our "successes" and our "failures." God reaches to us in both and encourages us not to remain stuck there, but to press on. Read Philippians 3:12 and journal about God's continuing work in you. Lingering too long over what has occurred will cause you to stagnate, preventing you from experiencing the grace that God has for you today, tomorrow, and beyond. Don't stay where you are, but "press on to take hold of that for which Christ Jesus took hold of [you]" (Philippians 3:12).

____
____
____
____

Knowing God by Heart

Find synonyms for the word "eternal" in a thesaurus or dictionary. How do these words give you a deeper understanding of God as eternal? Read 1 Timothy 1:17. What does this Scripture tell you about God?

____
____
____
____

Getting Practical

Continue adding to your list of changes. Note any other adjustments you have made in your eating. Do you see things other than your eating that are different? Give thanks to the Lord for He is good!

____
____
____
____

Memory Challenge

Review Philippians 3:13–14 until you can repeat it from memory.

Thin Within Tip

If you think "I'll never get this," practice saying, "I am a thin eater and can do all things through Christ who gives me strength." Walk in the confidence you have been given in Christ.

© 2003, Thin Within, All Rights Reserved

Day Four

Going Deeper

What is God's desire regarding your physical fitness? Prayerfully consider a reasonable goal and a date to accomplish it within a reasonable time frame. How can you rearrange your daily activity to incorporate this change? (Consider the list in the Physiological Information section of this week's lesson.)

____
____
____
____

Bible Study

What should our action be in this race toward God's prize for us (Philippians 3:13)? Are you beating yourself up because you didn't meet your goals for these twelve weeks? Or are you focused on all the success you have experienced during this time? Either way, what does Paul say you should do? "Straining toward what is ahead" implies that no one ever "arrives." There's always work that God intends to complete in us. Pray over these thoughts from Paul.

____
____
____
____

Knowing God by Heart—Review

Look over all the attributes of God that we have studied over these last three months. Journal about the character qualities that have spoken most to your heart.

____
____
____
____

Getting Practical

Add any other changes in your life since you have started Thin Within. Consider sending a note to Thin Within (e-mail joe@thinwithin.org) and letting us know how God is transforming you.

____
____
____
____

Memory Challenge

Repeat Philippians 3:13–14 from memory. Turn these verses into a prayer for yourself or someone you know.

© 2003, Thin Within, All Rights Reserved

EXERCISES

Day Five

Going Deeper

Journal about the blessings that God has given since you started *Thin Within*. Establish an "attitude of gratitude" by making thanksgiving a tangible part of every day. Pray about ways that you can do this.

____

____

____

Bible Study

You have set lots of goals in the last three months, but what does Paul say your ultimate goal is according to Philippians 3:14? How can you achieve that goal according to Hebrews 12:1–3?

____

____

____

Are you tempted to set your eyes on the scale, looser clothes, compliments from others, or a smaller body? Jesus is the author and perfecter of your faith and the only One on whom you are to gaze. Journal a prayer for God to turn your sights on Him and then on His goals for you.

____

____

____

Knowing God by Heart

How has this study of God changed you? How does the verse below ring true in your life?
We know also that the Son of God has come and has given us understanding,
so that we may know him who is true. And we are in him who is true—even in his Son Jesus Christ.
he is the true God and eternal life.
1 John 5:20

____

____

____

Getting Practical

Do you continue to find the Thin Within tools helpful? Use them as the Spirit leads. We have found that people will eventually reach a place where the tools are needed only on occasion in order to get back on track. Remain prayerful about their use and guard against making them the priority rather than God and His work in you that transforms you from within.

____

____

____

Memory Challenge

Meditate on Philippians 3:13–14 throughout the day and allow it to draw you closer to God. Ask Him to help you truly believe this Scripture so that it can set you free from all the deceptive lies of the world.

     © 2003, Thin Within, All Rights Reserved

Day Six – Optional Exercises

Going Deeper

First Corinthians 15:57 says, "But thanks be to God! He gives [you] the victory through our Lord Jesus Christ." Take some time to give thanks to God, who alone has given you the victory that you have seen these last twelve weeks.

____

____

____

____

Bible Study

Isaiah 58:11 says He will satisfy our needs, strengthen our frame, and make us like a well-watered garden. Journal about Jesus' provision for you to run the race each day and eventually to receive His heavenly prize.

____

____

____

____

Knowing God by Heart

List God's attributes and what they mean to you. Give thanks for all you have learned about Him in this study and how He has transformed you.

____

____

____

____

Getting Practical

From all you have learned in Thin Within, what can you do when you are tempted to go back to your old ways of eating?

____

____

____

____

Memory Challenge

Repeat Philippians 3:13–14 out loud and ask God to make these verses real in your life. What might God be leading you to "be" or to "do" in response to this passage?

Thin Within Tip

For those who like chocolate after a meal, buy your favorite candy bar and cut it into bite-size single serving pieces. Wrap each piece in foil, place them in a resealable bag, and store them in the freezer. (It takes longer to eat frozen candy.)

© 2003, Thin Within, All Rights Reserved

EXERCISES

Day Seven – Optional Exercises

Going Deeper

Review this week's exercises and reflect on the list of things the Lord has done through your Thin Within experience. Prayerfully submit to Him your decision about continuing on with the program or about starting a Thin Within Support Group. Is it possible the Lord would have you share with others what He has taught you?

____
____
____
____

Bible Study

Reread Philippians 3:12–14. Our earthly goal is to be conformed to the image of Christ. Let us adopt the same attitude as Paul and allow our walk of faith to propel us forward, remaining ever and always humbly dependent on our great Lord and Savior. Let us submit to Him and trust that He will continue His work in us. Let us throw off the bindings of past failures and successes and press on toward that which is yet ahead. Fix your eyes on Jesus. He will yet perfect your faith!

____
____
____
____

Getting Practical

Recall the past three months and rejoice in how God has transformed you.

____
____
____
____

Memory Challenge

Share your memory verse with a friend or family member, telling him or her how it relates to your Thin Within journey.

Thin Within Tip

Extend yourself some grace. We all have certain times when old habits come roaring back. However, God wants you to _quickly_ turn back to Him and press onward.

   © 2003, Thin Within, All Rights Reserved

Review of the Week

Take time at the end of each week to review what God has taught you and how it is impacting your life. This will give you a great overview to take to your Thin Within Support Group Meeting.

The most significant thing God taught me this week:

____
____
____
____

As I conclude the final phase of Thin Within, I have been led to take the following steps in order not to be mastered by anything:

____
____
____
____

With respect to 0-5 eating and making beneficial choices, I would describe my progress as:

____
____
____
____

My greatest victory during these twelve weeks has been:

____
____
____
____

The most significant thing I have learned about the character of God throughout this twelve-week study, and how I have come to know and be drawn closer to Him:

____
____
____
____

My prayer requests and praises:

____
____
____
____

© 2003, Thin Within, All Rights Reserved

© 2003, Thin Within, All Rights Reserved

What an amazing accomplishment! You have persevered through twelve weeks of this program that we hope has powerfully impacted your life. We recognize that it certainly has not been an easy process—in fact, it may be one of the most difficult things you have ever set out to do.

Take a moment and allow yourself to enjoy the fact that God loves you deeply and has been changing you from the inside out making you truly thin within. It is easy to become so focused on the scale that you lose track of all the other positive things that God may be doing during the program. Some of our most significant changes are not only physical, but spiritual and emotional. For instance, did you find a new capacity to forgive yourself and others that may not have been present before? What about coming to a new understanding of grace and how much God loves you unconditionally? These are life changes that will reap eternal rewards.

From a physical standpoint, if you have reached your goal weight, congratulations! One of your greatest challenges now is to make these new habits (waiting for 0, stopping at 5, observing and correcting, and others) a permanent part of your life. Set this point as a demarcation line in your life that you will not allow yourself to cross over again. In the future, you may observe weight returning to your body. Don't wait. Start correcting immediately using the principles you have learned. Most importantly, make sure you are seeking God in the process.

If you still have weight to release, don't despair. Remember that safe weight loss is about two pounds per week, and it can take up to a year or more for some people to reach their natural God-given size. As you continue to desire to glorify God in your body, His temple, never forget that He will be faithful to help you with the strength you need to persevere. Realize now that this journey is a long one and it will have its ups and downs. During the best of times and the worst of times, God's love for you remains constant. The only way the enemy will ultimately win is if you choose to give up in the race. Falling down and getting up over and over again is OK—just never forget to keep getting up. God will be there with open arms every time.

Whether you have reached your God-given goals, are looking for helpful ways to maintain your weight, or are still pressing onward, Thin Within will be here to help you. We have prepared an ongoing series of monthly lessons and exercises to continue to challenge and guide you. It never fails to amaze us that just when we think we have reached the end of something, we discover we are just at the beginning of something completely new. As this foundational material ends, we pray that it will be a new beginning for you—a beginning that sees you living life to the fullest, embracing all the potential God created in your life.

Yours in Christ,
Judy Halliday   Author and Founder

Joe Donaldson Director

© 2003, Thin Within, All Rights Reserved

© 2003, Thin Within, All Rights Reserved

thin within

Appendix

© 2003, Thin Within, All Rights Reserved

APPENDIX

Stop, Look, Listen, and Obey: Temptation Buster
A Battle Plan to Fight Temptation

- **How can we recognize temptation as an opportunity to choose that which is "good"?**
- **What is the biblical solution for dealing with thoughts and desires that are not from God?**
- **Is there a way to break free from a seemingly hopeless "sin pattern" that has enslaved us?**

God's Word provides an effective way to stop when tempted and turn from sin. Think of the childhood rhyme for safely crossing the street:

Stop, look, and listen before you cross the street.
First use your eyes and ears, then use your feet.

Take that simple verse and change it into a reminder of God's provision as you face temptation:

> ## Stop, look, and listen before you fall into sin.
> ## First use the Word of God, then obey and win.

Jesus responded to temptation by speaking the truth of God's Word. Matthew 4:1–11 says we are to resist the enemy by refocusing our attention on the truth rather than on the lies from Satan.

James 1:14–15 says that temptation starts with a desirous thought. Can you resist such a thought? The more you try to resist it, the more it will control and consume you. What is the answer? **Replace the tempting thought with Scripture and turn your mind to the truth**. The temptation will lose its power against God's living and active sword of the Spirit (Hebrews 4:12; Ephesians 6:17).

The following are some verses on which to focus when you face temptation. Memorize these verses and meditate on them in order to be prepared for daily spiritual warfare. Allow God to use His powerful Word to turn temptation into an opportunity to obey Him and experience the abundant life filled with the complete joy He promises.

Note: For your convenience there are Stop, Look, Listen, and Obey cards on a separate sheet in the Thin Within Foundation Materials for you to cut out and carry with you.

© 2003, Thin Within, All Rights Reserved

Stop, Look, Listen, and Obey

Stop – Stop and flee from evil desires.

- "Brothers, stop thinking like children. In regard to evil be infants, but in your thinking be adults." 1 Corinthians 14:20
- "Come back to your senses as you ought, and stop sinning." 1 Corinthians 15:34
- "Stop and consider God's wonders." Job 37:14

Look – Look for God's prepared path and turn away from temptation.

- "Stand at the crossroads and look . . . ask where the good way is, and walk in it, and you will find rest for your souls." Jeremiah 6:16
- "Look to the LORD and His strength; seek His face always." Psalm 105:4
- "When you are tempted, He will also provide a way out so that you can stand up under it." 1 Corinthians 10:13b

Listen – Listen to His voice as you draw on His grace and power to pursue godliness.

- "My sheep listen to My voice; I know them, and they follow Me." John 10:27
- "For the grace of God that brings salvation has appeared to all men. It teaches us to say "No" to ungodliness and worldly passions, and to live self-controlled, upright and godly lives." Titus 2:11–12
- "His divine power has given us everything we need for life and godliness through our knowledge of Him who called us by His own glory and goodness." 2 Peter 1:3

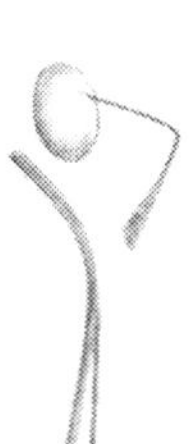

Obey – As you do what He asks you will experience complete joy!

- "If you obey My commands, you will remain in My love, just as I have obeyed My Father's commands and remain in His love. I have told you this so that My joy may be in you and that your joy may be complete." John 15:10–11
- "Do not merely listen to the word, and so deceive yourselves. Do what it says." James 1:22
- "But I say, walk by the Spirit and you will not carry out the desire of the flesh." Galatians 5:16 (NASB)

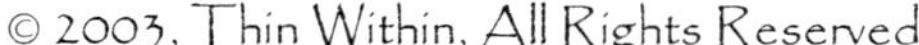

© 2003, Thin Within, All Rights Reserved

APPENDIX

Reentry after Fallout
Choosing Perseverance When the Going Gets Tough

The "Honeymoon"

Frequently when someone starts Thin Within, they experience a "honeymoon phase" where they find the new principles of hunger/satisfaction "easy" and the answer they have been looking for. Many experience weight loss and a refreshing new outlook on food, eating, and their bodies, as well as a closer relationship with God.

Naturally, participants expect to continue to soar in this newfound freedom. Many do. However, after a few weeks, it is not uncommon for some to encounter challenges along the way. The newness wears off and everyday life sets in. Holidays, birthdays, vacations, business trips, and weekends creep into the schedule and old habits rear their ugly heads.

You may have thoughts like these: "Why is this becoming difficult?" "Am I doing something wrong?" "What happened?" The road seems bumpy and some may experience disenchantment, discouragement, or even the temptation to "give up."

The Temptation to "Give Up"

First, stop and recall why you chose to participate in Thin Within. What were the godly goals you wanted to achieve? Consider some of the following:

- Peace with food, eating, and your body (Philippians 4:6–7)
- Reaching and maintaining your natural God-given size (1 Corinthians 6:19–20)
- Pleasing and honoring God in all that you do (1 Corinthians 6:19–20)
- Not being mastered by anything (1 Corinthians 6:12)
- Refraining from greed and self-indulgence (Colossians 3:1–5)
- Running in such a way as to "receive the prize" (1 Corinthians 9:24)
- Freedom from food rules and diet plans (Colossians 2:20–23)
- Choosing that which is most beneficial (1 Corinthians 6:12)

Remember, this is what the Thin Within program is all about.

Also, consider why we often "default" to giving up and quitting when things get tough. We are involved not only in a physical battle, but a spiritual battle as well (Ephesians 6:10–13). Satan's goal is to steal and destroy the things of God. However, he can't win the war because God has already established victory and nothing can separate us from His steadfast love.

So what is happening when you want to give up? Satan is doing all he can to place stumbling blocks along the way to try to pull your attention off of Jesus. His strategy is to get your focus on yourself and the things of this world. As a result, you might miss out on God's best for you. When you allow defeat to consume you to the point of quitting, Satan has won a victory. However, if you press on and take hold of the living Word of God, surrender your will unto the Lord, and trust in the finished work of Christ, the battle is won!

How effective are you for God's kingdom when "giving up" is part of your response? Jesus says in Matthew 6:33 that you are to "[s]eek first his kingdom and his righteousness, and all these things will be given to you as well."

Paul continually refers to our lives as a race where we are to press on to the finish line. He speaks of not giving up in this fight of faith. This requires a vigilance to "run with perseverance the race marked out for us" (Hebrews 12:1).

Don't give up! "Fix [your] eyes on Jesus, the author and perfecter of [your] faith" (Hebrews 12:2).

   © 2003, Thin Within, All Rights Reserved

How Do I Reenter Thin Within If...

I didn't make it past the first few weeks?

- If you stopped after just a lesson or two, you might want to reenter at the beginning to reaffirm and solidify your foundation and hope in Jesus Christ.

I felt it was too difficult and I couldn't do it anymore?

- Go back to the lesson that you were currently working on and ask God, through the power of the Holy Spirit, to give you a fresh perspective as well as the motivation and courage to continue.

I was doing great and suddenly it all got rather "fuzzy" and I just didn't "get it"?

- Start at the beginning of the lesson that went "fuzzy" and ask God for clarity and an ability to see the truth.

I got stuck on Lesson # _____ and just couldn't seem to work through it.

- First, make sure that you're not holding anything back from the Lord that He is asking of you. You may be at a tough crossroads, so pray for God's direction toward the next step.
- If you find a lesson too difficult to complete, then simply move on to the next lesson. Take comfort in the fact that you will revisit this topic several times in the supplementary curriculum. This will give you the opportunity to come back and review. Even if you postpone completing a lesson, you will come back to it further down the road.

I completed the foundational material and due to a busy schedule placed Thin Within aside for several months. I'm excited to begin again. Where do I start?

- If it has been several months, you may want to review the foundational material. Otherwise, feel free to jump in at any point.

- -

Take heart and have faith. You are on the right path. The bumps and obstacles are there for a purpose.

The Lord will meet you, instruct you, mold and change you into His likeness through the ups and downs of this process.

The main instruction from Paul is this: Don't give up. Press on. Take hold.

Not that I have already obtained all this, or have already been made perfect, but I press on to take hold of that for which Christ Jesus took hold of me. Brothers, I do not consider myself yet to have taken hold of it. But one thing I do: Forgetting what is behind and straining toward what is ahead, I press on toward the goal to win the prize for which God has called me heavenward in Christ Jesus.
Philippians 3:12–14

© 2003, Thin Within, All Rights Reserved

APPENDIX

© 2003, Thin Within, All Rights Reserved

Where to Get Support When You Need it Most

We know that the journey toward an abundant life in Christ is often very challenging. To be a member in Thin Within is to be part of a community of people who care for you. Here are a variety of resources available to you in those times when you have questions or need help.

Support Groups—Live

Support Groups are the best place to find encouragement, motivation, and support when you need it most. These weekly groups are hosted by some wonderful volunteers that have a heart to minister to others. You can search for local groups on our website or by calling us at 877.729.8932. If there are no groups close by, prayerfully consider starting one of your own. We will provide you with many helps to facilitate the leading of a group. If you are unable to start a group, consider asking one other person to join Thin Within and be an accountability partner with you. You'll find a support group or partner is invaluable as you learn to walk in obedience.

Member Community

The Member Community is a special place provided by and for Thin Within members. It offers a terrific opportunity to post your thoughts and questions in an environment of love and compassion. We at Thin Within have been overwhelmed by the support that members offer to one another. Stop by and take a look. We are sure you will be blessed by what you see.

Phone

Last, but certainly not least, Thin Within members are certainly welcome to pick up the phone and call us toll-free at **877.729.8932**. We may not have all of life's answers, but we will do our best to help you in any way that we can!

Please know you are never alone in this journey. Even if there are times when other members or Thin Within staff may not be available, Jesus said,

"...And surely I am with you always, to the very end of the age"
Matthew 28:20

© 2003, Thin Within, All Rights Reserved